'BOMBER' HARRIS
AND THE STRATEGIC BOMBING
OFFENSIVE, 1939–1945

Charles Messenger

'BOMBER' HARRIS
AND THE STRATEGIC BOMBING OFFENSIVE, 1939–1945

ST. MARTIN'S PRESS

New York

First published 1984.
For information, address St. Martin's Press,
175 Fifth Avenue, New York,
N.Y. 10010.

ISBN 0-312-08760-8

Maps and diagrams by Anthony A. Evans.

Jacket illustration:
Harris and Saundby discuss future 1,000 bomber raid
targets in June 1942 at Bomber Command HQ,
High Wycombe. (IWM)

Edited by Michael Boxall
Typeset by Typesetters (Birmingham) Limited
Printed and bound in Great Britain

CONTENTS

INTRODUCTION

Hindsight is the historian's greatest enemy, and the easiest trap in which to fall. This is particularly so when studying war, where often the intense stress on those responsible for its conduct is not appreciated, and there is a dangerous tendency to judge the actions of individuals in the light of information concerning the enemy which they would not have had at the time. If, too, the subject is controversial, there is the added danger of emotion overriding cold analysis. The Second World War provides no better example of these dangers than the Royal Air Force's bombing of Germany.

In 1961 the Official History of this campaign was published and, in its attempts to be impartial and objective, it was criticised by some who felt that it condemned Bomber Command and those who directed its activities, and by others who considered that criticism of the conduct of the campaign did not go far enough. That the History was so viewed is an indication of its balance. Compared to many other works of the same ilk, it stands out for its depth of research, the clarity of the writing and the meticulous examination of the various arguments. In this writer's view, its only failing is that it did not deal with some of the more emotive myths, which continue to be propagated. Two examples are the treatment of those aircrew who could no longer stand the intense strain of operational flying, and immediate post-war official attitudes to RAF Bomber Command and its role in the war. This omission has encouraged a number of writers unjustifiably to denigrate the conduct of the strategic bombing campaign. Apart from attacking it on moral grounds, some also portray those responsible for its conduct as being totally out of touch with reality, both in terms of the damage being inflicted on the enemy and the problems facing the aircrews who had to carry out the bombing. In this respect, no single individual has come in for greater punishment than the man who led Bomber Command for the greater part of the Second World War, Marshal of the Royal Air Force Sir Arthur Harris, GCB, OBE, AFC.

Called 'Bert' or 'Bud' by his friends, 'The Chief Bomber' by Churchill, 'Bomber' by the general public, 'Butch' by his crews and 'Butcher' by those who were opposed to what he stood for, these nicknames alone indicate something of the wide range of feelings about him that existed, even during the war. He has been pilloried on both operational and moral grounds, on the supposition that he cared little for those above and below him, and that he remained entirely inflexible in his attitudes from the beginning to the end. On the other hand, many of those who served under him remain to this day intensely loyal and very protective towards him, to such an extent that the author found it difficult to make contact with those who knew him well. It was clear that they assumed, as a result of past experience, that anything written about him and his Command was bound to be derogatory.

This book, therefore, endeavours to present a dispassionate picture of Harris and the strategic bombing campaign. It must be stressed, however, that it is not a biography. That has already been written by Dudley Saward, Harris's Chief Radar Officer for much of the war, and, with Sir Arthur's death, is now to be published. None the less, in order to understand Harris the wartime commander, it is necessary to include some biographical background in order to better comprehend his viewpoint. My aim, therefore, has been to judge him strictly on his merits as a commander and leader, against the backcloth of the most desperate struggle this country has ever experienced.

For sources, I have drawn heavily on the vast collection of official documents held by the Public Record Office in London, for it is only through a close study of these that one can begin to grasp how those in high authority perceived events at the time. Although corresponding use of German primary sources would in many ways give a more comprehensive picture, it would at the same time be misleading, because a true understanding of the circumstances in which decisions were made can only be achieved through knowledge of how the enemy's situation was judged and not as it actually stood. Thus, one cannot fault a decision or argument solely on the grounds of facts which were not and of necessity could not be appreciated at the time. By the same token, I have tried not to rely too heavily on interviews with those who served in Bomber Command or who had close connections with Harris during the war. Memory is very fickle, especially when forced back over forty years or more. Nevertheless, I have spoken over the years to a number of veteran aircrew and others, and have studied many written personal accounts, and something of their views is reflected in the narrative.

One other point needs to be stressed, and that is the pressure under which those in high office worked during the war years. A fifteen-hour day, seven days a week, was normal and would often be longer, especially at times of acute crisis. This reverberated on their staffs, who had constantly to keep their masters briefed on what was often a constantly changing situation. Much time was spent in committee or discussion, but there was, too, a constant deluge of paperwork covering a vast spectrum of subjects, which had to be read and digested. On top of all this was the constant realisation of being on a knife edge. If a decision were made too quickly, without full appraisal of the facts, or inordinately delayed, the result was the same – setback and the chance of ultimate victory receding farther into the distance. Given the high tempo of the strategic bombing campaign over a very long period, this pressure was intensified for those concerned in its conduct. It is in the light of these factors that this book should be read.

There remains but to single out some individuals who have given me particular assistance during the past year. First, there is Kelly Polanska. On my behalf, over a period of five months, she carried out very rigorous research in the Public Record Office. Although initially she knew little about the subject her keenness and ability to focus on the relevant, as opposed to the immaterial, has my unbounded gratitude and admiration. To Peter Tomlinson, too, I owe a very special debt. As Harris's personal assistant and pilot while he was AOC No 5 Group, and again (after he had been liberated from a POW camp) at the end of the war, as well as going into business with him afterwards, he knew Harris very intimately. Indeed, up to 1983 Sir Arthur spent part of every winter with him in South Africa. He was able to tell me much about Harris, of which I was not previously aware, and obtained answers from him to a number of my queries. Air Commodore Henry Probert and Humphrey Wynn of the Air Historical Branch, Ministry of Defence, London, also very kindly read the manuscript and corrected a number of points of fact. I thank them very much for their trouble. My thanks too, to Cecilia Weston-Baker for typing an untidy and, in places, illegible manuscript. I am more than grateful to her for her patience and cheerfulness in this tedious task. I should like to thank my publisher, Lionel Leventhal, and Editorial Director, David Gibbons, for their advice concerning my approach, for keeping me up to the mark and for their continual enthusiasm for the project; and last, but not least, Michael Boxall for his painstaking editing.

Charles Messenger, London, 1984

Stavanger

Edinburgh

Jurby

Dublin

100 Miles

400

300

200

NORTH SEA

Flensb

Hornum

Doncaster
Manby
Lincoln
Syerston
Lichfield
Newton
Marham
King's Lynn
Mildenhall
E. Harling
Gt. Yarmouth
Newmarket

London

Brunsbuttel
Bremerhaven
Wilhelmshaven
Emden
Wenzendo
D.E.C.
Bremen
Diepholz

Amsterdam
Ibbenburren
Osnab
Bie

Rotterdam
Zeeland
R. Rhine
The Ruhr
Pad
Göt

Flushing
Ostend
Eindhoven
Bruges
Hingene
K

Calais
Dunkirk
Aachen
Cologne
Esch
Boulogne
St. Omer
Wesseling
Bethune
Lille
Abbeville
Arras
Gembloux
Neuwied
We
Malmédy
Coblenz
Limbu

ENGLISH CHANNEL

Cherbourg
Bruneval
Amiens
Lutterade
Frankfurt
Billancourt
Sedan
Wiesbaden
Da
Trier
Mainz
We
Kreuznach
Ma
Dombasle
Oppau

R. Seine
Gennevilliers
Poissy
Paris
Saarfels
Villacoublay
Villeneuve
Karlsruhe
Stu
Offenb

Brest

Lorient

St. Nazaire

R. Loire

La Pallice

Berne

BAY OF BISCAY

La Rochelle

Bordeaux

Turin

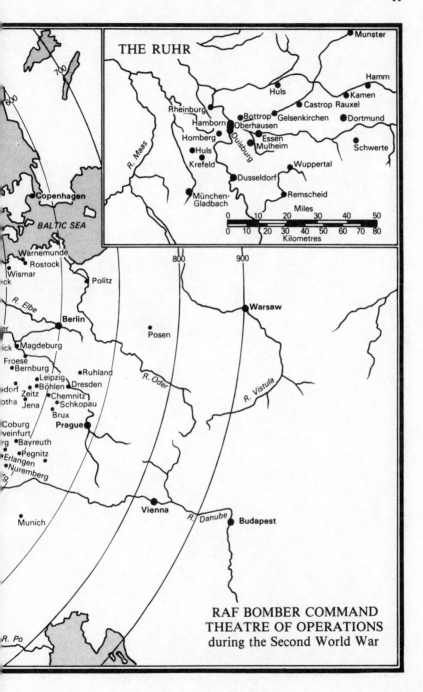

THE RUHR

Munster

Hamm

Huls

Kamen

Castrop Rauxel

Rheinburg

Bottrop

Gelsenkirchen

Dortmund

Hamborn

Oberhausen

Homberg

Duisburg

Essen

Mulheim

Schwerte

Huls

Krefeld

Wuppertal

Dusseldorf

München-Gladbach

Remscheid

R. Maas

Miles

0   10   20   30   40   50

0 10 20 30 40 50 60 70 80

Kilometres

Copenhagen

BALTIC SEA

Warnemunde

Rostock

Wismar

Politz

R. Elbe

Berlin

Posen

Warsaw

Magdeburg

Froese

Bernburg

Ruhland

Leipzig

R. Oder

Böhlen

Dresden

Zeitz

Chemnitz

Jena

Schkopau

R. Vistula

Brux

Prague

Coburg

weinfurt

Bayreuth

Pegnitz

Erlangen

Nuremberg

Vienna

R. Danube

Budapest

Munich

RAF BOMBER COMMAND
THEATRE OF OPERATIONS
during the Second World War

R. Po

CHAPTER ONE

ORIGINS

It is\on the bomber that we must rely for defence. It is on the destruction of enemy industries and, above all, on the lowering of morale . . . caused by bombing that ultimate victory rests. - Trenchard

---

On 22 September 1914 four aircraft of 3 Squadron Royal Naval Air Service (RNAS) took off from Belgium to attack the German Zeppelin sheds at Düsseldorf and Cologne. Although only one aircraft succeeded in locating its target and dropping bombs on it, the operation marked the first use of strategic bombing in war, and it was to be followed by three similar operations before the year was out. At the time, air forces, apart from the Zeppelins, were viewed as being strictly in direct support of navies and armies. Yet, the French did carry out some reprisal raids on Germany for Zeppelin attacks on French towns, and the Zeppelins carried out a number of night attacks on England during late 1915 and 1916, which resulted in the formation of Home Defence fighter squadrons and anti-aircraft gun detachments. In the early summer of 1917, however, the Germans switched their tactics and began raiding England using Gotha G IV bombers, and two of these attacks took place over London in broad daylight. As to the effect on Londoners themselves, here is an eyewitness account by an American airman:

> When we got down to the station it was already packed. We couldn't get down to the platform so camped on a landing halfway down. The air was as foul as the Black Hole of Calcutta and those people certainly were scared. We cheered the girls up and drank the whiskey and felt better. Every one had brought camp stools and it was sure a funny sight. I hadn't realized before how successful the raids are. It doesn't matter whether they hit anything or not as long as they put the wind up the civilian population so thoroughly. These people wanted peace and they wanted it quickly.[1]

A committee was set up under General Smuts to make recommendations on defence against attacks from the air. He himself had witnessed one of the daylight raids and its effects on civilian morale deeply impressed him as well. He wrote:

. . . the day may not be far off when aerial operations with their devastation of
enemy lands and destruction of industries and populous centres on a vast scale
may become the principal operations of war, to which the older forms of military
and naval operations may become secondary and subordinate.[2]

Believing that the Germans were now mounting a strategic
bombing campaign on England, Smuts recommended that similar
attacks be made on Germany, and that a new ministry be set up to
coordinate the bomber offensive. This resulted in the subsequent
formation of the Royal Air Force on 1 April 1918, a fusion of the
Royal Naval Air Service and Royal Flying Corps.

While the bulk of the new Service continued to devote its energies
to the traditional air roles of support to land and maritime forces,
the strategic bombing campaign against Germany had begun in
October 1917 when 41 Wing Royal Flying Corps at Nancy began to
carry out attacks by day and night, against industrial targets in the
Saar and Rhineland. Their operations, using DH4s, Handley Pages
and FE2s, were very much on an *ad hoc* basis, with makeshift
equipment and crews that had had no formal training. The
weather, too, severely restricted their activities. Not surprisingly,
results were meagre, but the infant Air Ministry, which began work
in January 1918, believed in the strategic policy and wanted to see
an Allied strategic bombing force set up. Consequently, 41 Wing
was expanded and on 6 June 1918 became the Independent Force to
stress that it was independent of land and maritime operations.
Appointed to command it was General (later Marshal of the RAF,
Viscount) Trenchard, who had commanded the RFC in France for
much of the war and who had, in fact, been opposed to strategic
bombing, seeing it as a dangerous diversion from the RFC's true
role of support of the armies in France. He had then been
appointed Chief of the Air Staff, but had resigned when he found
that he could not work with Lord Rothermere, the Secretary of
State for the Air Force.

The Independent Force concentrated its attacks against the
German munitions industry, especially chemical and iron and steel
works, but, as a means of supporting ground operations, railway
targets were also bombed, although this was often against the
wishes of the Air Staff. Similarly, in order to reduce German
fighter strength, Trenchard was forced to pay much attention to
enemy airfields. In May 1918 a decision was taken to form a wing in
East Anglia, which would be equipped with the new Handley Page
V-1500, which was expected to have the range to reach Hamburg
and Berlin, but the wing did not become operational in time. Also
in the last days of the war a plan was being set in motion for a
squadron to move from France to an airfield north of Prague in
order to bomb Berlin.

Immediately after the end of hostilities, the Air Ministry dispatched a commission to investigate the results of the Independent Force's attacks during 1918. Although material damage was found to be small, the Bombing Commission was deeply impressed by the effects on the morale of the civilian population, as well as the serious loss in industrial production, caused mainly by the fact that air raid warnings tended to be sounded over a wide area. The attacks also tied down a substantial element of aircraft, guns and searchlights.

THE TRENCHARD DOCTRINE

The end of the war, however, brought with it a wholesale reduction in the level of Britain's defences culminating in the 'Geddes Axe' of 1921, which pared all three fighting services to the bone. The two older Services were intensely jealous of the Royal Air Force, and throughout the 1920s its existence was under threat, and it was only thanks to Trenchard, who was Chief of the Air Staff throughout the period, that it survived. His policy was built on two platforms.

First, defence priority had reverted to protection of the Empire, and Trenchard saw that if the RAF could find a clear-cut role in this, its future would be very much more assured. The opportunity came at the Cairo Conference of March 1921, called by Winston Churchill, as Secretary of State for the Colonies, to discuss the conduct of military and political policy towards those territories which had been under Turkish control, but which under the terms of the Treaty of Versailles, had become a British responsibility. The Army garrisons in Mesopotamia and elsewhere were too costly to maintain, and Trenchard proposed that the RAF take them over, using aircraft, armoured cars and local levies, as a cheap and effective method of maintaining order. The value of the aircraft and armoured car, 'upon which we rely considerably', as the Civil Commissioner at Baghdad had stated the year before,[3] had already been recognised, and the Conference readily accepted Trenchard's idea.

Air power, or 'air control' as it was called, as a means of controlling unruly tribesmen had been demonstrated during the Third Afghan War in 1919, and one who had had experience of it was Squadron Leader Arthur Travers Harris, in command of a DH9a squadron. Born in 1892, he had left school at the age of sixteen and gone to Rhodesia, where he took on a variety of jobs ranging from gold-mining to farming. When war came in 1914, he joined the 1st Rhodesia Regiment as a Bugler and took part in General Botha's campaign in German South-West Africa. When this was over, Harris set sail for England and joined the Royal Flying Corps. His service during the rest of the war was in Home Defence fighter squadrons and in an artillery spotter squadron on the Western Front. However, he clearly made his mark and finished the war as a Major, with an Air Force Cross, and was offered a Permanent Commission as a Squadron Leader in the post-war RAF. He was posted to India, and recalled how 'one 20lb bomb in his palace grounds' deterred the Amir of Afghanistan from launching a holy war against India.[4] Harris also saw his service on the North-West Frontier as:

> . . . a bitter reminder of what happens when air forces, or any other forces with new weapons, are put under the control of another and older service and subordinated to the use of previously existing weapons. We lacked everything in the way of necessary accommodation and spares and materials for keeping our aircraft serviceable – the only thing there was never any shortage of were demands for our services when the trouble blew up on the frontier.[5]

Indeed, the situation got so bad that Harris at one point tendered his resignation. Then, in 1922 he was posted to Iraq to take command of 45 Squadron which was equipped with the Vickers Vernon and later the Victoria, which were troop transports. In order to convert them to what Harris claimed were 'the first of the post-war long-range heavy bombers', a sighting hole was cut in the nose and home-made bomb-racks were fitted.[6] His flight commanders were R. H. M. S. Saundby and R. A. Cochrane, both of whose names will crop up on later pages. Thus, Harris, like many others of his generation in the RAF, had experience of air control, and it provided a valuable means of giving aircrew operational experience between the wars. However, it would not be long before Harris would also become involved with the second plank of Trenchard's air policy.

It was the Italian General Guilio Douhet who first propounded the concept of the omnipotence of air power in wars of the future, when in 1921 he published his *The Command of the Air* which proposed that once his air force had been grounded, an enemy could be bombed into submission with little help from armies and navies. In the United States, too, General Billy Mitchell was propounding similar theories, although at this time he concentrated on demonstrating that air forces were a threat not just to land forces, but to fleets as well. Trenchard had begun to crystalise his own thoughts in his Official Dispatch on the Independent Force, which concluded, presumably using the evidence produced by the Bombing Commission, that '. . . the moral effect of bombing stands undoubtedly to the material effect in a proportion of twenty to one'.[7] This also appeared to be proved in the Middle East, where a few aircraft were achieving very much more than thousands of soldiers had done. By early 1923, however, with inter-service battles reaching a climax and the First Sea Lord, Admiral Beatty, threatening to resign if the Royal Navy did not get back its own aviation arm, a committee was set up under Lord Salisbury to investigate the role of air power in the defence of Britain. Trenchard laid his views before the committee: 'It is on the bomber that we must rely for defence. It is on the destruction of enemy industries and, above all, on the lowering of morale . . . caused by bombing that ultimate victory rests.'[8] Arthur Balfour, who was on the committee, also compared the strength of the RAF with that of the French Air Force, which, with France unconvinced that Germany would not threaten her again, had remained strong. In the hypothetical case of a war with France, bombers might attack London with 'a continuous torrent of high explosives at the rate of 75 tons a day for an infinite period', and since France was the only country which had bombers capable of attacking Britain, it was reasonable to match her strength.[9] This view was accepted, not only in the belief that the RAF was currently too weak, but also because many aircraft manufacturers, because of the Geddes Axe, were about to close down. Consequently, it was decided that a home-based or Metropolitan Air Force of 23 squadrons (nine fighter and fourteen bomber) should be formed, and later in the year, with Bonar Law's Conservative Government taking office, this was increased to 52 (17 fighter and 35 bomber) squadrons.

Harris arrived home from Iraq at the end of 1924, and in May 1925 assumed command of 58 Squadron. This had just been equipped with the Vickers Virginia, the first of the RAF's post-war heavy bombers. During the next two and a half years he worked his squadron very hard, with emphasis not just on day bombing, but night as well. Furthermore, Harris laid heavy stress on endurance flights and as early as September 1925, the Squadron Operational Record Book[10] records a flight made by eight machines, which set off from their base at Worthy Down near Winchester, flew to Leuchars in Scotland and returned without having landed en route. In all, they were in the air for more than eleven hours. Harris's efforts did not go without notice and, before relinquishing command in November 1927 to attend the Army Staff College as a student, he was made an Officer of the Order of the British Empire. As for his time at Camberley, he was appalled by the Army's conservatism and only Montgomery, then an instructor there, impressed him.

In the meantime, the Air Staff continued to propagate the power of the bomber. The Labour Government of 1924 considered it serious enough to set up the Air Raid Precautions Sub-Committee of the Committee for Imperial Defence (CID), and based their work on Air Staff calculations, founded on First World War experience, that 27,000 Londoners might be killed by bombing in the first month of a future war.*[11] In 1925, in view of the air threat, the Chief of the Imperial General Staff, Sir George Milne, declared that, '. . . the true strategic position of Great Britain is on the Rhine',[12] and even those arch protagonists of mechanised warfare, J. F. C. Fuller and Basil Liddell Hart, recognised the potential of the bomber. The former thought that the aeroplane might well replace armies and navies in the future, and argued that it was a humane way of waging war:

> If a future war can be won at the cost of two or three thousand of the enemy's men, women and children killed, in the place of over 1,000,000 men and incidently several thousands of women and children, as was the case in France during the recent war, surely an aerial attack is a more humane method than the existing traditional one?[13]

Liddell Hart, too, saw the aircraft as enabling 'us to jump over the army which shields the enemy government, industry, and the people and so strike direct and immediately at the seat of the opposing will and policy'. He painted a graphic picture of what might happen in a future war:

> Imagine for a moment London, Manchester, Birmingham and half a dozen other great centres simultaneously attacked, the business localities and Fleet Street wrecked, Whitehall a heap of ruins, the slum districts maddened into impulse to break loose and maraud, the railways cut, factories destroyed. Would not the general will to resist vanish, and what use would be the still determined factions of the nation, without organisation and central direction.[14]

Yet, in the Twenties the public as a whole did not look on aircraft as a threat. The pioneering endurance flights around the world were seen as a means of speeding up communications and as evidence that Twentieth-Century man was conquering his environment. There was wonderment, too, at the ever-increasing speeds at which aircraft could fly, especially as demonstrated in the Schneider Trophy Races, and the annual RAF Display at Hendon was one of the major events in the social calendar.

The Government, however, was bound by the Ten Year Rule, which, instituted in 1919, assumed, for defence planning purposes, that there would be no major war in Europe for ten years, and this was renewed annually every year up to 1932. This, financial stringency and the general atmosphere of disarmament meant that the original intention to produce a 52-squadron Metropolitan Air Force would not be met, and as early as 1924 this was recognised. Even so, by 1932, when, in view of the crisis in Manchuria, the Rule was rescinded, four-fifths of the plan had been accomplished. Manchuria and the global economic crisis precipitated by the Wall

*This estimate would rise to 66,000 in the first week of war when Germany became a potential enemy.

Street Crash of 1929 made people begin to realise that the world was perhaps not the safe place it had been thought to be during the previous decade. The economic situation also precipitated the formation of a National Government under Ramsay MacDonald, which had as one of its platforms the pursuance of global disarmament, especially through disarmament talks at Geneva.

During the winter of 1922–3 international jurists had met at The Hague in an attempt to draw up rules for the conduct of air warfare, and although they never went farther than a Draft, which was open to interpretation, the overall message that indiscriminate bombing was unlawful was generally respected. Indicative of this is correspondence which Trenchard had with his fellow Chiefs of Staff in 1928. They had disagreed with his view that in future wars aircraft would undoubtedly attack communications and munition centres, 'no matter where they are situated'. Trenchard believed that the aim of the RAF in war was 'to break down the enemy's means of resistance by attacks on objectives selected as most likely to achieve this end'. While accepting The Hague Draft Rules, he contended that factories and communications were military targets if they were involved with the manufacture and transport of munitions, and the fact that civilians might get killed in the process was analogous to a naval coastal bombardment. While he accepted that indiscriminate terror bombing was unlawful, it was an 'entirely different matter to terrorise munition workers (men and women) into absenting themselves from work or stevedores into abandoning the loading of a ship with munitions through fear of air attack upon the factory or dock concerned'. The other Chiefs of Staff disagreed with him, considering that the RAF's role in war, as he had defined it, allowed for too much latitude; their interpretation of the Commission of Jurists was that if bombing a target put innocent lives at risk, it should not be attacked,[15] and, as we shall see, this was the policy with which Britain went to war in 1939.

THIRTIES' DILEMMAS

Ramsay MacDonald approached the problem from a different angle, believing that bombers and bombing should be outlawed altogether. However, his Ministerial Committee on the Disarmament Conference, which was set up in early 1932 to prepare the Government's approach at Geneva, realised that such a convention would be very unlikely to be observed in war, especially since it would be easy enough to convert commercial aircraft to bombers. Nevertheless:

> . . . it was put forward strongly that public opinion at home took greater interest in this question of bombing, which might ultimately affect them, than in the

majority of the other qualitative disarmament proposals, and that the Government might find themselves in a position of some embarrassment if we did not
declare ourselves openly for the abolition of bombing.[16]

Thus, the Government found itself in an awkward if not impossible
position. The fear of the bomber, was not helped by Baldwin's
(then Lord President of the Council) celebrated statement in the
House of Commons that: 'No power on earth can protect that man
in the street from being bombed. Whatever people may tell him, the
bomber will always get through.'[17] Consequently, fear of the
bomber became a cornerstone of the growing peace movement in
the early 1930s. None the less, while both the Admiralty and War
Office also agreed that the bomber should be banned, the Air
Ministry pointed out that the 'moral knock-out blow' was very
much more likely if the country had no effective air defence, and
that, in any event, as long as aircraft existed, this danger was
always present. Furthermore, fighters on their own could not
defend London.[18] For a while, the Government continued to
struggle at Geneva to find a means of outlawing bombing, but by
the end of 1933, it was clear that their efforts were in vain, and there
was acknowledgement of the Air Ministry's arguments, which
resulted in a gnawing doubt that even if agreement were reached, it
might be at the cost of leaving Britain defenceless.

During much of this period Harris had been abroad, getting his
first experience of Staff work as Senior Air Staff Officer (SASO)
Egypt. He was then posted to Pembroke Dock to command 210
Squadron equipped with Southampton and later Singapore flying
boats. One of his pilots was an Australian, D. C. T. Bennett, who
was later, as we shall see, to have a distinguished career during the
Second World War. He recalls Pembroke Dock as 'one of the
happiest stations I have ever struck', and that Harris 'certainly
made things move'.[19] In 1933 Harris was posted as Deputy Director
of Operations and Intelligence at the Air Ministry in the rank of
Group Captain. In that same year Hitler came to power in
Germany, and in October 1933 she withdrew from the Geneva
Conference and from the League of Nations. Britain now had a
potential enemy in Europe.

In 1934 Harris was appointed Deputy Director of Plans in the
Air Ministry, and during his three years in post had the opportunity
to influence air policy. This, of course, coincided with the first steps
taken to expand the RAF in order to prepare it for the possibility of
war breaking out in five to eight years' time. In January 1934 the
Air Ministry Bombing Committee was set up, and the role of
bomber operations was defined as counter-offensive against
German factories and industries. Initially, after Baldwin's
announcement in the House of Commons on 8 March 1934 that 'in

strength and in air power this country shall no longer be in a position inferior to any country within striking distance of our shores',[20] Scheme A of July 1934 called for a force of 43 bomber, 28 fighter and 13 reconnaissance squadrons. More so, the bomber was viewed as a deterrent. A strong bomber force would dissuade Germany from launching the Luftwaffe against Britain because, if she did, she would suffer the same destruction in return. It was, in essence, nothing more than the doctrine of Mutually Assured Destruction that was to be propagated by the nuclear strategists in the late Sixties. This was in line with the generally held belief in the power of the bomber. However, the problem at the time was that the Air Staff believed that the bomber force must operate from Britain, since, if it were deployed to the Continent it was felt that the RAF, operating from an ally's bases, would lose much of its independence. On the other hand, the Harts, Hinds and Heyfords which made up the bombing force of the time hardly had the range and payload to be effective against Germany from home bases, especially as the first two types were designated light bombers. Both the Air Ministry and Cabinet were at one in wanting aircraft of much greater range and power, and by the end of 1934 the former was working on the assumption that by the end of the first year of the war the RAF would have expanded to a force of 260 squadrons, including 30 of heavy and 60 of medium bombers.[21]

Throughout 1935, spurred by the mistaken belief that the Luftwaffe had achieved parity with the RAF,* with the resultant deduction that Hitler had remained undeterred by Scheme A, further plans were drawn up. These resulted in Scheme C, which envisaged a force of 70 bomber and torpedo-bomber, 35 fighter and 18 reconnaissance squadrons to be produced by the spring of 1937. Apart from the optimistic time-frame, the problem still existed that nearly half the bombers were incapable of reaching the Ruhr from British territory. By now, the role of the bombing force had been refined to concentrating on the destruction of the German armaments industry, and hence it was clear that the types of aircraft involved in Scheme C were unsuitable. As a result, the future of the light bomber was called into question by the Chief of the Air Staff (CAS). One of those who was asked for his views was Harris, who argued strongly for the two-engined medium bomber, believing that the light bomber was only of use in the Army co-operation role. He concluded prophetically that:

> . . . we are not warranted in retaining the Light Bomber; that it is in fact a matter of emergency to place ourselves on a level with our potential enemies by adopting a policy of maximum range and/or bomb-carrying capacity obtainable within

*This was claimed by Hitler to Sir John Simon and Anthony Eden when they visited Germany in March 1935. See Eden, Anthony. *Facing the Dictators* (Cassell, 1962) p. 141.

the limits of our first-line numerical strength. As a corollary, it seems apparent that even the Medium Bomber will tend to disappear and that eventually a most economical size and type will be evolved, on the basis of Range and Total Striking-Power factors, into which all existing categories of bombers will tend to merge in order to obtain the maximum striking-power within the limits imposed by agreement or by resources.[22]

Nevertheless, although the light bomber was theoretically dispensed with, on 10 March 1936 the prototype replacement of the Hind and Hart, the notorious Fairey Battle, made its maiden flight, and fifteen squadrons would be equipped with it during the twelve months from May 1937. Quantity rather than quality dictated the expansion schemes, and even though service deliveries of the Bristol Blenheim began in November 1936, and the Armstrong Whitworth Whitley a few months later, the production rates were not fast enough to give the RAF the necessary numerical front-line strength to keep Germany at bay.

At the beginning of February 1936, however, Neville Chamberlain, in a memorandum to the Committee for Imperial Defence (CID), suggested that the bomber force might 'also be used as a frankly offensive weapon for reducing within manageable proportions the scale and intensity of a German land offensive'.[23] The Air Ministry had been thinking along much the same lines since the previous summer, and from this evolved Scheme F, which reflected the belief that Britain's security could only be upheld through offensive measures, which meant emphasis on medium and heavy bombers. Thus, the light bombers of Scheme C were replaced by medium, substantial provision was made for reserve aircraft, and the time-frame stretched to spring 1939. Although specifications for a new generation of heavy bombers – what were to become the Stirling, Manchester and Halifax – were drawn up in 1936, it was clear that they would not be in service by the spring 1939 deadline, hence the RAF, in order to fulfill its numerical quota had to rely on the Blenheim, Battle, Hampden, Whitley and Wellington as stopgaps. Then, in order to emphasise the offensive role of the bomber, the decision was taken in the summer of 1936 to reorganise the Metropolitan Air Force, dispensing with the existing Air Defence of Great Britain (ADGB) and forming in its place Bomber, Fighter and Coastal Commands. In view of the threat from Germany, Bomber Command's airfields were moved from southern to eastern England.

As to the envisaged shape of the coming war, Harris, in his capacity as DD Plans, also sat on the Joint Planning Committee (JPC), which was answerable to the CID. On this he worked with, among others, Captain Tom Phillips, who was to go down in the *Prince of Wales* off Singapore, and Colonel Ted Morris, who would command a division in Italy. One of their tasks was to draw up annual appreciations of the situation in the event of war with Germany, and that for October 1936 bore a covering note written by Harris, which explained that 'a picture of our "worst case" had been purposely painted. It was assumed that Belgium and France would co-operate with Britain, but the effectiveness of this would be 'an unreliable quantity'. Italy would remain neutral, at least in the early stages of the conflict, no Russian help to Britain or Spanish to Germany was assumed. The German ability to attack Britain by air was emphasised, with the conclusion that an air counter-offensive was the only answer. 'So long as we are compelled to adhere to the theory of the counter-offensive, we should invest it with the power of striking relatively so hard against the enemy that this will offset our greater vulnerability.' Contrary to the expansion schemes so far drawn up, the JPC emphasised that it was superiority in bomb load rather than parity in numbers which was the important factor, and that 'the offensive employment of our own and allied bombers is the only measure which could effect the same issue during the first weeks of the war'. During this opening phase they saw the role of Bomber Command as (1) to demoralise the German people, (2) to discover and attack some target whose security was regarded by the Germans as vital to their survival, and (3) to attack the bases, communications and maintenance organisation of the German bomber force. However, the first, in its implication of attacks on civilians, ran against The Hague Draft Rules on air warfare, and it was agreed that this role was unacceptable, just as the attack on a vital target was impracticable because of the problems of identifying it in time. This reduced Bomber Command's role to the attacking of the Luftwaffe's ground installations even though Bomber Command lacked both the navigation and aiming means to deliver its bombs accurately on such precision targets.[24] Indeed, as Harris's successor as DD Plans, Bennett noted in October 1937, 'we appear to be neglecting practical research and experiments . . . on the types of bombs and tactics which will bring about the destruction with the least expenditure of effort of each type of target'.[25]

At this time, a number of air plans, known as Western Air (WA) Plans, began to be drawn up to cater for possible Bomber Command targets. These reflected not just the recommendations in the 1936 Appreciation, but also operations in support of the Royal Navy (WA2, WA3, WA7, WA10, WA12, WA15, WA16), attacks on Germany's war industry (WA5, WA8) and communications (WA4), as well as attacks on forests (WA11), Government buildings in Berlin and elsewhere (WA13) and the dropping of propaganda leaflets (WA14). Thus, they covered any possible mission that Bomber Command might be called upon to undertake.

In midsummer 1937 Harris left the Air Ministry and took command of the newly formed No 4 Group, Bomber Command, being promoted Air Commodore. With headquarters at Linton-on-Ouse, No 4 Group was equipped with the Whitley, 10 Squadron at Dishforth being the first to receive them in the early months of that year. Although Harris was obviously pleased to be back 'in the field', his year in command did have its frustrations, especially in the restrictions placed on training. Availability of bombing ranges, for example, was a particularly difficult problem, and his efforts to find suitable spots were often blocked by conservationist arguments about wildlife and, in the case of Holy Island, the danger that 'we might disturb the shades of our less reputable ancestors'.[26] Nevertheless, as he had done with both 58 and 210 Squadrons, he placed considerable emphasis on night and long-distance flying, which in itself was worthwhile training.

In 1937, however, doubts began to grow as to whether British air policy was justified in relying on the bomber to deliver a knock-out blow at the outset of war. Inskip, appointed Minister for Coordination of Defence by Baldwin in early 1936, wrote to the Secretary of State for Air on 9 December 1937, expressing his reservations:

> I cannot . . . persuade myself that the dictum of the Chief of the Air Staff that we must give the enemy as much as he gives us is a sound principle . . . The *role* of our Air Force is not an early knock-out blow . . . but to prevent the Germans from knocking us out.

He believed that the numbers of heavy bombers should be reduced. Instead of attempting to knock the German Air Force out on the ground, which the Chiefs of Staff had admitted as being 'not a very satisfactory target for air attack', the RAF should concentrate on destroying it in the air. He went on to suggest that light and medium bombers might be used to supplement fighters in this role, possibly using 'special light bombs . . . designed . . . for . . . use against aircraft'.[27] Understandably, there was a certain amount of scepticism over the last point, but the need to ward off an attempt at a knock-out blow gained adherents, especially Kingsley Wood, who took over as Secretary of State for Air in May of the following year. Strongly supported by Dowding, Air Officer in Chief (AOCinC) Fighter Command, he urged that the fighter strength must be built up. By November, especially after the scare at Munich, a new expansion scheme, Scheme M, was evolved, which called for forty fighter and fifty bomber squadrons by the end of March 1939, rising to fifty and eighty-two two years later (1941), and this was approved by the Cabinet. To suggestions that this was making the RAF purely a defensive force, Kingsley Wood retorted that he did not accept the premise that 'the bomber will always get through', especially, although he could not speak of it in public, since developments in Radio Direction Finding (RDF), later known as radar, made it possible to prevent a surprise air attack. In fact, by 1939 the RAF was clearly developing into two wings, a defensive force equipped with multiple machine-gun armament and RDF capable of inflicting crippling losses on the enemy's offensive air force, and a striking force capable of causing as much damage to the enemy as the latter could to Britain, but which would be employed as a second phase war-winning, rather than first-phase defeat-averting weapon.

Bomber Command might seem impressive both on paper and in long-term potential, but two aspects continued to give cause for concern. Sir Edgar Ludlow-Hewitt, AOCinC Bomber Command from 1937, was another who did not share what seemed to be the Air Ministry's blind optimism that the bomber 'would get through'. He was concerned that rapid expansion in numbers of aircraft had been at the expense of crew training and navigation aids. In his Training Report for 1938[28] he pointed to the lack of equipment and the inexperience of his crews, and, although it had been 'a satisfactory year's work', the standard of advanced operational training was disappointing, and could only be improved once the squadrons had stable crews. Unfortunately, the rapid expansion meant an ever-increasing number of new squadrons, which could only be achieved by cadres removed from existing operational squadrons. Inability to navigate by day, let alone by night, and lack of effective bombing aids, made him doubt more and more as the months went by that Bomber Command could fulfil what was expected of it. He was also unhappy about the concept of the two independent forces within the RAF, and pointed out to the Air Staff that, especially with the limited armament with which the bombers were equipped:

> Experience in China and in Spain seems clearly to indicate that with the aircraft in use in these two theatres of war at present, Fighter Escorts are considered absolutely essential for the protection of Bomber aircraft. So as I am aware this policy runs counter to the view long heard by the Air Staff.[29]

Then, just before the outbreak of war, he warned the Air Ministry that if he were expected to undertake an all-out attack on Germany, his force would be entirely destroyed in less than eight weeks.[30]

However, any initial air offensive on Germany was not envisaged by the Air Staff as being an 'all-out' one. In the late summer of 1938 Ludlow-Hewitt had asked the Air Ministry whether attacks on aircraft factories were permissible on the outbreak of war, bearing in mind the danger of bombs falling on populated areas. This provoked much discussion. Bennett, Deputy Director of Plans, in a minute to the Chief of the Air Staff, reminded him of the Prime Minister's three publicly enunciated principles – that deliberate bombing of civilians was illegal, that targets must be capable of identification and that reasonable care must be taken in attacking these targets not to harm civilians in the neighbourhood. Although targets near populated areas might be militarily essential to attack, the political view was overriding, especially in that care must be taken not to alienate the sympathy of other countries, particularly the USA. Thus, although 'it seems hardly possible that in a war between major air powers it can be very long before the gloves come off . . . we certainly cannot be the first to take them off'. Newall, the Chief of the Air Staff, agreed with this, but was concerned that the French might be less discriminating. Ludlow-Hewitt was instructed 'to abstain from the bombardment of objectives in populated areas; even though those objectives may [be] . . . perfectly legitimate in themselves'.[31] Later in the month, it was also agreed that valuable aircraft, especially Blenheims, must not be risked in operations which were not vital to Britain's security,[32] an indication that the Air Staff were not wholly blind to Bomber Command's shortcomings.

These two factors, humanitarian and unpreparedness, were to restrict Bomber Command's scope of action severely, but at least they enabled the Government to reassure President Roosevelt at the outbreak of war that it had no intention of bombing civilians.

Harris missed this final period of heart-searching. After a short trip to the States to buy aircraft (Hudsons and Harvards) he was posted back to the Middle East, this time as AOC Palestine and TransJordan. Here he spent a frustrating year supporting the Army which had been coping with the Arab Rebellion since 1936. The only bright spot was that he was able to work for a short time with Montgomery, before the latter was invalided home. Harris too, would suffer this fate in summer 1939, when he developed an ulcer, but with war clouds looming, and the one 'faintest gleam of daylight' shining through them being the prospect of 'the bomber offensive', which he was certain would come 'after older methods had failed',[33] he was clearly pleased to get back to England, and quickly recovered.

CHAPTER TWO

THE BOMBER OFFENSIVE IS BORN

. . . there is one thing that will bring him . . . down and that is an absolutely devastating exterminating attack by very heavy bombers from this country upon the Nazi homeland. We must be able to overwhelm them by this means, without which I do not see a way through. – Churchill

EARLY FRUSTRATIONS

When Britain declared war on 3 September 1939, Bomber Command could boast 33 operational squadrons, of which ten, equipped with the Fairey Battle, were deployed to France as the Advanced Air Striking Force (AASF) to provide air support to the Allied forces in the event of a German invasion. Indeed, they and two squadrons of Hurricanes, also part of AASF, flew across on the day before the outbreak of war. A little later, the Air Component of the British Expeditionary Force (BEF), which included four squadrons of Blenheims, was also sent to the Continent. This left Bomber Command with six operational and one reserve squadrons of Blenheims (No 2 Group), six operational and two reserve of Wellingtons (No 3 Group), five operational and one reserve of Whitleys (No 4 Group) and six operational and two reserve of Hampdens (No 5 Group). To back these up were thirteen 'Group Pool' or training squadrons controlled by No 6 Group from Abingdon. Harris was to assume command of No 5 Group on 14 September.

Since almost all the bombing plans drawn up before the war were either set in the air counter-offensive scenario or had inherent dangers of casualties among civilians, Bomber Command initially had little scope in which to try out its theories of strategic bombing. Indeed, the only generally acceptable plan was WA7(b) which called for an attack on the naval base at Wilhelmshaven, or at least the shipping there. Consequently, one hour after Britain found herself in a state of war with Germany, a 139 Squadron Blenheim IV took off from RAF Wyton to check on the shipping in the Schillig Roads, and this marked the RAF's first operational sortie of the war. Unfortunately its radio froze up and it was unable to transmit any information. By the time it had landed back at base it was too late to mount an attack that day. Nevertheless, that night saw the first of what would be Bomber Command's 'stock in trade' during the Phoney War when the Whitleys from 51 and 58 Squadrons took off from Leconfield and dropped 13 tons of propaganda leaflets over the Ruhr, Bremen and Hamburg, with two aircraft having to make forced landings in France. These operations were codenamed NICKEL and the name stuck throughout the war. Next day saw further attempts to attack ships in the Schillig Roads: a raid by fifteen Blenheims of 107, 110 and 139 Squadrons, another by six Hampdens of 83 Squadron and then a third, this time on the entrance to the Kiel Canal, by Wellingtons of 9 and 149 Squadrons.

These three raids illustrated only too clearly how singularly ill-equipped Bomber Command was to mount a concerted bombing campaign. Bad weather forced the Blenheims to go in at low level, and five out of the ten which managed to get to the target were shot down by the flak defences, while the survivors had the frustration of seeing their 500lb bombs, set with 11½-second delay fuses, bounce harmlessly off the ships. The five aircraft from 139 Squadron never even found the target, and neither did the Hampdens. Worse still, none of the crews of the latter, as one of their number later wrote,[1] had ever taken off with a full bomb-load of 2,000 pounds and they doubted if the Hampden would actually get into the air. The Wellingtons, too, although they found the target, suffered two shot down in exchange for one possible hit on a ship. Nevertheless, making the best of it, the Ministry of Information announced that: 'Pilots and crews of the aircraft which took part in the successful attack on the German naval bases of Wilhelmshaven and Brunsbuttel . . . returned to their bases in fine fettle'. The Germans, on the other hand, claimed that thirty bombers had been shot down while attacking 'the civilian populations of several seaside towns in the North Sea areas' and both Goebbels and Goering warned of reprisal raids. This was enough to make the Air Ministry and Admiralty decide that in future only ships actually at sea would be attacked. This, then, was the situation when Harris arrived at Grantham to take over command of No 5 Group and it is hardly surprising that he later recorded that his mood was such that he had 'in the course of his lifetime rarely been so depressed'.[2]

In effect, these early disasters were the direct consequence of the expansion policies of the previous years. The policy of quantitative bomber parity with Germany had left Bomber Command with interim aircraft types inadequate for the role they were expected to perform. Indeed, although 1936 had seen the Air Ministry finally decide that it needed heavy bombers, these would not appear until 1941, and the declaration of war, so far as Bomber Command was concerned, had come at least eighteen months too early. Yet, it was not just the aircraft, but the overall efficiency of the crews that manned them and the ancillary equipment which were also of doubtful quality.

Almost as soon as Sir Edgar Ludlow-Hewitt assumed office as AOCinC Bomber Command in 1937, he began to warn the Air Ministry that rapid expansion would be to the detriment of efficiency. Individual aircrew members were not given sufficient training in the specialist tasks which they were expected to perform, especially navigation, air gunnery and bomb-aiming. With regard to the first, main responsibility for this was placed in the hands of the Air Observer who was expected to perform other tasks as well, yet was often of low, non-commissioned rank. It took Sir Edgar a year to get the Air Ministry to agree that observers should undergo a ten-week navigation course, the Air Ministry believing that this training could be done just as well within the squadrons, besides which, such a long course would slow down the rate of observers joining squadrons to the detriment of expansion. Consequently, in August 1939 it was found that more than 40 per cent of bomber crews were unable to find a target in a friendly city in broad daylight.[3]

The main system of navigation in use was 'dead reckoning'. The navigator plotted the aircraft's speed and course and then applied an estimated wind velocity in order to fix the aircraft's position in relation to the ground. From this he could work out the required course and speed in order to arrive over the target, but compasses and air speed indicators were still primitive and inaccurate. Combine this with the fact that pilots, especially if they were inexperienced or the weather was unsettled, often were not able to maintain a steady course and speed, and some idea of the difficulty of navigating becomes apparent. Of course, when flying below cloud, it was possible to use prominent landmarks, but during that first winter of the war, when cloud and fog were much in evidence, this often meant flying very low and, when over enemy territory, making oneself very vulnerable to flak and fighters. Above cloud, two additional techniques could be employed. The first was to use radio bearings from ground stations to the aircraft or vice versa, with the danger of betraying one's position to an ever-alert enemy, or one could use astro-navigation. In ideal conditions a skilled navigator could plot his position from a three star fix in about twenty minutes, but this was only accurate to within ten miles and, of course, the position was some twenty minutes late. It is understandable why in those early days so many aircraft failed to find the target.

At the outbreak of war, Bomber Command had three types of bombs: the 500lb GP high explosive (HE), the 250lb GP HE and the 40lb GP. All these were thick cased and streamlined, and relied on penetration and fragmentation for their effect, with the last named being considered as specifically an anti-personnel bomb. In order to aim them, the Course-Setting Bombsight was used, which had been developed as early as 1918, and relied on the aircraft flying on a straight and level course over the target, which was not easy to do in the face of flak. Combine this with the fact that only on the Whitley was a bomb-load of 4,000 pounds exceeded and it becomes apparent that accuracy and effect were likely to be low.

On the day that Harris took over command of No 5 Group a temporary halt was called to all bomber operations, which, after the abortive anti-shipping operations of 4 September, had been confined to NICKEL operations, to review progress this far. Many, including Harris, whose comment was that 'the only thing' which NICKELS achieved 'was largely to supply the Continent's requirements for toilet paper for the five long years of war',[4] questioned their value. However, it was decided to continue them, not so much for their propaganda value, but as a vehicle for reconnaissance of Germany and improving operational standards. For the time being, No 4 Group concentrated on these, with No 2 Group's Blenheims being mainly involved in photographic reconnaissance. The remaining groups were left with anti-shipping operations, which proved a frustrating business, as No 5 Group's Operations Record Book (ORB) shows.[5] Crews stood by for operations as a result of reports, often spurious, of enemy shipping in the North Sea, only to be stood down again at the last moment. Despite the problems of weather, however, Harris did institute a training programme, with emphasis on long-distance flying in preparation for the raids over Germany which he was confident would come.

Perhaps nothing illustrates the frustrations of this period more than an operation mounted by No 5 Group in late November. The German pocket battleship *Deutschland* was reported to have left Kiel and to be headed for the open waters off the Norwegian coast. As soon as it was light, 48 Hampdens, led by Wing Commander Sheen of 49 Squadron, took off to attack her. They reached the target area in two hours, but five hours' search revealed no signs of the ship and they turned for home, flying into an almost gale force head wind. After some hours, with no land in sight, it became clear that they were on the wrong course, the leading navigator being convinced that they were heading out into the Atlantic. Consequently they turned south-east, and the navigator came up with a position over the North Sea. They had now been flying for more than ten hours and fuel was very low, but fortuitously they came across a trawler, which indicated the direction of land and they eventually identified the Royal Naval Air Station at Montrose. They all got down safely, apart from one aircraft which ran out of fuel and crashed in a graveyard some three miles short of the runway, fortunately without casualties.

Of particular concern to Harris was the Hampden itself. Apart from the very cramped crew conditions, which hastened fatigue on long flights, the armament was inadequate, consisting of one fixed Vickers 0.303in firing straight ahead and three manually-operated Lewis guns. Their positioning left a number of blind spots and Harris, having failed to obtain any satisfaction through official channels, eventually took the law into his own hands and approached the family firm of Alfred Rose & Sons in Gainsborough, and arranged for them to manufacture twin Vickers mounts to take the place of the two rear-firing Lewis guns. He was also worried about the lack of self-sealing fuel tanks, something which applied to all bombers, even though this type of tank was used elsewhere. In a letter to Sir Edgar Ludlow-Hewitt dated 21 October 1939 he showed that it would be a comparatively simple task to modify existing aircraft[6] and they were eventually installed in all aircraft. However, neither this nor the armament problems were overcome in time to avoid a further series of setbacks in December 1939.

Apart from the Whitley, all bomber types were primarily for use by day, and the experiences of the First World War had convinced the Air Ministry that, provided the bombers maintained formation and coordinated their defensive fire, they could avoid being shot down by enemy fighters. The chance to prove this came at the beginning of December with an improvement in the weather and the fact that there was a growing concentration of naval shipping at Kiel. Urged on by Winston Churchill, First Lord of the Admiralty, 24 Wellingtons from 38, 115 and 149 Squadrons set out on 3 December to attack. Two aircraft were damaged by flak on the approach, but all bombed from 8,000 feet unscathed, although no hits were observed on the ships. The bombers were now attacked by Me 109s and 110s from astern. These attacks were driven off, and all returned safely, thus seeming to vindicate the concept. Then, on the 14th, twelve Wellingtons of 99 Squadron took off to attack the cruisers *Nurnberg* and *Leipzig*, reported badly damaged in the Jade Estuary after a British submarine attack. In appalling visibility, with the cloud base down to below 1,000 feet, the Wellingtons were forced to fly at 600 feet. On approaching the target they were fired at by flak, which scored several hits, and then attacked by Me 109s, which accounted for five bombers, with a sixth crashing on return to England. One German fighter was shot down. At the time, it was believed that it was flak rather than fighters which had caused the damage. As Air Commodore Bottomley, Senior Air Staff Officer (SASO) at HQ Bomber Command, commented:

> It is now by no means certain that enemy fighters did in fact succeed in shooting down any of the Wellingtons. Considering that enemy aircraft made most determined and continuous attacks for twenty-six minutes on the formation, the failure of the enemy must be ascribed to good formation flying. The maintenance of tight, unshaken formations in the face of the most powerful enemy actions is the test of fighting force efficiency and morale. In our Service it is the equivalent of the old 'Thin Red Line' or the 'Shoulder to Shoulder' of Cromwell's Ironsides.[7]

Although this was written on 28 December, events on the 18th must have raised doubts in his mind. On that day 24 Wellingtons of 9, 37 and 149 Squadrons were ordered to patrol Schillig Roads and surrounding areas and to attack shipping. In order to minimise the risk from flak, they were given a minimum bombing height of 10,000 feet. In a cloudless sky they set course and, although two aircraft returned early with engine trouble, found the target area without difficulty. However, German Freya radars, still in the experimental stage, had picked them up, and the fighter operations room at Jever was warned. Six Me 109s of 10/JG 26 under Johannes Steinhoff, later to become a renowned fighter ace, took off and intercepted the bombers near Wilhelmshaven. Two were immediately shot down and there was then a lull as the bombers passed through heavy flak from the naval base. Then, joined by further Me 109s and some Me 110s, the attacks were resumed, and within a few minutes ten more Wellingtons had been shot down, albeit at a cost of two Me 109s and several other fighters damaged. Air Vice-Marshal Baldwin, AOC No 3 Group, concluded that the main causes of this disaster were the lack of self-sealing tanks and the fact that the aircraft had not maintained formation. The German conclusion was that formation flying made it easier for the fighters to attack.

Indeed, on that same day, there had been much discussion on formations at a Group Commanders' Conference held at HQ Bomber Command, with Harris advocating the basic unit as being six aircraft (two sections of three each), and the general conclusion being drawn that 24 aircraft was the maximum that could be sent against a single target in view of the problems of control. Nevertheless, it is significant that at this same conference Ludlow-Hewitt stressed the importance of all groups devoting attention to night flying training. The loss of fifty per cent of the attacking force on that day, set against the need to conserve his limited resources for the main bombing campaign which would take place when the Germans invaded the Low Countries, saw the emphasis switch from day to night operations.[8]

THE SWITCH TO NIGHT BOMBING

In terms of Allied bombing operations, in the event of a German attack in the West, the original British view was that a daylight bomber offensive should be launched against the Ruhr, even though this might lead to heavy civilian casualties and might consequently have to be justified by the Germans inflicting such casualties on Allied populations beforehand. The French, however, made their feelings only too clear when Air Vice-Marshal Evill discussed the plan with General Gamelin, the Supreme Commander, and General Vuillemin, head of the French Air Force, on 23 October. The French regarded the bomber as a defensive weapon, to be used merely for support of ground forces, and felt that an attack on the Ruhr would lead to German retaliation on French industry, which they considered as being the more vulnerable. Another nail in the coffin for this plan came from Ludlow-Hewitt himself as a result of the December disasters, and in an appreciation dated 28 January 1940 he urged the Air Staff to think again, arguing that to attack the Ruhr by day was risking a 50 per cent loss rate. The Chief of the Air Staff, Sir Cyril Newall, consequently ruled at a conference in February that the Ruhr attack would only be mounted if the situation on the ground were critical, and that alternative plans should be considered.

The most prominent among these was oil, which along with the Ruhr offensive, had made up Plan WA5. The Directorate of Plans at the Air Ministry had considered the merits of this in a paper dated 16 October 1939, and had concluded that it had significant attractions over the Ruhr in that oil refineries tended to be away from centres of population. One advantage of this was that it would cause less bitterness among the civilian population – an important factor if at some stage in the future Britain found herself alongside Germany in a war against Russia. Also, a significant impact on the German economy would be achieved very much more quickly than by an attack on the Ruhr, which the paper viewed as relying 'for a rapid success largely on *moral** effect'.[9] Another type of target was transportation, which again had been considered before the war under WA4. Here, railways seemed particularly vulnerable since, as a report dated 6 November 1939 argued, trains were important to Germany because of her supposedly poor road system, and marshalling yards made especially good targets.[10] The Ministry of Economic Warfare (MEW) also supported this view.

Whichever plan was decided on, Ludlow-Hewitt became more and more convinced that Bomber Command would have to carry it

*Author's italics.

out by night in order to make his bombers less vulnerable to flak and fighters, and by the beginning of March priority in training was given over to precision bombing by night. So far as protection was concerned, he could draw comfort in the results of the NICKEL sorties. Up until the end of March 1940, 481 night sorties resulted in only ten aircraft failing to return, while during the same period 30 of 226 had failed to return from daylight sorties. This represented a loss rate of just over 2 per cent against some 13 per cent by day.[11] As for identifying targets by night, 'dry runs' undertaken during NICKEL raids seemed to indicate that the average crew, using astro-navigation, could get to within ten miles of the target, where it was assumed that they could pick up a prominent landmark to get themselves to the actual target. Except in perfect weather, however, it was acknowledged that some form of artificial illumination of the target would be required, but the existing 4.5in flare was inadequate, and Bomber Command had been pressing the Air Ministry for improved illuminating equipment since September 1938, without success. Bomb-aiming was not seen as a problem.[12]

The crews themselves found these early NICKEL operations a frustrating business:

> At 10,000 feet and several hours after take-off we were flying blind in miserable weather; the aircraft heating system had gone unserviceable, and, to make matters worse, Albert had dejectedly passed up a message to say that lightning which had struck the aircraft had burnt out the wireless installation in the process.
>
> The weather cleared momentarily as we turned south-east to cross into Germany, and there, just ahead, could be seen faintly silhouetted in the moon's filtered light row upon row of wharves and jetties of a great town which could be none other than Hamburg, our first objective. Passing directly over the built-up areas, we were puzzled by the flashes and blinking lights from the otherwise darkened city, but were quickly enlightened by the telltale puffs of black smoke and the thud of bursting flak – some of it much too close for comfort. Feeling our bundles of leaflets to be a quite inadequate response to such a warm but unfriendly welcome, we hurried on towards the target area and were soon releasing our propaganda leaflets with the thought that this indeed was a most peculiar war.[13]

The opportunity actually to test Bomber Command's ability to bomb accurately at night came soon. On the night of 16 March 1940, the Luftwaffe carried out an attack against the Fleet at Scapa Flow, and one civilian on the island of Hoy was killed. The War Cabinet decided that retaliation must take place and three nights later a force of thirty Whitleys and twenty Hampdens was sent to attack the German seaplane base at Hornum on the island of Sylt in the North Sea. Forty-one aircraft claimed to have identified the target, which was attacked with a mixture of HE and incendiaries. Certainly it was a bright moonlit night. As was the practice in those days, each crew was given much latitude as to when they set off and were responsible for finding their own way to the target – formation flying was a daylight tactic only. However, photographic reconaissance carried out on 6 April revealed no signs of damage, and it was assumed that this had either been repaired or hidden. Nevertheless, there was clearly some disquiet at HQ Bomber Command as the conclusion of the raid report indicated:

> The operation does not confirm that, as a general rule, the average crews of our heavy bombers can identify targets at night, even under the best conditions, nor does it prove that the average crew can bomb industrial or other enemy targets at night . . . Our general opinion is that under war conditions the average crew of a night bomber could not be relied on to identify and attack targets at night except under the very best conditions of visibility, even when the target is on the coast or on a large river like the Rhine. Under the latter conditions about 50% of the average crews might be expected to find and bomb the right target in good visibility; if the target has no conspicuous aids to its location, very few inexperienced crews would be likely to find it under any conditions.[14]

It would seem therefore that the pre-war policy of rapid expansion in terms of numbers of aircraft at the expense of all else was coming home to roost, with a force that was unable to protect itself by day or to bomb accurately at night. Three days before the photographic reconnaissance of Sylt, however, Ludlow-Hewitt had been replaced by Portal as AOCinC. Ludlow-Hewitt's views on the need to balance expansion with proper training and his realisation of the operational vulnerabilities and limitations of the force under his command had for long, in the eyes of the Air Staff, made him an uncomfortable bedfellow. Harris had held Ludlow-Hewitt in high esteem, and regarded his dismissal as 'a disaster, a catastrophe'.[15]

Before more thought could be given as to how Bomber Command should be employed, the ill-fated Norwegian campaign broke out and the Command found itself engaged once more on anti-shipping strikes and attacks on Norwegian airfields used by the Germans. In order to be able to carry a reasonable bomb-load these operations had to be mounted from bases in northern Scotland, and many were made in daylight. The weather made navigation difficult and what successes there were were few and far between. One particular disaster struck the No 5 Group Hampdens on 12 April. The day before, because of the very clear weather, Bomber Command had refused to sanction a daylight raid on enemy shipping at Christiansand, but on the 12th, as a result of reports that enemy capital ships were heading south across the Skagerrak, No 3 and No 5 Groups were ordered to locate and attack them. One formation of twelve Hampdens had two-thirds of its number shot down by fighters – despite Harris's efforts the defensive fire blind spots could not be eradicated – and from then on the Hampden was retained for night work only. However, it immediately collected another and what would become an increasingly important role – minelaying. Indeed, the first of these operations, known as GARDENING, was carried out by fifteen Hampdens from 44, 49, 50, 61 and 144 Squadrons on the night of 13/14 April, when they laid mines off the Danish coast. Harris who had urged the development of aerially delivered mines before the war and hence had a special interest in this type of attack, called it 'the one really bright spot in No 5 Group's operations' at this time.[16] Yet, the sands of time were now running out.

At 0530 hours on Friday 10 May the long-awaited German invasion of the Low Countries began. Two and a half hours later, at an emergency Cabinet meeting, the question of how the strategic bombing force should be used was discussed. It could either strike immediately at targets in Germany or be held back until the land battle had reached a critical juncture. In the end it was thought that: 'it would be preferable not to begin bombing operations in the Ruhr until we have definite news that the Germans have attacked targets . . . which would cause casualties to civilians'. In the meantime operations would be confined to west of the Rhine.[17] At 1130 hours the Cabinet met again and bombing policy was the main item on the agenda. A report from the British Ambassador at The Hague that a bomb had just dropped 600 yards from his residence and another from the Belgians that Brussels, in spite of being an open town, had been bombed, drew agreement from those present that 'we should be justified in starting bombing operations on military targets in the Ruhr this evening'. Nevertheless, a final decision would be deferred until that afternoon.[18] This, however, did not happen, for at the third Cabinet meeting that day Chamberlain tendered his resignation, Churchill took over, and it would be another five days before the decision was finally made. In the meantime the AASF and Air Component Blenheims and Battles, suffered severely in daylight operations in support of the ground forces, while on the night of the 10th, 36 Wellingtons raided Waalhaven aerodrome and eighty Whitleys attacked lines of communication in the Geldern, Goch, Aldekerk, Rees and Wesel areas – the first raid on mainland Germany. This was followed the next night by Whitley and Hampden sorties against communications in the München-Gladbach area. On the 14th, the Germans bombed Rotterdam, albeit after a breakdown in communications had prevented the attack being stopped. The War Cabinet, however, were more concerned about the German breakthrough across the Meuse, and it was not until the next morning that the bombing question was finally faced. Sir Archibald Sinclair, the newly appointed Secretary of State for Air argued:

The experience of the past few days in France points to the fact that, at the present rate, it will be extremely difficult for the RAF to maintain its present effort in support of the land battles by daylight bombing operations. . . The extent to which the Army can be supported in the immediate battle zone by night bombing is very limited. I therefore think that the right course will be to extend the activities of our long-range night bombers.

This view was supported by Dowding, AOCinC Fighter Command, who was present to defend his case for not sending more fighter squadrons to France. Churchill, however, expressed concern over the likely reaction of neutral countries, especially the USA, but Halifax also argued for an extension of Bomber Command's activities, and the decision to launch attacks east of the Rhine was taken.[19] That night 99 bombers took off for Hamburg and the Ruhr to mark the start of a campaign which would continue virtually unceasingly for almost five long years.

During the first month of this, the first phase of the strategic bombing campaign, Bomber Command, up to 15 June, launched 27 attacks against precision targets in Germany, mainly marshalling yards and oil installations. One striking aspect was the low loss rate, with only just 1 per cent of aircraft missing in more than 4,000 night sorties in May and June.[20] Furthermore, a remarkably high percentage of crews claimed to have successfully identified the target and dropped their bombs on it. Indeed, Harris in a report on the operations of No 5 Group during the second half of May claimed that 'the standard of navigation achieved has improved considerably as crews have gained experience, and the majority of aircraft can be expected to arrive within a few miles of their objective on D.R. [Dead Reckoning] and W/T [Wireless Telegraphy].' AOC No 4 Group, Air Commodore Coningham, agreed with him, and only AOC No 3 Group considered that 'Grave limitations are placed on night bombing of specific targets, particularly on moonless nights, owing to inexperience of pilots and navigators in map reading by night.'[21] Even so, it was not that Air Vice-Marshal Baldwin doubted that they would ever have the ability to do so, but merely that more experience was needed. Consequently, despite earlier misgivings, there was a generally held belief that Bomber Command could operate more effectively by night against precision targets. Further encouragement, too, had been gained from a spurious Intelligence report sent ten days after the 15 May raid, stating that it had caused consternation among the higher Nazi echelons, and this was followed by a succession of others in the same vein.

In the middle of July, with the threat of invasion building up, Bomber Command began to turn its attention to the German preparations for this, especially the barges being collected in the

Channel ports. The attacks on Germany continued in spite of this, but Portal was being ordered to cover a perplexing number of targets. On 4 July he was told to concentrate on German ports and shipping, on the 13th the aircraft industry, oil and communications, and then eleven days later aluminium plants were added. On the 16th, he complained that he was being asked to do too much, and pointed out that some of the specific targets which he had been given were hard to find, but the Air Staff thought him unduly pessimistic and ignored his pleas. Nevertheless, there was another factor which was causing concern: 'By the beginning of July most of the bomber crews were just about all in. Lack of sleep night after night has a cumulative effect, and soon tempers began to get frayed and quarrels were picked on the slightest pretext.'[22] This was something of which Harris himself was very aware. In contrast with his practice of later years, he was constantly visiting his squadrons and talking to the crews, whom he got to know very well and for whom he had a deep affection. His only proviso was that if he could possibly avoid it, he never spent a night away from home. In his Group report for the first half of June, he described how he was tackling the problem:

> The intensity of operational effort has increased, but there have been no increases in crews. When conditions of light and weather and the locality and type of the target make it difficult to find, I prefer to conserve crews, and latterly I have introduced a system whereby each crew normally has at least two nights rest between flights. Weather is apt to run in phases. When weather is good, or when the moon is of most value, it is preferable to take advantage by increasing the intensity of operations. It is a feasible proposition to call for an extra effort from crews if they are assured of consideration when occasions are not so favourable.[23]

The problem was that the fine summer of 1940, and the demands being placed on the Command meant that Harris's plan had little chance of being allowed to be put into operation. It must be remembered, too, that at this stage in the war the length of a tour had not been laid down, and air crews were only relieved on an individual basis when it was considered that they were 'war weary' and then only after Commanding Officers had consulted unit Medical Officers.[24] However, with replacements still in short supply, the high calibre and dedication of the crews meant that for the most part they just carried on until they were shot down.

With the opening of the Battle of Britain, attention naturally turned to the desperate efforts of Fighter Command, under Dowding's cool leadership, to prevent the Germans gaining air superiority over southern England. Bomber Command made a significant contribution in its successful campaign against the barges, and there were also some spectacular individual operations.

One of these was a No 5 Group attack mounted on the night of 12 August against the Dortmund-Ems Canal aqueduct over the River Ems. Five Hampdens from 49 and 83 Squadrons were selected for the attack, and they were carrying the 1,000lb bomb, which was making its operational début. Two were shot down and a further two badly damaged on the approach to the target, which was heavily defended. The final aircraft, skippered by Flight Lieutenant R. A. B. Learoyd, although hit repeatedly by flak, went into the attack at 150 feet and photographic reconnaissance later showed that he had succeeded in demolishing the aqueduct with his bomb. A week later he was awarded Bomber Command's first VC of the war, and a short time later, No 5 Group gained its second VC when Sergeant Hannah of 83 Squadron bravely fought a fire in his aircraft while on a barge attack at Antwerp. But, while Flight Lieutenant Learoyd's exploit demonstrated the Command's capability at precision bombing, albeit at a cost, a more significant event took place on the night of 25 August. The previous night the Luftwaffe had bombed London in error, although this was not known at the time. Churchill wanted revenge and insisted on a reprisal raid the following night. Consequently 81 aircraft from Nos 3, 4, and 5 Groups were sent against industrial targets on the outskirts of Berlin. The cloud was thick and only 29 crews claimed to have bombed the target, but the cloud did guard them from the heavy flak protecting the city and none was shot down. No civilians were injured and damage was negligible, but at least it made nonsense of Goering's boast that no enemy aircraft would ever bomb the capital.

THE COMING OF AREA BOMBING

It was now becoming clear, however, that Churchill had a slightly different view from that of the Air Staff as to how Bomber Command should be used. As early as 8 July, in a minute to Lord Beaverbrook, now Minister for Aircraft Production, he wrote:

> The blockade is broken and Hitler has Asia and probably Africa to draw from. Should he be repulsed here or not try invasion, he will recoil eastward, and we have nothing to stop him. But there is one thing that will bring him back and bring him down and that is an absolutely devastating exterminating attack by very heavy bombers from this country upon the Nazi homeland. We must be able to overwhelm them by this means, without which I do not see a way through.[25]

He wanted attacks on a wide range of cities, but Sir Richard Peirse, Vice-Chief of the Air Staff (VCAS) and soon to take over Bomber Command, told him: 'I think that there is little doubt that the reason for the effectiveness of our night bombing is that it is planned; and relentless until a particular target is knocked out or dislocated.'[26] Thus, when Portal was issued with a new directive on 21 September, the disruption of German oil supplies remained the top priority, with communications as the next, and the German aircraft industry, submarines and anti-invasion measures as secondary objectives. However, as a sop to the Prime Minister, Berlin, although it contained no targets connected with the above objectives, was included with the aim of causing 'the greatest possible disturbance and dislocation both to the industrial activities and to the *civil** population in the area'.[27] The question then of the traditional air power theorists' view that wars could be won by attacks on civilians was beginning to come into the open. Indeed, Portal himself had suggested in a minute dated 11 September that any indiscriminate attack on a British town should be followed by a retaliatory attack on a German one, with a wireless warning given. If this were not acceptable, a town like Essen should be chosen since it 'can for practical purposes be regarded as a military objective'. He followed this up with a canvass of views on the concept of diverting the attack from the enemy's means to his will to wage war. Clearly, Churchill was creeping towards this. In a minute to Sinclair dated 20 October, he wrote:

> On no account should the limited Bomber Force be diverted from accurate bombing of military objectives in Germany. But it is [*sic*-is it] not possible to organise a Second Line Bomber Force which, especially in the dark of the moon, would discharge bombs from a considerable and safe height upon the nearest built-up areas of Germany which contain military targets in abundance [?][28]

Then, at a War Cabinet meeting held ten days later, he crystallised his ideas even more clearly, stating that:

> . . . whilst we should adhere to the rule that our objectives should be military targets, at the same time the civilian population around the target areas must be made to feel the weight of the war. He regarded this as a somewhat broader interpretation of our present policy, and not as any fundamental change.[29]

At this time, however, there were changes in important RAF posts, the chief of which would suit Churchill's cause.

On 25 October 'Peter' Portal took over as Chief of the Air Staff (CAS), after Sir Richard Peirse had succeeded him as AOCinC Bomber Command. Harris's time, too, at No 5 Group was drawing to a close, but he bombarded his new superior mercilessly with suggestions, criticisms and comments. On 11 October, with Peirse hardly in the chair, he wrote complaining about the lack of publicity which Bomber Command was getting for its efforts:

> I am absolutely certain that both for the purpose of our war crews and still more for the heart of the nation as a whole, the most drastic steps are necessary to overhaul the Air Ministry Publicity Department and to get the stuff put out and

*Author's italics.

put across properly. Maybe the Department themselves have been bombed, are
all since dead and nobody's noticed it. Naturally enough, nobody would!

This was to be one of his constant themes throughout the war. On
the 17th, he wrote complaining about the 'IMP'* mine, pointing
out that it was effective when dropped at sea, but useless as a blast
weapon over land. Three days later he followed this with a missive
asking about progress at the Royal Aircraft Establishment (RAE)
Farnborough on investigations into an automatic navigator, which
had been developed pre-war and rescued from obscurity by Harris.
On the 22nd, it was a suggestion that aircraft involved in operations
against the Italian mainland should use Malta as a temporary base,
and it is interesting to note that he now believed in Churchill's 'eye
for an eye' principle – 'The day that Italian aircraft bomb London
we should bomb Rome.' Peirse in his reply said: 'I sincerely hope
and expect that Rome will be the first objective.' On 1 November he
was considering means of improving operational effort, suggesting
that tired crews could not all be absorbed by the Operational
Training Units (OTU) and that they should go to the Reserve
Squadrons and be used on GARDENING operations with not more
than one sortie per week, thereby allowing the operational
squadrons to concentrate on the bombing of Germany. He was also
concerned at experienced aircrew being posted outside the
Command and therefore being permanently lost to it. Apart from
the fact that the Reserve Squadrons had for some time now become
fully operational, and were, in effect, no more, the growing
demands of the training organisation made Harris's plan impossible to carry out. One interesting point about this letter was his
view that 'some 200 hours of operational flying, representing
between 30 and 35 sorties, is the maximum which can be expected
from a member of a crew prior to a long rest'. This may well have
prompted the Air Ministry to send out a letter to all Commands,
dated 29 November, asking for their views on the establishment of
fixed tour lengths.[30] On 4 November the subject was again aircrew,
and Harris wanted operational aircrew to have some form of distinguishing badge – 'say, a small star to be worn on the sleeve' – with,
perhaps additional marks for every one hundred hours' operational
flying. 'I think that it is only just to our fighting crews that they
should be entitled to some form of distinguishing mark and that it
would be, in fact, well earned'.[31] Three weeks later, however,
Harris found himself posted to the Air Ministry as Deputy Chief of

*The most common sea mine used during the war was the A Mark 1–4 MAGNUM which weighed 2,000 pounds and
contained some 750 pounds of explosives. The A Mark 5 or IMP was introduced in 1940 and was designed for any
aircraft capable of carrying a 1,000lb bomb. The A Mark 1–4 was replaced by the A Mark 6 MAGNUM in 1944 at
which time the IMP was succeeded by the A Mark 7 TIM. All were released by parachute. The IMP was used by
Flight Lieutenant Learoyd when he attacked the Dortmund-Ems Canal aqueduct.

the Air Staff (DCAS). His successes with No 5 Group had already been recognised by his being made a CB in July, but the prospect of returning to the Air Ministry 'horrified' him.[32]

Portal's arrival as CAS was marked by a fresh directive to Bomber Command. On 15 September came the climax of the Battle of Britain, but also two daylight raids on London by the Luftwaffe. From then on the Luftwaffe attacked the city by night. This prompted further raids on Berlin, and the 21 September directive laid down that, from experience gained from the raids on London, electricity and gas plants were to be the main targets as 'not only the quickest but most lasting and effective means of dislocating the life of the community'. Portal's directive took the campaign a stage farther, and reflected both his and Churchill's views on the wholesale bombing of German cities. While oil remained a prime target on nights when visibility was good enough to permit precision bombing, and aluminium plants and component factories were to continue to receive attention, subsidiary attacks were to include a continuation of attacks on northern Italy (these had been taking place spasmodically since mid June) and marshalling yards, as well as submarine pens and airfields in northern France. Most significant, however, was the suggestion that 20–30 towns and cities be selected as targets which Portal said should have the 'primary aim of causing very heavy material destruction which will demonstrate to the enemy the power and severity of air bombardment and the hardship and dislocation which will result from it'.[33] The Air Staff also felt that Bomber Command must strive for a greater concentration of effort against oil and morale. Peirse, when asked to comment on the directive, took a more sanguine attitude. His limited resources and his doubts, which went against the generally held view at the time on the ability of crews to find the target, caused him to feel that he was being asked to do too much, but when a revised directive was issued on 30 October it was clear that his objections had been ignored. Indeed, it spoke of the need to adopt the German technique of fire-raising attacks, with follow-up sorties focussing 'their attacks to a large extent on the fires with a view to preventing the fire-fighting services from dealing with them and giving the fires every opportunity to spread'. As the Official History commented: 'Thus, the fiction that the bombers were attacking "military objectives" in towns was officially abandoned. This was the technique which was to become known as area bombing.'[34] It did not come into being so much through Bomber Command's inability to carry out precision bombing, for most had not recognised this as yet, but more as a conscious decision by the War Cabinet to hit back at the enemy with every means possible, fair or foul. However, in view of the desperate war situation and the fact that London was being bombed night after night, it is difficult to condemn this policy in hindsight.

Indeed, much of the rationale behind it lay in the desire for retaliation, and there was no means of knowing at the time that the Luftwaffe had not attacked non-military targets intentionally. In fact, it was this again which caused the next escalation in area bombing. On the night of 14/15 November 499 bombers raided Coventry, as part of the Luftwaffe's new plan for attacking British industrial centres outside London, and caused more than 1,400 civilian casualties, as well as untold destruction to the city. This was followed during the next few months by attacks on other industrial centres as well as a continuation of the attacks on London. Although there was an outcry from the War Cabinet and the population at large, and a demand for immediate retaliation, Churchill had become concerned about Bomber Command's losses. Although they had dropped from 3.8 per cent in July to 2.4 per cent in October, November saw a significant rise to over 4 per cent[35] and in a minute dated 17 November to Portal he wrote:

> I watch these figures [of RAF losses] every day with much concern. My diagrams show that we are not now even keeping level, and there is a marked downward turn this week, especially in the Bomber Command. Painful as it is not to be able to strike heavy blows after Coventry, yet I feel that we should for the present nurse Bomber Command a little more.[36]

This certainly echoed Peirse's views, and came the night after Bomber Command's largest raid to date, when 127 aircraft were sent against Hamburg. Consequently, it was not until a month later that a retaliatory raid for Coventry was sanctioned with an attack on Mannheim, the bombers, for the first time, being ordered to aim for the centre of the town. Preceded by Wellingtons armed with incendiaries to mark the target and manned by experienced crews, a new technique, in all, 134 aircraft took off, with 102 claiming to have successfully attacked, and the operation appeared to have been a complete success. Subsequent investigations, however, were to result in a shadow being cast over the Command's performance to date.

Up until this time, post-raid photographic reconnaissance had been mainly the province of the Blenheims of No 2 Group, although a few rather indifferent cameras were carried by aircraft of the other Groups. The Blenheims, however, often had problems in getting good pictures, and the tendency was to rely mainly on the crews' reports. On 16 November, however, Bomber Command began to receive cooperation from the Spitfire Photographic Reconnaissance Unit (PRU) and photographs taken by them after the Mannheim raid revealed how inaccurate the bombing had been.

Although it was felt that part of the cause was inaccuracy by the fire-raising Wellingtons, there is no doubt that it did send a tremor of shock through the higher echelons of Bomber Command. Bottomley, who had taken over from Harris at No 5 Group, saw these photographs as 'the first of any real evidence we have had as to the general standard of bombing accuracy which characterises our present night operations', while AOC No 4 Group admitted, 'For my part I have little idea of what the Whitleys do, and it causes me considerable anxiety.'[37] Further disquiet was generated by a report from the British Embassy in Budapest, which reported the US Naval Attaché in Berlin as stating that the raids on Berlin had caused little damage, to which the Prime Minister commented in a minute to Sinclair dated 31 December that, 'this is the most serious and precise of the many melancholy reports we are having of our bombing . . . the matter causes me a great deal of anxiety, and also the Cabinet'.[38]

The main concern was, however, as to how the bomber strength could be increased. In November 1940 Churchill had written to Portal expressing his concern at the 'pitifully small' bomb tonnage being dropped on Germany, and followed this up on 30 December with a minute to Sinclair, Portal and Beaverbrook: 'I am deeply concerned at the stagnant condition of our Bomber Force . . . I consider the rapid expansion of the Bomber Force one of the greatest military objectives now before us.'[39] In reply, CAS stated that the reason for this was 'the large-scale expansion of the training organisation, resources being diverted to Middle East and the rapid development of Fighter and Coastal Commands', and saw the solution as being in speeding up crew training and reducing Middle East reinforcement.[40] There was, however, another factor, the long-awaited introduction of the new range of 'heavies' – Short Stirling, Avro Manchester and Handley Page Halifax. These had just begun to enter squadron service, but crew conversion took time, which meant that eight squadrons had been stood down and they would not be operational again until February 1941.

Harris, who had spent the first few weeks of his new appointment 'cleansing the Augean Stable' of the Air Ministry by getting rid of waste and reducing the size of the staff so that the essential did not drown in a sea of trivia, watched the German assault on the capital. 'If we could keep ahead of the Germans, I was convinced, having watched the burning of London, that a bomber offensive of adequate weight and the right kind of bombs would, if continued for long enough, be something that no country in the world could endure.'[41] It was now a question of whether Bomber Command could make an effective start to such an offensive.

1941 - A YEAR OF DISAPPOINTMENT

Shortly after the outbreak of war, the Chief of the Air Staff had set up a special Intelligence sub-committee under Geoffrey Lloyd, the Secretary for Petroleum, in order to monitor Germany's oil stocks and the effects of bombing them. Naturally, with oil remaining the prime objective during the 1940 bombing campaign, much importance was attached to the work of this committee, and in December it concluded that a 15 per cent reduction in German oil output had been achieved and this at a cost of only 6.7 per cent of Bomber Command's total effort. So encouraging was this that Portal could not resist extrapolating these figures, and concluding that if seventeen synthetic oil plants were destroyed, the Axis would suffer a grievous blow. Working on the basis of the bomb-load required to knock out one plant for four months, he calculated that 3,400 sorties would be required every four months, and assuming nine clear nights per month, considered that this was well within Bomber Command's capabilities. Thus, he recommended to the Chiefs of Staff that oil remain the prime objective. This was endorsed by the War Cabinet, and Peirse was issued with a directive along these lines on 15 January. When weather and tactical conditions made oil plants an unsuitable target, the harassment of towns and communications was to be carried out. In other words, in spite of the revelations over bombing accuracy of December 1940, Portal had fixed his colours to the mast of precision bombing. Indeed, even a report circulated by the Photographic Interpretation Section at the end of December, which demonstrated clearly that the twin oil plants at Gelsenkirchen had suffered little damage despite attack by 296 aircraft with 262 tons of bombs, failed to move either Portal or Peirse, who was also confident that the directive would be successfully carried out. On weather alone Portal's estimate proved to be very over-optimistic and by the end of February only two attacks on oil had been carried out. One of these, on oil storage tanks in Rotterdam on the night of 10/11 February marked the operational début of the Stirling, while that for the Manchester came two weeks later. The Halifax dropped its first bombs in anger on the night of 11/12 March, but one of the six involved in this raid on Le Havre was unfortunately mistaken for an enemy aircraft and was shot down by a night fighter over Surrey on its way back.

    In the meantime, raids on German towns continued to be mounted on nights when there was no moon, but inability to find the target resulted in little damage, although Peirse and his Group Commanders remained remarkably confident. Portal, however, quickly became disenchanted and expressed 'serious doubts about the soundness of the calculations upon which our oil policy is based', and was drawn back to 'mass attacks on industrial areas'.[42] However, another problem was now threatening to engulf all else.

The twin menaces of the U-boat and the Focke-Wulf Condor were again making their presence felt in the Atlantic after a comparative lull because of bad weather during the preceding months. In February more than 350,000 tons of Allied and neutral shipping were sunk in the Atlantic alone, and this rose to more than 500,000 tons in March. The War Cabinet expressed increasing concern, and as early as 1 March Portal warned Peirse that he might have to deflect his main effort in order to ease the crisis. Eight days later Peirse was sent a fresh directive. The main aim now was to concentrate on 'defeating the attempt of the enemy to strangle our food supplies and our connection with the United States'. To this end, effort was to be directed towards submarines, aircraft and surface shipping, which was also playing a significant role in the toll of Allied merchantmen. Nevertheless, oil was to be continued to be attacked when conditions allowed, as were towns, although some like Hamburg, it was argued, were naval targets as well, representing centres of maritime industry. Indeed, the directive spoke of priority of submarine and long-range aircraft connected targets being given 'to those in Germany which lie in congested areas where the greatest moral effect was likely to result'. Peirse, however, quickly became disillusioned, especially with repeated attacks on German cruisers at Brest. On 15 April he asked Portal:

Is not too much emphasis being put on the Battle of the Atlantic and too little on the forthcoming battle for our vital industries and the staying power of our civilian population? . . . Our only defence is the counter attack in Germany. We ought now to be piling up the damage in Germany.[43]

Portal agreed, but Churchill's comment was: 'It must be recognised that the inability of Bomber Command to hit enemy cruisers in Brest constitutes a very definite failure of this arm.'[44] Harris, too, in a minute dated 1 April when commenting on the German invasion of Yugoslavia wrote:

I feel that the best support we can give . . . is from our main air offensive against Germany from this country. We have seen how our people can stand up under the German blitzkrieg so long as they know that our own counter offensive is being developed in a like manner against Germany in ever increasing strength. The same applies indirectly to our Allies and Neutrals; the cry is always for a demonstration of the power of our air offensive to sustain the resolution and will to resist.

He went on to suggest that Berlin, or a nearer target such as Hamburg or Cologne should be selected and that:

Our objective should be to do the maximum damage and destruction to the populated areas, as a demonstration of that ruthless force which we shall have to employ against Germany sooner or later if we are to get the full moral effects out of our air defensive.[45]

Trenchard, still regarded as the 'Grand Old Man' of the RAF, also gave his views to the Prime Minister in a paper dated 19 May. He believed the Germans to be particularly susceptible to bombing, and argued that attacks against ships at sea were uneconomic in that 99 per cent of bombs would miss the target, while if against German cities 99 per cent would damage German morale. Everything therefore should be concentrated to this end. He appreciated that, with casualties likely to be high, a very large bomber force would be needed, but that the other two services would have to recognise that they could contribute nothing towards victory until German morale had been broken. Churchill circulated this among the Chiefs of Staff, who, while they accepted the Trenchard premise of the vulnerability of German civilian morale to bombing, realised, as did even Portal, that it was impossible to give unconditional priority to the strategic bombing campaign and that Bomber Command could not devote all its attention to German cities alone. Instead, they recommended that, in the short term, bombing policy should be directed against transportation, coupled with morale, and that, once the bombing force was large enough, the priority should switch to morale *per se*. Eventually, after further deliberations, a fresh directive was issued to Peirse on 9 July, which continued to reflect a mixture of precision and area bombing. In the former category were nine railway targets in the Ruhr, two synthetic rubber plants (a means of striking indirectly at road transport) and the Dortmund–Ems and Ems–Weser Canals, with the idea of breaking their banks, together with mine laying on the Rhine. During non-moonlit nights, six cities would be attacked, which would represent attacks on morale. Nevertheless, there were dissenters to the switch of priority from oil to transportation, notably Lord Hankey, who bombarded the War Cabinet with minutes during June and July 1941, putting forward the case for oil. However, the Air Staff remained adamant that railway targets were easier to hit and that, especially with the German invasion of Russia, transportation attacks would 'bite' more quickly.

By this time Harris had left the Air Ministry and had been sent to the United States to head the RAF Delegation there, arriving in Washington in mid June. As a result of the secret Anglo-American Staff talks held at the beginning of the year to discuss joint strategy should the USA enter the war, and the passing of the Lend-Lease Act in March, the USA consented under what was called the 'Slessor Agreement' to supply Britain with much needed aircraft. Whereas it was the task of the British Air Commission (BAC) actually to procure these, the RAF Delegation was, as an agent of the Air Ministry, to maintain the RAF's case for aircraft, which was urgent in terms of the need to expand the strength of the RAF, both in terms of front-line and training aircraft. Because America was still technically neutral and a large section of her population wished her to remain so, the Delegation had to operate in a semi-surreptitious way. Harris, was not a stranger to the country, having been there in 1938 on a purchasing commission, but he found his task far from easy. As the chief civil servant in the Delegation wrote at the end of June,

> Harris has been very energetic since his arrival but I think he is suffering a little disillusion from the discovery, which is past experience among our predecessors that promises in high quarters do not always materialise in the face of the many obstacles to be surmounted in forcing schemes through the machine.[46]

Besides Russia's forced entry into the war, and the sending of Lord Beaverbrook and Averell Harriman on a joint UK/US mission to Moscow to establish Russian requirements for military aid, there were the expansion of the US forces and the demands of China to be catered for, as well as doubts that the US production schedules actually could be achieved. Nevertheless, Harris did have some success and, as far as Bomber Command was concerned, one manifestation of this was the delivery of twenty Boeing B-17C Fortresses in the early summer of 1941. These arrived in time to take part in daylight operations mounted against German capital ships in French ports. With the reduction in German fighter strength in France, a significant part of which had been moved to the Eastern Front, it was thought that daylight attacks by heavy bombers would prove effective against precision targets. Casualties proved high, however, with the Fortress being found to have poor armament, even though it was used at heights of more than 30,000ft. After a number had been lost, the remainder were sent in the autumn to the Middle East where they operated by night only.

As far as bombing accuracy by night was concerned, there was still disquiet, albeit outside Air Ministry circles. This culminated in Churchill's scientific adviser, Lord Cherwell, commissioning a study of raid photographs for attacks carried out during June and July. This was conducted by a member of the War Cabinet secretariat, D. M. Butt. The raids involved 6,105 sorties, with two-thirds of the crews claiming to have attacked the target. A study of some 630 associated photographs revealed, however, that only two-thirds of crews attacking French ports had dropped their bombs within five miles of the target, while over the Ruhr it was as low as one-tenth. Bomber Command remained unconvinced by the infallibility of the Butt Report, but Cherwell pointed out that, if nothing else, it emphasised 'the supreme importance of improving our navigational methods',[47] which Portal conceded. As for Churchill, he was moved to remark: 'It is an awful thought that perhaps three-quarters of our bombs go astray. If we could make it half and half we should have virtually doubled our bombing power.'[48]

Although, as will be related in the next chapter, aids to bombing accuracy were under development, they were not yet ready for service. It was clear that in the meantime precision bombing would have to be put on one side. There was, too, a growing agitation from the public at large and even some sections of the American community. Thus, William L. Shirer, one of the most prominent of the US foreign correspondents in Europe at the time, wrote in *The Daily Telegraph* in mid September 1941, that the RAF bombing of German war industries and supply depots was not enough:

> What they must do is to keep the German people in their damp, cold cellars at night, prevent them from sleeping and wear down their nerves. Those nerves are already very thin after seven years of belt-tightening Nazi mobilisation for total war. The British ought to do this every night.[49]

Further implied support came in a Chiefs of Staff memorandum dated 31 July:

> We must first destroy the foundations upon which the German war machine rests – the economy that feeds it, the morale which sustains it, the supplies which nourish it and the hopes of victory which inspire it. Then only shall we be able to return to the continent and control portions of his territory and impose our will upon the enemy . . . It is in bombing, on a scale undreamt of in the last war, that we find the new weapon on which we must principally depend for the destruction of German economic life and morale.

It set no limits on the size of the force to carry this out, apart from recognising that security of the United Kingdom was uppermost, and then went on to say that: 'After meeting the needs of our own security, therefore, we give the heavy bomber first priority in production, for only the heavy bomber can produce the conditions under which other offensive forces can be employed.'[50] In many ways it echoed Trenchard's views. As far as the size of the force was concerned, the Air Staff had for some months been basing their calculations on the figure of 4,000 heavy bombers. Using this figure as a base, and arguing again why it should be so, the Directorate of Bomber Operations at the Air Ministry spent the first part of September working on a new plan.

Instead of basing it on the theoretical capabilities of the Command, they took as their starting-point the damage done by the Luftwaffe to British cities. Using evidence provided by the RE8 Branch of the Ministry of Home Security, whose task it was to monitor the effects of the German blitz on the population, combined with studies of the physical damage caused, they concluded that a town in Germany, equatable to Coventry, could be rendered totally destroyed after six raids of equivalent intensity to that of 14 November 1940. Since it was not feasible to mount these on successive nights, it was believed, bearing in mind that to get Coventry functioning at a reasonable level again took 35 days, they would be almost as effective if spread over six months. A list of 43 German centres having populations of more than 100,000 was drawn up, and the proposal was placed in front of Portal, who supported it to the hilt, and having stated that with 4,000 bombers Germany could be forced to her knees in six months, sent it to the Prime Minister.

Churchill's view on this was summed up in a minute dated 27 September:

It is very disputable whether bombing by itself will be a decisive factor in the present war. On the contrary, all that we have learnt since the war shows that its effects, both physical and moral, are greatly exaggerated. There is no doubt that the British people have been stimulated and strengthened by the attack made upon them so far. Secondly, it seems very likely that the ground defences and night fighters will overtake the Air attack. Thirdly, in calculating the number of bombers necessary to achieve hypothetical and indefinite tasks, it should be noted that only a quarter of our bombs hit the targets. Consequently an increase in the accuracy of bombing to 100% would in fact raise our bombing to four times its strength. The most we can say is that it will be a heavy and I trust a seriously increasing annoyance.

Clearly, the Butt Report and theoretical extrapolatory calculations had disillusioned him, and he had lost much of his faith in the ability of the bomber to 'get through'. Portal, however, in his reply dated 2 October, took Churchill to task, in a way which Sinclair thought was 'masterly' and 'audacious'.[51] He reminded the Prime Minister of his previous statements on the efficacy of the bomber, as well as the Chiefs of Staff paper of 31 July. 'Production has already been planned to conform with this strategic conception and we are already committed to it.' Pointing out that it was 'hard to reconcile' the statements of policy with Churchill's minute, he said that, if Churchill now disagreed with the Chiefs of Staff view, another plan would have to be found. Bombing techniques were certain to improve, and he did not see the bomber as 'a weapon of declining importance'. Furthermore:

The effect of bombing on morale depends, I believe, on the weight of attack. Light attacks may well stimulate morale, but this can scarcely be said of attacks on the Coventry model. Judging from our own experience it is difficult to believe that any country could withstand indefinitely the scale of attack contemplated in the Air Staff Plan. Civilian casualties alone would be a major feature. German attacks on this country over the past year have caused the death or serious injury of 93,000 civilians. This result was achieved with a small fraction of the bomb load we hope to employ in 1943. Moreover, the consensus of opinion is that German morale is much more vulnerable to bombing than our own.

What concerned him most, however, was that Churchill might be changing his mind with regard to the role of the strategic bombing force:

... existing directives ... give a clear cut definition of the kind of Air Force we must create if victory is to be won. But these directives rest on the assumption that – given the necessary production – the Royal Air Force is capable by itself of carrying the disruption of Germany to a very advanced stage. If that assumption is no longer tenable we must produce a new plan. The worst plan of all would be to continue our present preparations after we had ceased to believe in the efficacy of the bomber as a war-winning weapon.

Churchill replied to this on 7 October, stressing that there was no intention not to carry out the expansion plans for the bombing force and that the air offensive over Germany would continue. 'I deprecate, however, placing unbounded confidence in this means of attack, and still more in expressing that confidence in terms of arithmetic.' In particular, he pointed to the pre-war exaggerations on the number of likely civilian casualties in the event of a German air offensive over Britain. He had, too, in reply to another Portal minute of 28 September, expressed doubts over the popularly-held belief that German morale would wilt under bombing more than the British had. In conclusion, he wrote: 'One has to do the best one can, but he is an unwise man who thinks there is any *certain* method of winning this war, or indeed any other war between equals in strength. The only plan is to persevere.'[52] Still, after a conversation with the Prime Minister, Portal was reassured, but also felt the need to demonstrate Bomber Command's potential before Churchill's doubts became more entrenched.

The result was a multiple operation mounted on the night of 7/8 November 1941. A total of 169 aircraft raided Berlin, with 21 failing to return; seven out of 55 were lost over Mannheim, nine out of 43 while mine-laying over the Ruhr, and only the 133 operating over Cologne, Ostend and Boulogne got away without casualties. Much of the problem lay with the weather, which, contrary to the Met forecast, had been appalling over Germany, and this, combined with the ever-improving German defences, had been largely responsible for the toll. Indeed, compared to 1940, although half as many sorties again had been carried out (30,608 as compared to 20,809) the loss of aircraft on operations in terms of missing and crashed had risen from 3.2 per cent to 4.1 per cent.[53] Clearly no expansion of the Command could take place with this level of casualty rate, and on the next evening Churchill summoned Peirse to Chequers. The outcome was that, despite Peirse's insistence that damage was being done to Germany, a new policy of conservation was to be implemented. The object would be 'to build-up a strong force to be available by the spring of next year'. In the meantime, operations would be concentrated on nearer targets, and 'in the normal course of operations' attacks were not to be 'pressed unduly especially if weather conditions were unfavourable or if aircraft were likely to be exposed to extreme hazard'.[54]

The year 1941 had thus been a frustrating one for Bomber Command, and to all intents and purposes it had failed to fulfil the high hopes of the earlier part of the year. As D. C. T. Bennett, now commanding 77 Squadron, wrote:

> . . . my faith in the bomber offensive had been seriously shaken. Like many other Air Force officers, I had looked at this great offensive as the only means of victory. Admittedly, America was now in the war on our side, as indeed was Russia. On the other hand, the operation of getting a foothold back on the Continent of Europe without first weakening the enormous unprecedented military might of Germany seemed to me to be quite insurmountable.[55]

Yet, with the land forces still biting at the Axis periphery, Bomber Command was still the only weapon available to strike directly at Germany. This was important, not just to prepare the way for eventual re-entry to the Continent of Europe, but also to give positive assistance to the hard-pressed Russians, who even now were struggling with their backs against the gates of Moscow. Bomber Command must therefore be made stronger and more effective, and the fact that conservation did not mean the abandonment of the strategic bombing offensive, but merely a pause for breath while gathering and increasing its strength, gave hope for the future. In addition, new technical aids to increase its capabilities were on their way, as well as a new commander equipped with the necessary forcefulness and determination to see that Bomber Command did succeed.

CHAPTER THREE

HARRIS TAKES CHARGE

Let him have it, right on the chin. – Harris

On 23 February 1942 Arthur Harris took over as Commander-in-Chief Bomber Command. Before going any further, it would be as well to describe the way in which he exercised command over an ever-expanding force during three years of war. Throughout those years only very seldom would there be a night on which Bomber Command was not involved in some type of operation, if only GARDENING or NICKELS. Consequently, every day there were plans to be made and considered, and this was done at Harris's daily 0900 hours conference. Crucial to any operation was the weather, and the meeting always opened with a forecast by Magnus Spence, Bomber Command's Chief Meteorological Officer. From this Harris could decide the area on which the forthcoming night's operations would concentrate, and Intelligence and navigation representatives would advise on enemy defences, and possible routes. Harris then detailed targets within the framework of the Air Staff's current directive, the force required and the bomb-loads. These details were then passed out to the Groups on secure tele-printer, and they had the opportunity to raise objections or ask questions by means of a secure telephone system. In the meantime, the SASO, Saundby, who knew Harris well from air control days in the Middle East, would supervise the detailed planning, out of which would appear the operation order. Once Groups had this, they would pass the details down to the stations under their control, who would in turn inform the squadrons. The latter would have already known that an operation had been scheduled for that night, and would have drawn up the necessary bomb-load. This would be put on board the aircraft once the crews had carried out their Night Flying Tests (NFT). Finally, the crews would be briefed. The fact that they would often take off less than ten hours after Harris had made his decision illustrates how impressive the mechanics of command and control were, a fact that is not often recognised.

Harris would spend the rest of his day in his office. His years of experience in the Air Ministry had given him a virtually limitless capacity for paperwork and the sheer volume he produced each day was impressive by any standards. As we have already seen, he had his own individual style of writing and an ability to express himself, which made his views on even the most technical subjects entertaining to read. He had, too, an impressive grasp of detail, both technical and non-technical, gleaned through his own experience, his reading and numerous discussions with his Staff and others. Once a week he would chair a Group Commanders' conference at High Wycombe, and similarly he would attend Portal's weekly conference in London. There were, too, a large number of other meetings to be attended, either by him or Saundby, as his deputy, and a constant stream of visitors to be seen at his headquarters – some 5,000 over the three years and more of Harris's time in command. For these reasons, he did not, contrary to the accepted practice for a successful commander and leader, show himself to his crews, yet they all felt his presence. He had been well known for his characteristics of bluntness and single-mindedness in the peacetime RAF, and those No 5 Group aircrew who had survived from his time there also recognised the value of these traits. Thus, word got round very quickly and, after the setbacks of the previous months, there was a feeling throughout the Command that Harris, with his positive approach to life, would put an end to the, at least from the perspective of the crews, idea of attacks with no clear-cut overall aim.

Harris's gruffness and cold, penetrating stare made him a difficult man to get to know well, and the names by which his crews called him, 'Chopper', 'Killer', but more usually 'Butch' (short for Butcher) seem to indicate that they felt he cared nothing for them and cold-bloodedly sent them to their deaths. This was not so. With the spectre of death always at their side, the crews had developed a fatalistic and 'sick' sense of humour, an example of which is:

> They tell us the story today in our Squadron of the mid-upper gunner who did not fire his guns while the rear gunner was blasting away at a night fighter attacking from abeam. The gunner called out, 'Why aren't you firing?' and the mid-upper gunner replied, 'What, and have to clean my guns tomorrow? Not bloody likely!'[1]

Harris was thus called by these names more in humour and as a token of their respect and, perhaps, in some cases, even admiration. In return, although it was not in his nature to wear his concern on his sleeve, Harris did care deeply for his crews, especially for the veterans or 'old lags', as he called them, who were the backbone of his command.

Apart from his determination to see the war won, Harris drew his strength very much from his family. His first marriage, which had taken place in 1916, ended in divorce, and he had married again in 1938. His second wife, Thérèse, always known as Jill, was much younger than he, but they were devoted to each other. His happiness had been completed by the birth of a daughter,* Jacqueline or Jackie, as she is called, and the two of them provided his solace during the war. It was his love for them that made him avoid spending nights away from home. The only other individuals who were close to him were the others who lived in his house, 'Springfield' at High Wycombe: his Personal Staff Officer, Personal Assistant/Pilot, and Saundby. Robert Saundby, called Sandy by his friends, was to spend longer at HQ Bomber Command than any other officer. Having taken over as SASO from Bottomley in 1940, he was to remain at High Wycombe for the remainder of the war, latterly as Deputy CinC. A mild and genial man of many hobbies, he was the very antithesis of Harris in character. He was to be very much a bridge between his Chief and the remainder of the Staff, and although there is no evidence to indicate that he ever violently disagreed with Harris, he undoubtedly smoothed paths and soothed friction.

Harris was an incessant smoker (American Camels) and his Personal Assistant constantly had to be on hand to light his cigarettes. He took no exercise, a long-standing trait going back to his experiences during the campaign in German South-West Africa, when the long and arduous marches through the bush gave him, he said, enough exercise to last him a lifetime. He also took not a single day's leave during his time at Bomber Command. Yet, in spite of all this and the fact that he had been invalided from Palestine, he never had a day's serious illness. He had little in the way of hobbies, although he did on occasion enjoy cooking and liked his food and occasionally played with a model railway set given to his daughter by the American airman General Ira Eaker, who stayed in his house for his first three months in England. Otherwise, his mind was constantly on the job in hand, the waging of the strategic bombing campaign.

Harris took over at a dark time for the Allies. Admittedly the Japanese attack on Pearl Harbor had precipitated America's entry into the war and Britain no longer stood alone, but otherwise the outlook was bleak. In the Far East the Japanese were sweeping all before them, while in North Africa, the British had been forced back to the Gazala Line. Merchant shipping losses in the Atlantic were also once again on the increase. Although the Russians were

---

*He had a son and two daughters by his first marriage.

on the counter-offensive and regaining some of their territory, they were clamouring for munitions from the Western Allies and increasingly agitating for the opening of a Second Front. Everywhere resources seemed to be spread too thin, and the sorting out of priorities was a constant bugbear for the War Cabinet.

As for Bomber Command, the last three months had been spent in an attempt to get its house in order. As Harris himself wrote:

> When I took up my Command the bomber force had played its very great part in stopping the projected invasion of England, but had done nothing else worth mentioning to injure the enemy. The force had been too small for that, and was still, in February 1942, much too small to achieve anything lasting, it was also poorly equipped.[2]

Indeed, its operational strength on 23 February revealed that it had 408 aircraft with crews available for operations, of which by far the greatest proportion were Wellingtons, 184 in number. As for heavies, there were only 70 available, of which five were the new Lancaster, now coming into service with 44 and 97 Squadrons of No 5 Group. This aircraft, a direct development of the Manchester, would in time become the mainstay of the bomber offensive, and eventually no less than 55 squadrons would be equipped with it, but in February 1942, this happy state of affairs was a long way off. The Stirling, in spite of its large bomb-load, was a sluggish aircraft, except at low level, and had a poor ceiling. The Halifax, once its initial teething troubles had been eradicated, was to prove a reliable, if unspectacular aircraft. As for the Manchester, by the beginning of 1942 it had an evil reputation with its crews. Engine overheating problems, its poor handling characteristics when fully loaded, and its unnecessarily complicated hydraulic system all combined to make it very unreliable, and it is significant that 65 per cent of all Manchesters built were lost, and two-thirds of these on operations.

Aircraft production presented problems. In order to achieve a first-line strength of 4,000 medium and heavy bombers, it was calculated that 22,000 would be required between July 1941 and July 1943, of which it was hoped that the Americans, through Lend-Lease, would provide 5,500. Yet, by September 1941, it was clear that Britain, under existing arrangements, could produce at most only 11,000 of the balance. Churchill had therefore ordered Beaverbrook to produce a plan increasing this to 14,500, even if it meant slowing up Admiralty and War Office programmes. 'Other long-term projects must give way to the overriding need for more bomber aircraft.'[3] This meant a massive factory expansion programme which, given even Beaverbrook's dynamism, took time to implement. In terms of heavies, therefore, the average production for 1940 was four per quarter, rising to 67 during 1942 and 428 during 1943.[4] Furthermore, America's entry into the war brought about a temporary break in her aircraft supplies since naturally she needed to accelerate her own re-equipment and expansion programme. Thus, during 1942 at least, Harris still had to husband his force.

Allied to this were the demands on aircraft resources from elsewhere. Continuing crises in the Atlantic led to Admiralty pressure for more aircraft to be given to Coastal Command, which was under the former's operational control. The Army, too, begrudged any weakening of Army Co-operation Command, and the development of airborne forces meant yet another drain on aircraft. Furthermore, there was continual pressure from other theatres of war, the Middle and Far East, for increased air support, especially during time of intense enemy pressure. Thus, a typical comment was that of Wavell, who was conducting a desperate defence in South-East Asia in the face of the Japanese drive:

When, after trying with less than 20 light bombers to meet an attack which has cost us three important warships and several others and nearly 100,000 tons of merchant shipping, we see that over 200 bombers attacked one town in Germany.[5]

Indeed, it was a problem of strategic priorities and whether attack should take precedence over defence, and those commanders engaged in the latter were understandably resentful when they were seemingly denied resources which they perceived as vital to swing the balance from defeat to victory in their own theatres, and the securing of the overall Allied position so that offensive operations could be launched from a firm base. Yet, to dissipate Bomber Command's strength overseas would be to remove the only weapon in the British armoury which could strike the enemy directly and go some way towards placating Stalin as well as maintaining Home Front morale.

If aircraft availability was a problem, so was that of crews. Thus, the Bomber Command operational strength of 23 February 1942 showed that there were 518 crews available, but only 408 crews with aircraft. There were a number of reasons for this shortfall. For a start, at this stage of the war, conversion from mediums to heavies was being carried out, which meant squadrons, or at least elements of them, being stood down for weeks. As for the crews themselves, there was a constant drain from two sources. First, there were those who were shot down (running now at well over 3 per cent per month) and those lost during training flights. Then, there were the lucky ones who had reached the end of their tour.

As a result of the Air Ministry canvass of the Commands at the end of 1940, it had been laid down in March 1941 that an operational tour should be 200 hours. This would be followed by six

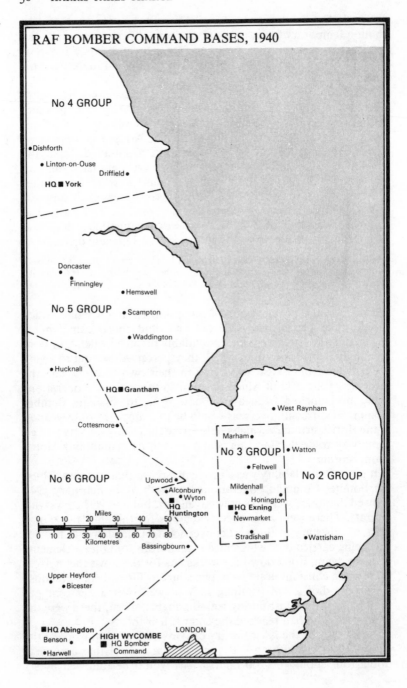

RAF BOMBER COMMAND BASES, 1940

No 4 GROUP

• Dishforth
• Linton-on-Ouse
Driffield •
HQ ■ York

Doncaster •
Finningley •
• Hemswell
No 5 GROUP
• Scampton
• Waddington
• Hucknall
HQ ■ Grantham
Cottesmore •

• West Raynham
Marham •
No 3 GROUP • Watton
• Feltwell
No 6 GROUP   Upwood •   Mildenhall •   No 2 GROUP
• Alconbury   Honington •
■ Wyton   ■ HQ Exning
■ HQ   Newmarket
Huntington
Stradishall •   • Wattisham
Bassingbourn •

Miles
0   10   20   30   40   50
0 10 20 30 40 50 60 70 80
Kilometres

Upper Heyford •
• Bicester

■ HQ Abingdon
Benson •   HIGH WYCOMBE   LONDON
• Harwell   ■ HQ Bomber
Command

months' rest, which would normally be spent instructing at an OTU, after which a second 200-hour tour would be undertaken.[6] As we have already seen, in Harris's estimation, when he was AOC No 5 Group, this length of tour equated to some 30–35 operational sorties. These crews had to be replaced from those graduating from the OTUs. Crews arriving at the latter – each Command ran its own, and those for Bomber Command were controlled by Nos 6 and 7 Groups (to be renamed Nos 91 and 92 Groups in May 1942) – came only after a lengthy initial period of training. First, there was the initial three-day aircrew selection board at which those who passed were categorised into pilot/navigator/bomb-aimer and wireless operator/flight engineer/gunner, and this was followed by ten days kitting-out at the Air Crew Reception Centre in Regent's Park, London. Twelve weeks were spent on ground training at an Initial Training Wing, and then came flying school. That for pilots and navigators took the longest and often they would do their training in the USA, Canada, South Africa or Rhodesia. After it had been decided which Command they would be posted to, all met up at the OTU, where they were formed into crews to carry out operational training on the type of aircraft they would fly in an operational squadron. Naturally enough, some fell by the wayside during training, through unsuitability, injury or death. Indeed, 5,327 were killed and 3,113 injured during training in Bomber Command throughout the war.[7] For a pilot, the total time between induction and his first operational sortie could be as long as eighteen months, and at this stage the policy was for heavies to have two pilots in each crew, one 'second tour' and one 'fresher' pilot, although this was under review when Harris arrived at Bomber Command HQ at High Wycombe.

A further drain on crews came from those who lost their will to continue operational flying, although these were a relatively small proportion. 'Lack of Morale Fibre' (LMF) is a subject which has aroused much emotion among aircrew and air historians alike, but very little account has yet been taken of official policy on the matter. The basic guidelines had been laid down by the Air Ministry in a directive dated 22 April 1940. This did not cover flagrant cowardice, which was a court-martial offence, but those aircrew 'whose conduct may cause them to forfeit the confidence of their commanding officers in their determination and reliability in the face of danger'. Two categories of what the Air Ministry termed 'Waverers' or Category W cases were defined – those who maintained a show of carrying out their duties, but had lost the confidence of their COs, and those who made no secret of their intention 'not to carry out dangerous duties'. If they could not be 'cured' by 'encouragement' or 'suitably dealt with by disciplinary means', their cases were to be referred to the Director of Postings at the Air Ministry, with the recommendation that their 'services be dispensed with' or that they would receive no further advancement until they had regained their confidence. A month later (22 May), a further directive covering aircrew suffering from 'war strain' stated that they were to be sent to a non-operational flying or ground job, and then to an OTU if necessary, before posting back to an operational unit, but squadron commanders had first to consult their medical officers, who either referred the individual to a specialist or recommended specialist action along the lines of the 22 April directive. The latter was revised on 28 September, when crews unable to stand up to the strain of operational flying were to be categorised into medical and non-medical cases. It was appreciated that this might not be easy because 'the individual, though physically fit, must be proved to be lacking in morale fibre'. Hence, the CO, if he had any doubts about a man, had initially to refer him to the MO, who could recommend treatment on station, leave, admission to hospital or a medical board, if he were convinced that the man was a medical case, or refer him to a neuropsychiatrist if he were in doubt. If no medical condition could be established, the case was referred back to the CO, who sent his own report, initialled by the man concerned, together with the medical reports, to Group, who after the AOC had made his personal recommendation, passed it to the Director of Postings. Those who were officially placed in Category W were, if non-commissioned,

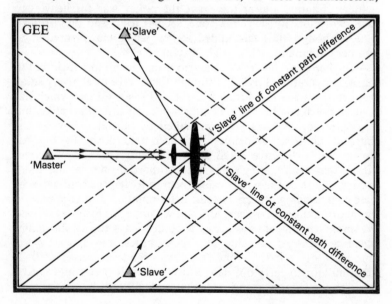

remustered in ground trades or, if officers, discharged and made liable for conscription in another service. Initially, the Air Ministry considered the retention of the flying brevet or badge on an individual basis, but by mid 1941 removal of it became automatic. As we shall see, however, LMF was a problem which was to cause concern throughout the war.[8]

So much for some of the background problems facing the Command in February 1942, but, apart from the arrival of the Lancaster, there was another technical development which gave much optimism for the future. The experiences of the early months of the war had prompted technical research into an improved navigational aid. This had begun at the Telecommunications Research Establishment (TRE) at Worth Maltravers, near Swanage in Dorset in spring 1940, and by October that year a prototype was in being. TR 1335, or GEE, as it was called from mid 1942 onwards, used three ground transmitters set along a baseline, some 200 miles long, to send a stream of pulses to an aircraft. The centre station was known as the 'Master' and the others as 'Slaves', and the time difference between the Master and each Slave were displayed on a cathode-ray tube in the aircraft. With this and a special chart with a grid showing lines of constant difference, the navigator could identify the latter relevant to his position on the tube and then refer to his grid. Where these lines crossed was his position. The advantages of the system were that the readings were accurate to a mile or less, and that it took only two minutes to pinpoint the aircraft's position. However, it was dependent on line of sight, which gave a range of 400 miles only, and was also possible to jam.

During the winter of 1940–41 there had been debate as to the best moment to introduce it into service, and the conclusion was that it would be better to delay until sufficient sets had been produced to equip a significant proportion of aircraft, since the Germans were bound to introduce counter-measures, which might well come in before it had had a chance to make an impact. There was also a technical problem in the manufacture of one of the valves. Thus, not until May 1941 did service trials start, and it is significant that it was already being thought of as a blind bombing device as well as a navigation aid. In July, Wellingtons of 115 Squadron were equipped with it, and two of these took part in a raid on München-Gladbach on 11 August, with encouraging results. The following night, two further GEE-equipped aircraft were involved in a raid on Hannover, which was optimistically calculated as being at extreme range for the equipment. However, one was shot down, and although it had a self-destruct device, there was concern that GEE might have fallen into German hands. A third operational test demonstrated GEE's qualities as a homing device, and then trials were halted with the decision that it would not be further employed until 300 bombers were equipped with it. By the time Harris assumed command, there were nine GEE-equipped squadrons – five Wellington and two Stirling in No 3 Group, one Halifax in No 4 Group and one Lancaster in No 5 Group. This was still a long way short of 300 aircraft, but the Air Staff believed it sufficient for Bomber Command to make its presence felt once more.

During the period December–February, Bomber Command had found itself, at Admiralty instigation, devoting much energy to attacking German capital ships in harbour, especially the *Scharnhorst, Gneisenau* and *Prinz Eugen* at Brest. Success against them was just as elusive as it had been earlier, and this was demonstrated in their 'Channel Dash' of mid February, although, significantly, the two first-named ships were damaged during the last leg of their voyage to the Elbe by mines dropped by Bomber Command. Churchill's reaction to the failure to intercept them was that now they were all bottled up in one place, Bomber Command could resume its attacks on Germany, provided that losses were contained. In the meantime, Bottomley, as DCAS, had presented a draft on bombing policy to Portal on 4 February. He saw the introduction of GEE as 'not merely an aid to normal navigation but as a means of removing many of the tactical limitations which have been imposed on our bombing operations in the past'. He stressed the importance of employing it to the full as its life 'may be of short duration', and envisaged GEE-equipped aircraft employing 'fire-raising tactics, and flare concentration' against their targets, which, in view of the GEE range, were to be the Ruhr and Rhineland. Portal latched on to this, seeing GEE as a means of cancelling the conservation policy,[9] and the result was Directive No 22 which was issued to Bomber Command on 14 February.

DIRECTIVE No 22

Although Harris's return from the United States was still awaited at the time of issue of Directive No 22, and Baldwin, AOC No 3 Group, had been 'minding the shop' since Peirse's departure for India in January, Harris was enjoined 'to employ your effort without restriction until further notice'. However, attacks were still not to be pressed in the face of bad weather or 'extreme hazards'. He was to regard GEE as a 'revolutionary advance in bombing technique', and there was likely to be six months' use to be had of it until the enemy had effective counter-measures.* Hence, it was 'of first importance to exploit the advantages that it confers to the full'.

---

*This would prove to be a very accurate forecast.

Incendiary attacks were emphasised, in that it was the best time of the year for them, and Harris was also reminded that his efforts would be of help to the Russians. Most significant, however, was the prime aim of his operations, which was to be 'focussed on the morale of the enemy civil population and in particular of the industrial workers'. Four primary GEE targets were selected – Essen, Duisburg, Düsseldorf and Cologne – with north German dockyards as alternatives. On clear nights, targets beyond GEE range were to be attacked, particularly Hamburg, Lübeck, Rostock and Berlin. Once experience with GEE had been gained, precision targets, notably factories (a list was given), were to be taken on, and these included French factories producing items for the German war effort, but, so as to avoid civilian casualties in this case, on clear nights only. German fighter strength in France was to be kept tied down and No 2 Group were to resume their daylight 'Circuses' in conjunction with Fighter Command and to undertake Intruder operations (attacks by night on aircraft on enemy airfields). However, Harris was warned that he would continue to be called upon to assist the Royal Navy, as well as Combined Operations and must be prepared to carry out other 'diversionary attacks on objectives, the destruction of which is of immediate importance in the light of the current strategic situation'.[10] The Directive would remain in force, with few amendments, for the next year. Harris's view on this was that, although he lacked the resources at this stage to carry out a decisive campaign, he had 'the only force in the West which then could take any offensive action at all against Germany' and that at least it would force the Germans to keep their fighters at home rather than use them against the Russians. Indeed, it would tie down a significant proportion of enemy manpower on defence of the homeland, as GARDENING 'could put a large part of the German Navy on the work of minesweeping, and many workers on to the repair of ships'.[11]

Harris was no sooner ensconced at High Wycombe, however, when bombing policy was questioned and aired once again, this time in public. During 24/25 February, a two-day debate on the conduct of the war was held in the House of Commons. A number of MPs complained of the seeming independence of Bomber Command, and Hore-Belisha, Secretary of State for War in the early months of the war, argued that the escape of *Scharnhorst* and *Gneisenau* after the incessant pounding which Bomber Command had given them 'does suggest that we are putting too much energy and too much of our manpower into the long-distance bombing policy'. He was not, of course, aware that the Air Staff had complained about the unsuitability of this type of target for heavy bombers. However, a more specific criticism was put by Professor

A. V. Bull, a distinguished scientist and the Member for Cambridge University. Pointing out that the blitz had had no significant effect on Britain, either in terms of lowering morale or reducing war production, and the fact that attacks on Germany involved longer distances, which meant the need of better aircraft, he said that Bomber Command's navigation accuracy was less than that of the Luftwaffe, consequently:

> The net result of bombing has long been known to be singularly small. The reports issued by the Air Ministry have been . . . far too optimistic. Everyone now knows that the idea of bombing a well defended enemy into submission . . . is an illusion . . . We know that most of the bombs we drop hit nothing of importance. We know that German devices for leading us astray are multiplying, and the quality of their defence . . . is, like ours, improving. The disaster of this policy is not only is it futile but that it is extremely wasteful, and will become increasingly wasteful as time goes by.

What, in RAF eyes, made the situation worse, was the new Lord Privy Seal, Sir Stafford Cripps's winding up speech for the Government. He reminded the House that the bombing policy had been initiated when Britain stood alone, but now she had allies. Hence circumstances were different and the original policy was now under review.

> I can assure the House that the Government are fully aware of the other uses to which our resources could be put, and the moment that they arrive at a decision that the circumstances warrant a change, a change in policy will be made.[12]

What concerned the Air Staff was not so much that the Government might be changing its mind over bombing policy, but more over the effect that this public dissension was having on the Americans, whose material contribution to the bombing offensive the Air Staff were now relying on to come to fruition in the near future. Portal wrote in the minute to Sinclair dated 27 February:

> Our mission in Washington have already informed us of serious repercussions which Government policy is likely to have. Will almost certainly be maintained that we have begun to weaken in our belief in bomber offensive and that this will be seized on by Naval and Army staffs to upset priorities at present given to heavy bomber program. It may also fortify US Navy's argument for concentrating whole of America's available heavy bomber squadrons in SW Pacific.[13]

Harris, however, was more concerned over what criticism of the conduct of the bombing campaign would do to the morale of his crews. In a long letter to Portal, he spoke of 'the fearful effects on the morale of crews, which will rise to crescendo unless these mischievous tongues are bridled', although he accepted that morale was as yet unshaken. He saw much of the criticism as unjustified, and commented that:

... when such attacks, coupled with wholesale charges of incompetent command and incompetent execution, are made on the Air Force purely as a smoke screen to cover the incompetence or irresolution of the other Services, the last straw is added to the camel's back, e.g., Singapore.*

Clearly, this remark was unjustified and misplaced, and serves as an important indicator to one of Harris's weaknesses. Too often, as we shall see, he would put pen to paper or utter in the heat of the moment without thought as to the adverse effect it might have on others, and it was a major reason why he was unpopular among some of his fellow commanders. Furthermore, it illustrates something of his scepticism towards the other two fighting services, which made relations between Bomber Command and them continually difficult. Indeed, the very next day (6 March), Portal wrote to him, with regard to co-operation with the Army, stressing '. . . how much depends in these difficult times on mutual help and understanding between the two Services'.[14]

With regard to the implementation of Directive No 22, Harris's first opportunity to improve the standing of the Command came on the night of 3/4 March, and this was against a precision target. During January 1942 HQ Bomber Command and the Air Ministry had between them evolved a technique of target marking using flares, and Bottomley had invited Baldwin, as Acting AOCinC, to try this out against the Renault factory at Billancourt near Paris. Consequently, 235 bombers were sent to attack in three waves. The first, consisting of experienced crews, identified and marked the target (GEE was not used), attacked with 1,000lb bombs, and then continued to drop flares from windward of the target, while the second wave, also armed with 1,000-pounders bombed. Finally, heavies, armed with 4,000lb bombs went in. All this was carried out below 6,000ft since it was known that the anti-aircraft defences were light. Indeed, only one Wellington failed to return and 224 aircraft claimed to have bombed the target. Photographic reconnaissance next day showed that considerable damage had been caused, and accuracy had been high. Furthermore, the attack had been carried out in under two hours, a far higher concentration of aircraft over the target than had ever been achieved before. Although, in terms of challenge, it did not compare to an operation over the Ruhr, it was a most encouraging début for Harris, and undoubtedly a good morale raiser for his crews. Another, who was grateful for its success was Sinclair, who had to defend Bomber Command in the House of Commons on the 4th, and was able to use it as an example of how effective Bomber Command could be. As for inter-service co-operation, he emphasised the support being

*Singapore had fallen to the Japanese on 15 February 1942.

given to the Army in the Middle East, and to the Navy in the Atlantic and the numerous attacks on *Scharnhorst* and *Gneisenau*. He reiterated, too, that Bomber Command was '. . . the only force upon which we can call in this year, 1942, to strike deadly blows at the heart of Germany'.[15]

Five nights later, Harris went two steps further forward when he launched an attack on Essen, this time using GEE-equipped aircraft to mark the target with flares, in what became known as the SHAKER technique. Although, the marker aircraft were instructed to use GEE and drop their flares 'blind', only eleven out of twenty did so, the others attempting to do it visually. However, Essen was notorious for the strength of its defences and the industrial haze which surrounded it. The Germans, too, used dummy flares and fires to good effect, and the results, for an attack by 211 bombers, were disappointing. Next night, it was Essen again, and this time, only nine out of 23 marker crews used GEE – clearly unfamiliarity with the equipment prevented wholesale confidence in it. This time, considerable damage was done to Hamborn and Duisburg, but no bombs dropped on Essen. Harris, however, in a report which he wrote to the Prime Minister said:

> The crews are enthusiastic especially with the result of the 2nd night's operation on Essen and the gain so far is not only an excellent means of navigation and especially of bombing within the immediate neighbourhood of the selected target, which was far greater than on similar types of operation prior to GEE . . . We are all enthusiastic as to the utility and efficiency of GEE.

Nevertheless, he accepted that Essen did not 'get it in the neck', although there were numerous fires in the southern part of the town.[16] An attack on Cologne on 13/14 March, this time with 134 aircraft, produced better results, with daylight reconnaissance revealing that some 50 per cent had dropped their bombs within five miles of the target centre. One interesting aspect of this raid is brought out by one participant, a rear-gunner in an 83 Squadron Manchester:

> Across the centre of the city I saw flares illuminating every detail of the towers, turrets and buttresses of the cathedral. Here let me say at once that Whitey and Bill had previously discussed their run-in with care to avoid bombing this ancient building, and as far as I could find out so did every other crew who attacked Cologne that night.[17]

Within a matter of weeks such sensitivities would be laid to rest. Two nights later, it was Essen again. The tempo of operations was stepping up.

To maintain this level of operations was difficult with the limited resources at Harris's disposal. However, with aircraft available in operational squadrons being greater than the number of crews, the first requirement, as he saw it, was to try and increase the latter. The two-pilot policy on heavies was under review by the time he arrived at High Wycombe. The AOC No 6 Group had argued in a paper to HQ Bomber Command dated 9 January 1942 that one well-trained pilot would produce better efficiency than two less well-trained ones, apart from increasing the flow of fresher crews from OTUs to operational squadrons. Furthermore, he wrote:

> I venture to recall a lament which was often heard from Air Marshal Harris. He frequently complained that the shaft of all our training organisation in the RAF was very thick and the actual spearhead of operational effort was very small. I believe this analogy to have been extremely well-founded, and it will be found that the proposal which has now been submitted will result in the shaft becoming much more slender and the spearhead more sharp.[18]

Indeed, Harris raised the issue with Portal very shortly after he assumed command, and the result was that an Air Council meeting, presided over by Portal, agreed (on 29 March), that from now on heavies and mediums would have a crew consisting of one pilot and one wireless operator/air gunner, a front gunner/bomb-aimer, who would vacate his turret position when bombing, a flight engineer on heavies, who would be trained as a 'pilot's mate', and that on mediums, where the latter crew position did not exist, the bomb-aimer or wireless operator would be trained in these duties. Harris, however, had already 'jumped the gun' in that he had certainly instructed No 1 Group, at least, to convert to a one-pilot crew at the beginning of March.[19]

Two other steps which he took to improve crew availability, concerned leave and the retention of trained crews. He was convinced that operations in poor weather brought a poor return:

> It is my view . . . that we should aim at intensifying to the utmost our operations in good weather, and reducing as far as possible our attempts to operate in doubtful or bad weather . . . During such fine periods, unless we become favoured with a spell of fine weather of exceptional duration, crews must be expected to work 2 or even 3 nights running . . . Conversely, during bad weather everything possible should be done to rest the personnel concerned.

Crews were therefore not to take leave during good weather, and those who were on leave when fine weather arrived might well find themselves called back.[20] He was also aghast at the number of trained crews who slipped out of the Command's clutches. As he wrote to his Group Commanders on 23 March:

> The outlook now and for the future is desperate. This is directly due to inexcusable, heedless and fantastic extravagance in posting broadcast [sic] throughout the world, for every conceivable job except bombing, vast numbers of OTU trained bomber crews many of whom have never started, let alone completed an operational tour. I propose to see to it that without exception . . . every bomber crew is employed on the job for which he has been trained until he has completed the full compass of 2 operational tours and 2 OTU tours.[21]

As we shall see, his main concern was the diversion of crews to the Middle East and Coastal Command.

There is no doubt that Harris had already made an impact on those under and immediately above him, but what of Churchill's impressions? On 13 March, the Prime Minister had written to Sinclair saying that he hoped he realised 'how widely the existing policy of the Air Ministry is challenged by opinion', and that he saw the bombing of Germany as 'not decisive but better than doing nothing'. He felt, too, that priority of production should be given to shore-based torpedo-bombers over that of high-level bombers and that he was concerned that the Royal Navy was not getting the aircraft that they needed.[22] Then, it appears that on the evening of 22 March Harris went to Chequers for the first of what would be many visits. The object was to discuss a persistent Admiralty request for Bomber Command to attack the *Tirpitz* in Trondheim Fjord.* There is no doubt that Harris made an immediate impression on Churchill – perhaps he saw much of his own bulldog tenacity in Harris – and this was indicated in a letter which Churchill wrote to Roosevelt the following day. Speaking of the need to transfer Bomber Command squadrons to Coastal Command, he wrote 'I find it very hard to take away these extra six squadrons from Bomber Command in which Harris is doing so well. Our new methods of finding targets is [*sic*] yielding most remarkable results.'[23] Indeed, this was the start of Churchill's restoration of faith in the bomber, and Harris now had direct access to him, which would help him immeasurably in his conduct of the bombing campaign.

The question of the transfer of squadrons to Coastal Command had been pursued by the Admiralty for some time. They wanted six and a half squadrons to assist in the Battle of the Atlantic and two for long-range work in the Indian Ocean. At a Chiefs of Staff Meeting on 27 March, however, the First Sea Lord asked for four Lancaster squadrons, to replace four of Catalinas which had been sent to the Indian Ocean. Harris complained that of his forty front-line squadrons, four were day bomber only, three were Whitley, and no longer suitable for operations over Germany, and four were grounded Lancaster squadrons, either through conversion from other types or GEE installation. This left him with 29 operational squadrons or three less than Bomber Command's operational strength at the outbreak of war. However, the situation in the Battle of the Atlantic was serious and the Air Staff in the end struck a bargain whereby Coastal Command would receive a total of six

*This took place on 27 March and was mounted by Halifaxes of No 4 Group, who succeeded, at a cost, in causing some, but hardly fatal, damage. Wing Commander Bennett, later AOC No 8 (Pathfinder) Group was shot down on this raid, but managed to make his way home via Sweden some weeks later.

squadrons – two Wellington, three Whitley and one Hampden. Thus, at least Harris was able to retain his heavies intact.

FURTHER EXPERIMENTS

He now turned to that part of Directive No 22 which dealt with incendiary attacks. The main object was to establish if the leading wave could guide subsequent waves onto the target by starting a conflagration. For a target, he selected Lübeck, which, although out of GEE range, was on the coast and relatively easy to find. It was also built largely of wood. Although not a vital target, 'it seemed to me better to destroy an industrial town of moderate importance than to fail to destroy a large industrial city'.[24] A total of 234 aircraft took off on the night of 28 March, in three waves. The first two were mainly loaded with incendiaries, while the third, which was to be over the target an hour after the second wave, would carry high explosives. Although thirteen aircraft were posted missing, one of which enabled the Germans to obtain their first GEE equipment, 190 crews claimed to have successfully attacked, and half the town was found to have been laid waste. Again, morale, both among the crews and the public at large, received another boost, and Hitler's reaction was to launch his Baedeker Raids* on English towns during the last part of April and May.

Two days after this raid there was another debate on the higher direction of the bombing offensive, this time conducted in private. On 30 March Lord Cherwell addressed a minute to the Prime Minister. Extrapolating on the evidence of bomb damage to British towns and cities, which indicated that one ton of bombs destroyed '20–40 dwellings and turns 100–200 people homeless',which he argued had a greater effect on civilian morale than the actual casualties caused, he proposed a de-housing campaign on Germany's 58 largest cities and towns. Estimating that bomber production during the next twelve months would be of the order of 10,000, that each bomber had a three-ton bomb-load and survived on average 13–14 sorties, he believed that the German spirit could be broken.[25] Both Sinclair and Portal were much taken by the force of his argument, although they pointed out to Churchill that success was dependent on sufficient production rate of heavies, the development of navigational and bomb-aiming accuracy to ensure that 50 per cent of all bombs dropped in target area, and that further diversions from the bomber offensive against Germany would have to be avoided. One who violently disagreed with this was Cherwell's great scientific rival, Sir Henry Tizard, who at this

*After the tourist guidebooks of that name.

stage represented the Ministry of Aircraft Production (MAP) on the Air Council. As early as December 1941 he had serious doubts over the efficacy of the bombing policy, commenting to MAP of the heavy bomber production plans: 'The war is not going to be won by night bombing. This programme assumes that it is.'[26] By mid February he was convinced that top priority should be given to 'operating aircraft over the sea on a very much larger scale than we have done hitherto, and that we shall be forced to use much longer-range aircraft' – a prophetic view. He did accept that the bombing of Germany forced the enemy to put more resources into home defence, but 'this end could be achieved by steady bombing on a much smaller scale than is at present contemplated by the Air Staff'.[27] Now, in a memorandum dated 20 April to Sinclair and Cherwell, he set out to demolish Cherwell's arguments. First, existing production plans allowed for only just over 8,000 aircraft for Bomber Command up to the end of June 1943, of which some 40 per cent were Wellingtons, and past experience showed that in real terms Bomber Command would only receive some 7,000. Secondly, if each bomber were only to survive a certain number of operations, this meant that they would all be destroyed and that 'we should be left at the end of the period with a front-line strength no greater than it is at present, which is surely quite unthinkable'. He also doubted whether Bomber Command would attain sufficient accuracy in time and felt that it would be able to drop only 25 per cent of its bombs on target. Hence, he concluded that the Cherwell plan could not have a decisive effect by mid 1943, and would only work, in any event, on a very much larger scale than that envisaged by Cherwell. He also stressed to Sinclair his belief in priority of effort going into attacks on the German Navy.[28]

In the meantime, however, the War Cabinet had decided to put the matter in the hands of an independent arbiter, and on 16 April Mr. Justice Singleton was called upon to undertake an inquiry with the following terms of reference:

> In the light of our experience of the German bombing of this country, and of such information as is available of the results of our bombing of Germany, what results we are likely to achieve from continuing our air attacks on Germany at the greatest possible strength during the next six, twelve and eighteen months respectively.[29]

The following day Harris produced another 'rabbit out of his hat'.

THE AUGSBURG RAID

This operation related to that part of Directive No 22 which called for both Bomber and Fighter Commands to tie down as much as possible of the German fighter strength in northern France in order to prevent it being used to reinforce other fronts. This implied, so far as Bomber Command was concerned, daylight operations. At the same time, Harris wanted to force the Germans to spread their anti-aircraft defences as widely as possible in order to reduce their concentrations in the Ruhr and other prominent and important targets. It was then a question of finding a point in the enemy's air defence crust through which the bombers could be escorted by fighters and then choosing a route inland where they were unlikely to meet heavy fighter opposition. This led Harris to think of southern Germany. Here he needed a suitable and worthwhile target which could be easily located, and which could be attacked in daylight with the bombers returning in darkness before entering any heavily protected areas of Germany. Also, the nature of the route should be such as to keep the Germans guessing as to the actual target until the last moment. The aircraft would fly at minimum height and, since it was to be a daylight attack, would go for a precision target. Harris came up with three possibilities. Schweinfurt, although its ball-bearing factory was a vital part of the German war industry, was dismissed since the route would force the bombers, because of range problems, over the Rhine in daylight, and also because there were few prominent landmarks to aid navigation. Nuremberg was discarded because of the very heavy defences around it, and this left Augsburg, and in particular the MAN factory which produced diesel-engines, and was reputed to be the largest of its kind in Germany. The aiming-point was to be the machine assembly shop.[30]

Seven crews each from the first two Lancaster squadrons in service, Nos 44 and 97, from Waddington and Woodhall respectively, were chosen, under the command of Squadron Leader J. D. Nettleton. They began practising low-level formation flying on 14 April, and three days later twelve of them took off in the mid afternoon intending to arrive over the target just before dusk. They had no fighter escort, but thirty Boston and more than five hundred Fighter Command sorties were mounted over northern France as a diversion. This was insufficient and four Lancasters were shot down by Me 109s over France. The others pressed on and attacked, but three more were shot down over the target; the remainder, all damaged, eventually made it back, including Nettleton himself, who was subsequently awarded the Victoria Cross. While all applauded the gallantry shown and the fact that the machine assembly shop had been hit, it was quite clear to Harris that such raids, although spectacular, were too costly to be pursued in daylight with heavy bombers. Nettleton, who would later be killed leading his squadron over Turin in July 1943, said in a wireless broadcast delivered some days later: 'The war can't be finished without attacking the enemy.'[31] No clearer echo of the Air Staff's and Harris's views could have been given.

THE SINGLETON REPORT

Night attacks against Essen were maintained, and encountered the same problems of industrial haze and stiff defences, and there was another attack on the *Tirpitz* on 27 April. GARDENING sorties, too, continued to be sent out each night. However, the other 'spectacular' that month was the attacking of Rostock on four successive nights between the 23rd and 28th. This was, so far as technique went, in the same mould as the Lübeck attack, with incendiaries making up the major part of the bomb-load. Also, as happened at Lübeck, when a machine tool factory had been singled out, Harris laid down the Heinkel aircraft factory at Marienehe as a precise target within the area zone. The results of the first attack of 142 bombers were very disappointing, with most bombs falling south-east of the main target and the Heinkel factory remaining untouched. Of the 91 aircraft sent out the next night, 83 claimed to have successfully attacked and an analysis of photographs revealed a fair degree of success, although the bombing was somewhat scattered. It is also significant that all except five aircraft attacked within one hour – the attack concentration was improving. This, however, was easily surpassed on the third night when 99 out of 128 aircraft attacked within half an hour and 110 claimed to have hit the target. Again the photographs revealed steady improvement. Finally, Nos 1 and 4 Groups sent 52 aircraft against the town, and Nos 3 and 5 Groups' 55 aircraft attacked the Heinkel works. All the photographs showed the target area, and post-raid photographic reconnaissance confirmed a resounding success. To Harris, the main lesson was that crews were being too easily misled by fires which were not on target, and not determined enough to find the aiming-up point on their own. 'Only when it became obvious to crews that they were going on with Rostock until Rostock was completed did they seem to make a really determined effort to find their precise objective and hit it.'[32]

Mr. Justice Singleton for one was impressed with Bomber Command's efforts, as he indicated in his report dated 20 May 1942. Whereas in the past there had been no clear demonstration of what Bomber Command could do, and indeed bombing policy was 'not well directed', the change of policy and what had been done to Lübeck, Rostock and the Renault works gave a much better picture. He did not consider morale was a worthwhile target in itself, but preferred 'to think of the effect of morale combined with the other factors and to envisage the bombing of an industrial area with important factories in the centre rather than the bombing of houses, and I think better results will be achieved thereby'. He was strongly of the opinion that bombing accuracy must be improved, and felt that GEE was not achieving as much as was hoped, especially in view of the short period of time before the Germans were likely to find an answer to it. He believed that more successes would be achieved with a new aid, H2S, which was then under development, but was unlikely to be available before the end of 1942. In conclusion, he saw the next six months as hardly decisive on their own and that they should be regarded 'as leading up to, and forming part of a longer and more sustained effort . . .' Much would depend on what happened on the Eastern front and 'the effects of a reverse for Germany, or of lack of success would be greatly increased by an intensified bombing campaign in the autumn and winter.' It would certainly effect morale in these circumstances.

> And if this was coupled with knowledge in Germany that the bombing would now be on an increasing scale until the end, and the realisation of the fact that the German Air Force could not again achieve equality, I think might well prove the turning point – provided always that greater accuracy can be achieved.

On this last point on accuracy, there is a telling remark in the comments on the report by Air Commodore Baker, Director of Bomber Operations at the Air Ministry.

> It comes as something of a shock even to the initiated to realise that our night bombing accuracy has not only forced us to regard the target area as normally falling within a radius of five miles from the aiming point but that, except under very favourable conditions of weather, visibility and geographical location, we can seldom expect to get more than 20% of our despatched effort within this area.

This certainly echoed the Tizard, as opposed to the Cherwell view. Baker also took up the recommendation made in the report that each operation must be organised and controlled at Command level, and agreed with it. Bottomley thought that, though it was cautiously worded, it did indicate that bombing was going to be the main ingredient of final victory and that, as such, it was another argument for not allowing more than the very minimum diversion of bomber potential to strategically defensive operations.[33] However, Portal viewed it as having no clear-cut conclusions, and Pound, the First Sea Lord, used it as an argument for more RAF participation in the war at sea.[34] Indeed, the language was vague and it seemed to 'mean all things to all men'. Not surprisingly, no positive policy was formulated from it.

What was clear to Harris, however, was that Bomber Command could only get the aircraft and the support it needed by continuing to produce positive results through action rather than by merely presenting its case theoretically. So far his operations had been encouraging in their success, but were too small in scale to make the necessary impact on those who questioned the concept of the strategic bombing campaign as a war winner. His slender force was not large enough to begin to knock out cities either in the Cherwell or Singleton vein. If, however, he could somehow bring together a significantly large force, even for one operation, perhaps he could wreak devastating damage. During April, he turned this over in his mind, and set Saundby the task of investigating the feasibility of gathering one thousand bombers for a raid on a German city.

THE FIRST THOUSAND RAID

By the beginning of May, Saundby had reported that by using OTU aircraft and crews, who were, in any event, being used on GARDENING and NICKEL operations as part of their training, and calling on other Commands, especially Coastal, it was possible. The target would need to be within GEE range, which meant the Ruhr, or near the coast, and it had to be of maximum economic and political importance. Furthermore, in order to ensure maximum possible bomb-load on target it needed to be carried out during a full moon period, the next of which would be at the end of May. Having worked out his plan in some detail, choosing Hamburg, as Germany's second largest city and the centre of the submarine construction industry (to placate the Admiralty), and Cologne as the alternative should the weather be unsuitable over Hamburg, Harris now had to sell his plan.

Harris's relationship with Churchill was burgeoning, and it seemed logical to try the proposal out on him first, which he did at Chequers, where Harris was becoming a regular guest, on the evening of Sunday 17 May. Churchill was enthusiastic, and next day Harris saw Portal, asking him to seek assurance from the Admiralty that a sizeable Coastal Command contribution would be made. This Portal achieved and on 20 May Harris informed his Group Commanders and Coastal, Flying Training and Army Co-operation Commands of the plan.

> The idea of the operation is so to saturate the ARP [Air Raid Precautions] at the objective as to cause a complete and uncontrollable conflagration throughout the target area. To that end the maximum number of incendiary bombs would comprise the load, HE being used only when essential as a make-weight towards an economical load.[35]

The date was fixed at 28 May or the first suitable night thereafter. Groups and other Commands came back with estimates on what they would be able to produce. From his four operational groups (No 2 Group, together with Army Cooperation Command would be used on INTRUDER operations to damp down night fighter activity on the night) he could muster 485 aircraft, his two training groups – now Nos 91 and 92 Groups – could provide 330 between them, Joubert AOCinC Coastal Command came back with 250, and Flying Training Command offered up 21 Wellingtons and Hampdens of doubtful calibre. Thus, Harris had his 1,000 bombers and more, and Fighter Command had also agreed to some INTRUDER sorties. The operation order went out dated 23 May. A significant amount of redeployment of aircraft was needed, especially of those from the other Commands and OTUs. It was essential, however, that maximum secrecy be maintained, so the deployment of aircraft was ordered under the guise of Operation BANQUET, an RAF contingency plan in the event of German invasion of Britain, periodically practised under various guises. The crews quickly sensed that something big was brewing. For the OTUs, the tell-tale sign was 'the arrival of the Incendiary Bombs at stations' and 'the spirits and morale of the OTUs rose out of all proportion, as it was obvious that the "Exercise" was going to be a practical one'.[36]

On 25 May, in the midst of the preparations, Harris was hit by a bombshell. The Admiralty suddenly stepped in and removed the whole of the Coastal Command contribution. No reasons appear to have been given.* A further dredging of the Bomber Command Groups managed to raise the aircraft availability figure to 916, which still was not enough to reach the magic figure of one thousand. Harris decreed that all training and conversion flights within the operational groups would also be used. Next day, a revised operation order was issued.

For such a large operation, the written orders were surprisingly concise, but what is more significant was the way in which the attack was to be carried out. Although, as we have seen, the concentration of bombers over a target had been steadily increasing, there was now to be a 'quantum leap', with more than 1,000 bombers expected to deliver their loads in a period of only 90 minutes. By this stage, a fair amount of detail was known about the German defences, especially the notorious Kammhuber Line, a belt of radars, anti-aircraft guns, and night fighter operational zones, which stretched from Switzerland to the Baltic. In particular, the successful Bruneval raid of February 1942 had brought back details of the Würzburg radar, one of its cornerstones. On the theory that each radar could only cover and direct night fighters onto one aircraft at a time, the Operational Research Section (ORS) at Bomber Command had developed the technique of streaming,

*No published account gives one, and the author's search of RAF and Naval files at the PRO failed to reveal anything in writing on this decision.

whereby the bombers passed over a given point in a concentrated stream. However, there was the risk of collision, and as Dr. Basil Dickins, Head of the ORS, said:

> We had to reduce it all to mathematics, and work out the actual chance of a collision. And it became quite obvious to us at ORS that while a collision was a half per cent risk, the chances of being shot down by flak or fighters was a three or four per cent risk. So we could allow the collision risk to mount quite a bit, provided that in doing so we could bring down the losses from other causes.[37]

He envisaged ten bombers crossing a given point every minute, which meant ten aircraft scattered randomly in a box of sky three miles long by five or more miles wide and nearly two miles deep. Naturally enough there was some apprehension among the crews over his calculations, but, in the event he was proved right; there were only two mid-air collisions, one over the target and the other over England on return. Once again, three waves were to be used. The crews of the first wave of GEE-equipped aircraft from Nos 1 and 3 Groups were told, as No 3 Group's operation order put it, that 'bombs would be released visually on the homing run when the target is identified and the position confirmed by TR1335'.[38] The heavies of Nos 4 and 5 Groups would attack next, followed by the remainder. It was also decided, in view of the fact that the weather during May had been unseasonably bad, to bring the first possible night forward to 27 May in order to give more leeway. As it happened, bad weather on the 27th and 28th brought about stand downs, but the next day looked slightly more promising. By lunchtime, however, although reasonable over England and France, it appeared to be closing in over Germany, and the raid was postponed again. Harris was now in a dilemma. Apart from GARDENING operations, there had not been an operation since 19 May, when 197 bombers had attacked Mannheim and a further 65 had bombed Saint-Nazaire. With the weather fair over France, the Germans might become suspicious if he did not take advantage of it. On the other hand, possible loss of aircraft and the fact that crews would be operating two nights running would detract from the Thousand Plan. Harris decided that the risk had to be taken, and 120 aircraft were sent against objectives in France, while a further 24 carried out GARDENING operations, eight of them failing to return.

Next morning, at his daily 0900 hours conference, Harris heard from Group Captain Spence, that although there was much thundery cloud over north-west Germany, it was dispersed and decreasing over the Rhine. He decided that he could wait no longer, and Cologne was selected for that night.[39]

Fortified by a message from Harris reminding them of the significance of the operation and exhorting them to 'let him have it, right on the chin',[40] no less than 1,050 bombers[41] took off from 55 airfields. When the first aircraft, Stirlings of 15 Squadron, arrived over the target, flak was light and they noticed that dummy fires had been lit outside the city. They dropped their incendiaries on each of three aiming-points in the centre of Cologne and then turned away, while the second wave began their attacks. Soon, there was an enormous conflagration, and the later aircraft had little difficulty in identifying the target. As a Halifax pilot in 76 Squadron recalled: 'We took off at about 10pm – the final wave to bomb – and I could not simply believe my eyes at the Dutch coast at what I saw 100 miles ahead of us. It was a gigantic fire that an hour before had been the city of Cologne. There it was on fire from end to end, with still another 300 bombers to deliver their load.'[42] Indeed, it was this aspect which made the deepest impression, not least on Air Vice-Marshal Baldwin, AOC No 3 Group, who was flying in a 218 Squadron Stirling. The following extract is from a letter from a Wellington rear gunner from 27 OTU at Lichfield, written a few days after the raid:

> On the Cologne show we had a nice quiet journey all the way out. Coming into Cologne you knew exactly where you were, the place was absolutely lit up and huge fires all over the show. We were running into bomb when we were caught by searchlights & then the flak started all around us. We dodged and dived till we got out of it at 7,000ft & then ran up & bombed then stooged as hard as we could for home. Everything was quiet for about 10 minutes when suddenly a master searchlight suddenly came straight on us followed immediately by flak absolutely all round us. The plane went straight into a power dive and I nearly thought we were hit till the cool voice of the pilot came over 'OK Chaps?' Anyway we dived & weaved down to 3000 & managed to get out of it and stooged the rest of the way over occupied Europe at that height. The plane had four shell holes in it & we thought it an exciting trip.[43]

Others were not so fortunate. A Manchester from 50 Squadron was hit in the bomb bay over Cologne, having been 'coned' by searchlights. The pilot, Flying Officer L. T. Manser, climbed to evade, but that ever-present danger of engine overheating in the Manchester resulted in his port engine catching fire. He limped his way across the Belgian border, and the other engine began to falter. Manser ordered his crew to bale out, and by the time they had done so he was too low to save himself and he died in the resultant crash. Four members of the crew eventually got back to England via the underground, and when the full story of Manser's self-sacrifice became known he was awarded a posthumous VC in October 1942.

For most, however, it was a reasonably uneventful trip, and when the figures were correlated, it was found that forty aircraft only were missing (Churchill had been prepared for a loss of one hundred and Harris sixty), although a further twelve were so seriously damaged that they had to be written off and another 33 were categorised as seriously damaged. Even more encouraging was the fact that no less than 890 claimed to have hit the target, representing 540 tons of HE and 915 tons of incendiaries. Because of the enormous pall of smoke over the city, it was to be some days before the damage could be accurately assessed, but it was clear that Bomber Command had had a spectacular success. As the Bomber Command Quarterly Review put it: 'the greatest air operation ever planned and undoubtedly achieved the greatest single success in aerial warfare'.[44] The Press had a field-day – the normally sober headline of *The Times* proclaiming: 'OVER 1,000 BOMBERS RAID COLOGNE: Biggest Air Attack of the War. 2,000 Tons of Bombs in 40 Minutes'.[45] The German official communiqué also bore out the success of the raid: 'Great damage was done by the effect of explosions and fires, particularly in the residential quarters.'[46]

Of the many tributes which flowed into HQ Bomber Command, two meant more to Harris than any other. From Churchill:

> I congratulate you and the whole of Bomber Command upon the remarkable feat of organisation which enabled you to despatch over a thousand bombers to Cologne area in a single night and without confusion to concentrate their action over the target into so short a time as one hour and a half. The proof of the growing power of the British Bomber Force is also the herald of what Germany will receive, city by city, from now on.

And from General 'Hap' Arnold:

> As Commanding General of the US Army Air Forces I desire to extend my congratulations to you, your staff and combat crews for the great raid last night on Cologne. It was bold in conception and superlative in execution. Please convey to your officers and men my admiration for their courage and skill, and say that our air forces hope very soon to fly and fight beside them in their decisive blows against our common enemy.[47]

On 14 June it was announced that Harris had been advanced to a KCB. Bomber Command had shown what it could do if it had the aircraft, but was the euphoria over its success to be lasting or merely of the moment?

CHAPTER FOUR

THE COMING OF THE PATHFINDERS

What we need to aim at is an effective degree of illumination and incendiarism in the right place and only the right place - Portal

---

FURTHER THOUSAND RAIDS

With two nights of the full moon left, and his 'Thousand Force' still concentrated, Harris determined to capitalise immediately on the success of Cologne. The crews were therefore warned of a repeat operation for the following night, 31 May. He had hoped to attack his original primary target, Hamburg, but, by 1830 hours, with bad weather persisting over the city and no time to plan for an alternative, operations were cancelled. Two GEE-equipped Wellingtons from 57 and 75 Squadrons were sent to check the damage at Cologne, but failed to take any photographs because of the continued pall of smoke. Accordingly, with only one night left, he decided to go for the Ruhr again, this time to infamous Essen, using the SHAKER technique. A total of 956 bombers took off, all except two from Bomber Command, but, although 767 crews claimed to have attacked, few of them asserted this with much confidence, and subsequent analysis showed little damage to Essen, although Oberhausen, Mulheim and Duisburg had suffered. Once again haze had defeated the efforts of the bombers, and the raid showed, if nothing else, that GEE, although a useful navigation aid, was unsatisfactory as a blind-bombing device. The Force was therefore stood down for the time being.

On 13 June Harris told the Prime Minister that he intended to mount another 1,000-bomber operation during the June full moon and urged him to apply pressure to the Admiralty to release Coastal Command aircraft for it. Next day, Harris informed Portal of his plans, and Churchill in a minute of 15 June spoke of Harris 'using the June moon for another edition of "ARABIAN NIGHTS"'.[1] On the same day he wrote to the First Lord and First Sea Lord one of his 'Action this Day' memoranda informing them of further 1,000 raids. 'On the coming occasions it will be necessary that Coastal

Command should participate and I must ask definitely for compliance with this request.'[2] The Admiralty came back with an offer of 100 Hudsons and a Polish Wellington Squadron, which they wanted to hand back to Bomber Command in exchange for another squadron, as the Poles were too 'wild' for Coastal Command work.[3] Harris had hoped for 250 aircraft, but, the Admiralty being adamant, he had again to draw heavily on OTUs, which he had hoped to leave alone, for the third 1,000 Raid, which took place on 25 June.

This time the target was Bremen, and 1,006 aircraft took off, all from Bomber Command except for 102 Coastal Command Hudsons and five Army Cooperation Command Blenheims. It was hoped to compress the raid into 65 minutes, but, once again a gamble had to be taken on the weather, which was marginal. As it was, there was an abrupt change of wind, and the cloud which had been forecast to disperse did not do so. Although some damage was caused to the town, especially to the Focke-Wulf factory, which was No 5 Group's aiming-point, the results were disappointing. Worse, 49 aircraft failed to return, including a high proportion of the OTU student crews (21 of No 91 Group's 24 aircraft were lost), who found the conditions too much for them.

After the success of Cologne, Harris had hoped to make the Thousand raids the cornerstone of his campaign. Indeed, he had written to Portal on 20 June suggesting that the Thousand Force be concentrated for two raids twice a month, 'while devoting the rest of the month and more of the resources of the operational units to training crews'. He accepted that 'a minimum force' would be needed during the rest of the time 'on most fine nights to keep the pot boiling, to fill *ad hoc* requirements and to carry on with the mining': 'But I have personally a strong feeling that four raids a month by one thousand aircraft might prove to be very much more effective than one Thousand Plan a month plus ordinary every day hum-drum operations in the interim.'

On the evidence of the Cologne damage analysis, he believed that two to four successive raids of this size on a similar city would knock it out 'for any forseeable duration of the war', and suggested that a list of 20–30 such towns be drawn up. It would seem that Portal was in favour of this, and a list was being compiled,[4] but the comparative failure of the Bremen raid gave pause to the plan.

The problem was that Bremen had demonstrated that the 1,000 Raids, although spectacular, were self-defeating, given the present slender strength of Bomber Command. The Admiralty was not prepared to countenance a contribution from Coastal Command large enough as to obviate the need to draw on the OTUs. Indeed, on 16 June, the First Sea Lord had stated that while he had 'no wish to stop the bombing of Germany' he was 'anxious that priority be given to the improvement of our position at sea which, in his opinion, was more vital and of greater urgency, particularly since the bombing of Germany was a long-term project'.[5] The fact that Churchill, in the end, was not prepared to force him to increase his contribution to the Bremen raid indicates that he was of two minds. Besides which, the Battle of the Atlantic was no longer of purely British interest, but affected the Americans equally now that they were beginning to transport men and *matériel* across to Britain. If Britain were not seen to be pulling her weight in the Atlantic, this fact would play into the 'Japan First' lobby in the States. Thus, in order to mount the 1,000 Raids, OTU crews had to be used. However, although AOC No 91 Group had, after Cologne, stated himself in favour of such operations in the future, listing several reasons in support of them, he did accept that ten to eleven days' training had been lost as a result. Combined with the possible level of OTU casualties as demonstrated by Bremen, Harris's concept put a question mark over the ability of the OTUs to continue to provide sufficient crews to man the ever-increasing number of aircraft which Bomber Command was expecting to receive. The truth of the matter was that Harris had mistaken 'the wood for the trees', forgetting that the present period was a build-up to a more positive campaign in 1943, and his initial success at Cologne had temporarily blinded him to the limitations of his Force. He had set out to demonstrate what he could do, given sufficient aircraft, but now wanted 'to run before he could walk'. Yet it is clear that Portal, in his initial acquiescence to Harris's proposal, must take some of the blame.

There were, however, two other aspects. The first was the use of OTU crews who had already completed an operational tour (known as 'screened' crews as opposed to 'fresher' crews who were about to embark on their operational tours). They had gone to OTUs in order to have a well-deserved rest from operations, but how much of a rest was it when they were expected to take part in major raids over Germany? This question was graphically answered in a minute by the Under-Secretary of State to VCAS dated 2 October 1942. Discussing the case of some Royal Canadian Air Force (RCAF) Sergeant Instructors at an OTU, he wrote:

> Three of these are under arrest for being absent without leave – and this deliberately. They did not wish to refuse to operate because they would have become 'Ws'. Absenting themselves without leave did not bring their personal courage into question but enabled them to register a protest against going to war on old aircraft, which they considered inferior to those of their late operational units, during a period when they were supposed to be at rest.[6]

The message was plain.

There was also a moral aspect. A censor's analysis of letters opened in the wake of Cologne noted:

> There are those who are pleased and those who regret that so much suffering should have to be inflicted. There are those who fear reprisals. Many of the letters contain two or three of these elements. Predominant is satisfaction, but many women express regret . . .[7]

However, an open attack on the concept came from the eminent military theorist, Basil Liddell Hart, who opposed the strategic bombing campaign throughout the war. In a reflection written just after Cologne he remarked:

> If our pounding of German cities, by massed night bombing, proves the decisive factor, it should be a sobering thought that but for Hitler's folly in tackling Russia (and consequently using up his bomber force there, as well as diverting his resources mainly into other weapons), we *and* the Germans would now be 'Cologning' each other's cities – with the advantage on Germany's side, in this mad competition in mutual devastation.[8]

Not all the seeds of moral conscience had been blown away, but the Press were quite clear as to what these raids were about. Thus *The Times*, in an article on 'The Bombing of Germany' by its Aeronautical Correspondent, asked how long it was going to be before the Germans publicly accepted that the RAF was causing material damage to industry, communications and docks, instead of merely complaining about the deaths of civilians.

> It is certain, however, that at no time have the RAF deliberately attacked either civilians or non-military objectives. It would not be worth the while of Bomber Command to send valuable aircraft and highly skilled and equally valuable trained men such long distances merely to knock down a few inoffensive houses.[9]

Meanwhile, Harris relentlessly continued his battle to make Bomber Command the decisive weapon of the war, and bombarded Churchill with his views. In a long minute dated 17 June, he complained of the diversions from his force to 'the comparatively futile purpose of carrying a few paratroopers on one side show' and 'the already over-swollen establishments of the purely defensive Coastal Command'. He asserted that 'The success of the 1,000 Plan has proved beyond doubt in the minds of all but wilful men that we can today dispose of a weight of air attack which no country on which it can be brought to bear could survive.' As for Coastal Command, 'it achieves nothing essential either to our survival or to the defeat of the enemy'. Indeed, its very defensiveness made it 'merely an obstacle to victory'. He called for the return of all bomber types from Coastal Command, Army Co-operation Command, the Middle East, once the current situation had stabilised (at this stage Rommel was driving the Eighth Army in disarray back towards Cairo, and Tobruk was about to fall), the procurement of the maximum number of bombers from the States, for Stalin to use his heavy bombers to bomb Germany, and for the 'highest possible priority' for heavy bomber production. Then, he would knock out the German Baltic and North Sea ports, which would put paid to the U-boat threat, destroy Berlin and the Ruhr and then turn on Japan. Finally he stressed that 'premature landing on the Continent, before the bomber has done its work and the landing becomes a mere police action, spells disaster'.[10] Having read this, Churchill asked Harris to write a paper on the role and work of Bomber Command for consideration by the War Cabinet. This he submitted on 28 June, although it was another two months before it was circulated. He began by pointing out the numerous misconceptions that people appeared to have, and then went on to stress the work, in terms of GARDENING and attacks on U-boat installations, Bomber Command was doing in support of the Royal Navy. Once again, he stressed that 'the purely defensive use of air power is grossly wasteful', and likened the Naval use of it to 'picking at the fringes of enemy power, of waiting for opportunities which may never occur, and indeed probably never will occur, of looking for needles in a haystack'. Finally he spoke of:

> . . . an extraordinary lack of sense of proportion [which] affects outside appreciation of the meaning, extent and results of Bomber Command's operations. What shouts of victory would arise if a Commando wrecked the entire Renault factory in a night, with a loss of seven men! What credible assumptions of an early end to the war would follow upon the destruction of a third of Cologne in an hour and a half by some swift moving mechanised force which with but 200 casualties, withdrew and was ready to repeat the operations 24 hours later! What acclaim would greet the virtual destruction of Rostock and the Heinkel main and subsidiary factories by a Naval bombardment! All this and far more, has been achieved by Bomber Command: yet there are many who still avert their gaze, pass on the other side, and question whether the 30 squadrons of night bombers make any worth-while contribution to the war.[11]

Furthermore, as he pointed out in another minute to Churchill, this time arguing his case for his four 1,000 Raids per month, which Churchill, in order to clear misapprehensions in the public's mind, had warned would be the exception rather than the rule until the bomber force was considerably larger:

> The Army fights half-a-dozen battles a year. The Navy half-a-dozen a war. But poor Bomber Command! Every night that the weather gives us a breather even though our monthly sortie ration is always attained, every night that for such reasons we fail to stage and win a major battle, the critics rise in their wrath and accuse us of doing nothing yet again![12]

However, with the Admiralty sticking to its guns, and the Army viewing the bombing of Germany as only 'one of the many ways in which we will bring Germany to her knees',[13] Harris and Portal had little chance of getting their ideas whole-heartedly accepted.

Meanwhile, as the Bremen 1,000 Raid had only too amply demonstrated, the need to improve bombing accuracy was paramount. This was being tackled in two ways – by the formation of a specialist target marking force, and the introduction of new technical aids.

THE PATHFINDER CONCEPT

The idea of forming a special target marking force appears to have been first officially mooted in the Air Ministry in March 1942, when Group Captain Bufton, Deputy Director of Bomber Operations, suggested in a minute to Harris that he should designate six squadrons for this task, which could then concentrate on developing effective tactics. Bufton himself had commanded a Whitley squadron in 1940–41 and then a Halifax squadron, and hence had plenty of operational experience, and he was undoubtedly in close contact with those still on operations.[14] Mr. Justice Singleton had

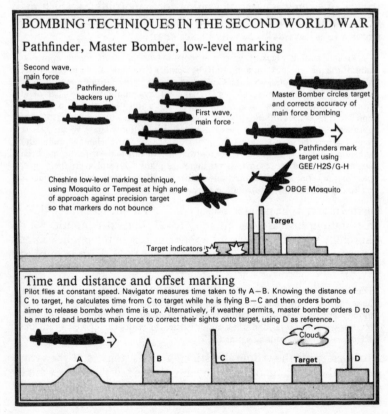

BOMBING TECHNIQUES IN THE SECOND WORLD WAR

Pathfinder, Master Bomber, low-level marking

Second wave, main force

Pathfinders, backers up

First wave, main force

Master Bomber circles target and corrects accuracy of main force bombing

Pathfinders mark target using GEE/H2S/G-H

Cheshire low-level marking technique, using Mosquito or Tempest at high angle of approach against precision target so that markers do not bounce

OBOE Mosquito

Target

Target indicators

Time and distance and offset marking

Pilot flies at constant speed. Navigator measures time taken to fly A–B. Knowing the distance of C to target, he calculates time from C to target while he is flying B–C and then orders bomb aimer to release bombs when time is up. Alternatively, if weather permits, master bomber orders D to be marked and instructs main force to correct their sights onto target, using D as reference.

A   B   C   Cloud   Target   D

interviewed two officers who had used GEE operationally, and their view was that they were satisfied with its accuracy 'provided that it was used by a specially-trained crew' and 'were firmly convinced of the desirability of a specially-trained Target Finding Force.'[15] Thus, it is very likely that the idea sprang from the grass roots of Bomber Command, the crews themselves, and was given official backing by Bufton. Harris considered the proposal and discussed it with his Group Commanders. While he had 'a fairly open mind on the subject of the Target Finding Force', he and his Commanders were 'against the formation of such a force'. Instead he proposed to institute a monthly competition among the squadrons, with those producing the best raid photographs being responsible for target finding the following month, which he believed would instill an atmosphere of healthy competition, thereby raising bombing standards throughout the Operational Groups as a whole. Furthermore, he believed that the standard of GEE operating was improving, and finally:

> . . . I am not prepared to accept all the very serious disadvantages of a Corps d'Elite in order to secure possibly some improvement of methods which are already proving reasonably satisfactory and certainly very costly to the enemy – at a serious loss of morale and efficiency to the other squadrons.[16]

Although Harris might seem to have been contented with the fact that any bombs landing within five miles of the aiming-point were considered to be on target, and to have felt that on this basis results were steadily improving, within his Command he was concerned about the lack of accuracy. During the summer of 1942 he rebuked his Group Commanders when analysis of raid and post-raid photographs did not reveal a sufficiently high standard of bombing. The subject was also frequently discussed at his Group Commanders' Conference. Thus, he did have to come round to Bufton's views that some form of permanent force should be set up, but resisted its becoming a separate entity. As Portal, who fully supported Bufton's suggestion, wrote to Harris on 11 June:

> Over a period of three months your attitude seems to have progressed from the complete rejection of the Target Finding Force proposal, through a Target Finding Squadron phase to this present raid leader suggestion. I can not feel that it is logical that you should now reject the final and essential step of welding the selected crews into one closely knit organisation which, as I see it, is the only way to make their leadership and direction effective.

He was convinced that the more effective the illumination the easier it would be to penetrate the industrial haze of the Ruhr, which was causing such problems at the time:

> What we need to aim at is an effective degree of illumination and incendiarism in the right place and *only the right place*. It is our opinion that this admittedly difficult task can only be done by a force which concentrates upon it as a

specialised role, and which *excludes those less expert crews whose less discriminating use of flares or incendiaries in the vicinity of the target have recently led so many of our attacks astray.*

He also reminded Harris that the Singleton Report, with its strong recommendation to increase accuracy, was before the Chiefs of Staff and 'any failure on our part to effect a radical improvement may well endanger the whole of our bomber policy'.[17] The force of Portal's argument was difficult to resist, and after fighting a rearguard action during a conference at the Air Ministry, Harris was forced, albeit reluctantly, to try out the idea. In a letter dated 20 June he ordered AOC No 3 Group to set aside four squadrons – two Wellington and two Stirling – for this purpose, with the warning that it might have to be increased to six in the future. These squadrons were to be known as Pathfinders, and their crews were to be of proven high calibre. If necessary, crews from other Groups were to be posted in.* Crews would wear a special badge, which Harris had originally envisaged as being worn by his Squadron Raid Leaders, the RAF 'eagle' worn below medal ribands. Those coming to the end of their tour were expected to carry straight on with a second tour, and Harris hoped that all Pathfinders would be given a step up in rank.[18]

He almost 'jumped the gun' on this last point and had to add a 'PS' stating that this had not yet been formally sanctioned. Indeed, the Treasury proved intransigent, in spite of the Air Ministry's and Harris's combined efforts to sway them. Eventually in desperation, Harris addressed a long and impassioned minute to the Prime Minister. In it, he expressed his reservations once again, this time arguing that he considered his force too small to support such a large specialist organisation, but stressed the need to make the prospect of volunteering for the Pathfinders attractive, especially as it had now been decided that promising crews would be invited to do so after their fifteenth operation.

> Well will they know what it means to continue straight through as Pathfinders to their sixtieth operational flight. They will always be in the forefront of the battle. The fully fury of untouched defences will always confront them. Tied to their 'aids' they will have to restrict evasive action to the minimum. We shall ask indeed much of these young men.[19]

Churchill asked the Chancellor of the Exchequer, Sir Kingsley Wood, what he could do about it. Wood considered that it was setting a dangerous precedent. Flying personnel, along with submariners, airborne troops and others, received special pay because

---

*Because Groups expressed concern at the thought of losing their best crews to the Pathfinders, it was agreed shortly afterwards that each Group would provide one squadron: No 1 Group (156 Squadron); No 3 Group (7 Squadron); No 4 Group (35 Squadron); No 5 Group (83 Squadron). They were later joined by No 2 Group's 109 Squadron, flying Mosquitoes.

what they did was dangerous anyway, irrespective of the enemy. 'But to recognise even continuous and acute danger arising from the actions of the enemy by the grant of added rank or pay is a very different matter.'[20] The Air Ministry then came back with compromise proposals, fixing a special establishment for Pathfinder squadrons, which would give good promotion prospects, and there the matter rested.

Harris personally selected D. C. T. Bennett, who had just got back from Sweden after being shot down during the attack on the *Tirpitz*, to command the new force. Bennett recalls his interview with Harris:

> He categorically refused to allow it to be called a Target Finding Force, because that was the name which had been put forward by the Directorate of Bomber Operations, and which he, therefore, automatically opposed. He did not put it quite in those words, but that was obviously the implication. He told me that whilst he was opposed to the Path Finder Force and would waste no effort on it, he would support me personally in every way. This assurance was carried out to the letter and in the spirit from then on to the end of the war.[21]

This was reflected at a Group Commanders' Conference at High Wycombe on 17 August, the day before the Pathfinders, who had been formally established on the 11th of that month, flew their first operation against Flensburg. Harris stated that he still did not consider the Pathfinder concept to be a practicable proposition and insisted that further emphasis be placed on every crew accurately identifying the target.[22] Even more significant was the fact that at this very time the Germans began jamming GEE. The new technical aids were still under development, so for the rest of the year the Pathfinder Force was to be reliant on merely their own experience and natural ability to identify targets.

THE NEW TECHNICAL AIDS

The two devices on which Bomber Command was pinning its hopes for the future were OBOE and H2S. The former was a development of the *Lorenz* beams used by the Germans in 1940. It was essentially a blind-bombing device, which relied on two ground stations, the 'Cat' and the 'Mouse'. The aircraft flew on a circle at constant range from the Cat, the navigator receiving audio signals to keep the aircraft on the correct course. The Mouse noted the aircraft's position on that circle and, when it was over the target, gave it the signal to bomb. It was first tried operationally by the Stirlings of 7 and 15 Squadrons in attacks on *Scharnhorst* and *Gneisenau* at Brest in December 1941, with reasonable results, but the equipment was found to be not yet reliable enough, and further development was required by TRE. It had been hoped that it might come into service in July 1942, but it was not ready until the end of the year. Although it had good potential for accurate blind-bombing, it did have drawbacks. Once again, it relied on line of sight, which, of course, limited its range, but even more so than GEE, in that the pulses travelled tangentially to the earth. The range of the system could only be increased by flying higher. Even so, when attacking targets in the Ruhr, where the aircraft's distance from the Cat was 270 miles, it would need to fly at 28,000 feet. This, of course, severely limited its use in heavily laden bombers, and at this time (August 1942), as Harris wrote in a minute comparing the advantages and disadvantages of it and H2S: 'At present all our heavies are unable in general to reach much above 21,000ft.'[23] Furthermore, a Cat and Mouse combination could control only one aircraft at a time, and the system was also sensitive to jamming.

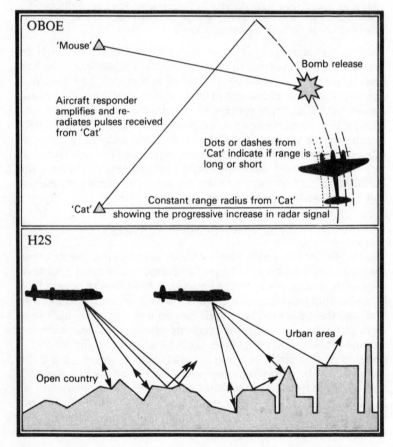

OBOE

'Mouse'

Bomb release

Aircraft responder amplifies and re-radiates pulses received from 'Cat'

Dots or dashes from 'Cat' indicate if range is long or short

'Cat'

Constant range radius from 'Cat' showing the progressive increase in radar signal

H2S

Urban area

Open country

The problem of limited range brought about the development of H2S, originally known as 'Home, Sweet Home'. A downwards-looking rotating radar transmitter scanned the ground over which the aircraft was flying. Different types of terrain, water, built-up areas, etc., produced different echoes, which gave a display, or at least an image, on a cathode-ray tube, of the country over which the aircraft was passing. In this way, H2S could be used both as a navigation aid and as a bombing device, but it took a skilled navigator to identify ground features from his display, and this was a disadvantage of the system. Another was that, since it depended on transmitters within the aircraft, the Germans could pick up the bomber stream and direct their night fighters to it with ease. Curiously, H2S was the very first radar aid to be put under development for bombers. Flight trials had begun in 1937, but the defensive role assigned to radar had forced it to take a back seat, and it was not seriously considered as an aid to bombing until about the end of 1941. Another factor was the type of valve used. The original development had used the klystron valve, which was well known to the Germans, but Coastal Command were interested in the newer magnetron valve and, as Harris pointed out at a meeting on the co-ordination of the bomber offensive held at the Air Ministry in mid July 1942, the latter had several advantages, especially in terms of range. The klystron valve had a range of only eight to twelve miles, and, if a bomber had to take evasive action over or near its target, it was difficult to pick it up again. Magnetron, although there were wrinkles still to be ironed out, had a forty-mile range, and was infinitely preferable. He therefore pressed that this type be fitted to two of the Pathfinder Squadrons for use during the winter, and it was agreed that manufacture would be concentrated on the magnetron type.[24]

This led to yet another clash with the Admiralty as to where strategic priorities lay. The magnetron H2S had been developed for Coastal Command, and yet here was Bomber Command trying to muscle in. Joubert wrote to Harris asking for his support in the Coastal Command drive to get 200 sets by Christmas, instead of by June 1943 as originally planned, so that the tempo of the anti-U-boat war could be maintained. This indeed had reached a crucial stage in that the Germans had developed the Metox receiver which was capable of detecting the metric klystron ASV radar and, with U-boat sightings falling off, Coastal Command urgently needed to switch to magnetron, or centimetric radar. Harris, not surprisingly, refused to agree if it was to be at the expense of his Command. 'Our casualties increase and the way to maintain pressure [on Germany] without an intolerable increase of casualties is to provide us with much of the equipment we have always shouted for and never been able to obtain because everybody else always had the priorities.'[25] In the event, neither was satisfied since manufacturing difficulties delayed the introduction of H2S until the end of the year. In the meantime, the Pathfinder Force had to continue as it was, and it was perhaps its notable ability over that of the average crews to find the target that gradually brought Harris round in favour of it.

CREW PROBLEMS

With GEE now being jammed, although great efforts were being made to modify it, which were generally successful, and the Pathfinder Force still, so far as High Wycombe was concerned, of questionable value, the drive to improve the bombing accuracy of individual crews was continued. By this stage the introduction of cameras into bombers had become widespread, and by the beginning of August HQ Bomber Command had instituted a scheme whereby, after each operation, the individual raid photographs were plotted on a chart with the name of the aircraft captain beside each one. Harris, however, was concerned that, while there were a large number of determined crews who did everything possible to get within the target area, there were others who 'consistently failed to get anywhere near the target'. The more of these there were, the more attacks would have to be made on that target.

> The peculiarity of night bombardment is that it is individualistic, no matter what the number of aircraft employed on an objective. There is, therefore, every latitude for the inefficient or the irresolute to 'get away with it', and to keep on doing so, at the expense of those who are determined to go right in, and to the depreciation of the effort as a whole.

He therefore proposed that the operational tour should be thirty operations, as opposed to 200 hours, and that for a particular trip to count, a crew would have to produce photographic proof that it had bombed the target. His argument for making the tour a specific number of trips was that:

> . . . towards the end of the tour crews become tired and stale. It has even been indicated that some of them are inclined to put in air time deliberately on the way to and from objectives.

He considered that crews of 'proved efficiency and resolution' be permitted to 'clock-up non-photo failure [sic] sorties at the discretion of squadron commanders', and that perhaps two-thirds of sorties would require photographic proof, including the last few of the tour. He accepted that 'this rule is a harsh step but it is becoming increasingly apparent that from every point of view it is an essential one'.[26] Certainly, this appears to have found favour with the Group Commanders. Indeed, Cochrane, who had just taken over No 3 Group, wrote to Harris on 19 September giving his first impressions, and was particularly concerned over lack of determination in pressing home attacks, which he put down to a high percentage of inexperienced crews within the squadrons, brought about by 'fairly heavy casualties over a long period'. He quoted a recent raid on Essen in which, of 72 crews detailed, four failed to take off and 19 turned back before reaching the target. Of the latter, having interviewed the captains, he found only two who had turned back for justifiable reasons. The most common and suspect reason for turning back was 'Intercom U/S' and those who made a habit of this were liable to be investigated as Waverers. Cochrane felt, after talking to his station commanders, that much of the problem lay in those crews that were skippered by NCOs, especially if there were no commissioned officer in the crew; he suspected that decisions were made in council rather than by the captain. The answer, he believed, was to ensure that the captain was of commissioned rank, even though he might not be the pilot.[27] This suggestion, however, cut across the basic principle enshrouded in RAF law, that the pilot was always the captain of the aircraft, and was rejected. Indeed, NCO skippers would continue to operate in large numbers for the rest of the war and just as effectively as their commissioned counterparts.

By this stage a fair amount was beginning to be known about the effects of stress on operational aircrew. In terms of casualties, a crew was at its most vulnerable at the beginning of their tour. Although they carried out GARDENING and NICKEL operations while still at OTU, it was not until they had had some five trips over Germany that they became properly *au fait* with operational flying. During 1942, however, it began to be noticed that too many experienced crews were being lost towards the end of their tours. The Senior Medical Officer (SMO) at RAF Marham, the home of 115 and 218 Squadrons of No 3 Group, in June 1942 reported that:

Until this year, 1942, it seemed that, generally speaking, if a crew survived their first 8 or 10 operational sorties, they would finish their tour safely. Now, however, they are lost as frequently towards the end of their tours as at the beginning. Many of these 'late' losses have occurred amongst crews who showed no sign of emotional and physical stress, and one suspects that perhaps they have become sluggish mentally. On the other hand these particular losses may be due to over confidence or great determination . . . these causes being more dangerous than they used to be.[28]

Or, as a crewman flying at the time remembers it:

Dick was at thirty, I was at twenty-seven and the others were knocking on in the late twenties and we had all reached that delightful state of being 'flak-happy'. This manifested itself in a feeling that since we had come so far along the road by which so many had fallen what was to stop us from going on to the end?[29]

Bomber Command ORS made a number of investigations, but could find no concrete evidence that there was a significant increase in crew casualties towards the end of a tour. However, after an investigation resulting from a high Halifax casualty rate in autumn 1942, which led to Halifaxes being grounded for four weeks, they did establish that the number of sorties which a pilot survived depended on the number of 'fresher' trips he made sitting in the Engineer's seat alongside an experienced captain. If he had three or under, his average life was two main operational trips, otherwise it went up to eight.[30] Even so, these were grim figures. Indeed, the Halifax was beginning to get as bad a name for itself as the Manchester. The same was so with the Stirling whose limitations were such that, it was decided to phase it out of Bomber Command in favour of increased Lancaster production. Harris himself was constantly complaining about both aircraft, and in a letter to Sinclair dated 30 December, he vented his spleen on the management of both Short's and Handley Page, speaking of 'the incompetent drunk' who ran the former and the fact that the Halifax situation would not improve until 'H.-P. and his gang are also kicked out, lock, stock and barrel'.[31] The Halifax situation did improve significantly with the introduction of the Series 1A in early 1943, although Harris continued to be dissatisfied. Yet both types could absorb a surprising amount of punishment, as this description of a trip in a Stirling shows:

I came back from Kiel Bay one night after having one engine blown clean out of its mountings by a direct hit from heavy flak when we were over the target. Then we were attacked by fighters on our way home – the bastards always went for the stragglers. One airscrew parted company from its engine as we crossed the Dutch coast and I saw it for an instant, shining like a scimitar, 400 yards ahead of us before it flashed into the sea. By the time we had shaken off the swarms of fighters we had 10,000ft on the clock, but we gradually lost height as we limped across the ditch towards the English coast. Soon it became obvious that one of our two remaining engines had absorbed a good deal of tracer before we had realised what was happening. The engine began to run rough and this got worse and worse until it was vibrating like an organ pipe. The only thing to do was to throttle back gently. This meant losing still more power and yet she still kept going – going like a bird – on one engine and the remains of the other just keeping her in the air. There wasn't a chance of bailing out when we had crossed the English coast; we hadn't enough height for that. Our rear gunner was dead, and the mid-upper was severely wounded. The flaps and undercarriage were more absent than present, and to this day I've never rightly understood how the aircraft held together let alone kept airborne. We put down in a stubble field not far from Brandon Heath and, as the aircraft came to rest, she simply fell apart as if she were tired of life.[32]

The other worrying aspect with regard to crews was over those who were embarking on their second tour. The SMO at RAF Wyton, also a No 3 Group station, noted in June 1942 that these displayed:

. . . a tendency to try and push themselves along as they fear the opinions of their fellows and a tendency on the part of the squadron commander to screen such men from Medical Section as there is still an unfortunate feeling in GD [General Duties] Branch that some slur attaches to flying stress.[33]

At this time, a man could be categorised as a Waverer in his second and subsequent tours, although this was rescinded in March 1943, but the Air Ministry were concerned enough about these veterans to put out a discussion paper to AOCinCs of all Home Commands at the end of November 1942. This asked for their views on reducing current tour lengths, then resting crews at their peak and making a second tour mandatory, extending the first tour to the maximum which crews were capable of and excusing crews a subsequent tour, or maintaining the existing scheme. They did stress, however, that:

Whichever system is adopted there is much to be said for allowing a degree of latitude to Squadron and Station Commanders and their medical advisers in deciding when any individual is reaching the limit of his physical or mental endurance and recommending the withdrawal from operations.

Both Coastal and Fighter Commands felt that the present system should remain, as did Harris, and only Army Co-operation Command argued for a shorter first tour. Indeed, Harris pointed to his ORS's conclusion that there was not a dramatic increase in the casualty rate towards the end of the first tour, and repeated their calculation that crews were asked to face a 1 in 20 risk of failing to return sixty times (two tours) in their operational careers, and that the risk of being killed was less than that of becoming a POW. He accepted that the overall risk was not small, but there was '. . . no indication that a majority or even a substantial proportion of the crews concerned is unequal to the strain'. Thus, the existing system was maintained.[34]

Meanwhile, the Pathfinder Force was cutting its teeth, and during the period August 1942 – January 1943 took part in 26 attacks, of which six were in bad weather when the target could not be identified, eleven were in moderate weather with the target being found in six of them, and the remainder in good conditions. Nine of these attacks, the ORS concluded, showed a significant improvement over pre-Pathfinder days, and, with the introduction of OBOE and H2S, there was every reason to suppose that Bomber Command's offensive against Germany would really begin to bite in 1943, especially with ever more Lancasters coming off the production line, and the United States Army Air Force adding its weight to the fray.

CHAPTER FIVE

TOWARDS A COMBINED OFFENSIVE

My American friends are despondent . . . The US Navy/Army faction are . . . determined to stop the bombing of French inland targets by the US Fortresses. – Harris

THE AMERICANS ARRIVE

On 17 August 1942 the US Eighth Air Force flew its first operational mission from England, when Brigadier-General Ira C. Eaker, commanding the first elements of the Eighth Air Force, personally led twelve B-17Es of the 97th Bombardment Group in an attack on the marshalling yards at Sotteville-les-Rouen. It was a daylight raid, with Spitfires providing the escort and a further six B-17Es flying a diversionary sweep. All returned safely, having bombed the target with reasonable accuracy, and an encouraging start had been made to the Americans' part in the strategic bombing campaign.* During the next few weeks a further ten American operations were mounted with fair success and only two aircraft were reported missing.

It had been agreed at the Washington Conference in January 1942 that the USAAF would join Bomber Command in an air offensive over Germany, but the US Air Staff had its own ideas as to how it should be carried out. Before America had entered the war, many of her nationals – journalists, businessmen, diplomats – had had the opportunity to see the results of the RAF's early efforts to attack Germany from the air, and, in general, had not been very impressed. The conclusion was that area bombing was ineffective, and better results would be gained by precision bombing by day. Pinning their faith on the heavy armament of the B-17 and its Norden bombsight, the Eighth Air Force arrived in Britain with this intention firmly in mind. However, apart from these gentle

---

*The first US attack on the Continent from Britain, using light bombers, had taken place on 4 July when six Bostons of 15th Bombardment Squadron (Separate) had joined six from No 2 Group's 226 Squadron in a raid on Dutch airfields. Two US and one RAF Boston failed to return.

'warm up' attacks the main effort was delayed by the diversion of resources to Operation TORCH, the Anglo-American landings in North Africa, which were to take place in November 1942. This would postpone any positive contribution by the USAAF until the new year. In the meantime there was a continuing debate as to how the Eighth Air Force should be employed when its time came.

Churchill was impatient at the delays over getting the Eighth Air Force into action. In a telegram to Roosevelt he congratulated him on the 'most encouraging' results of the first Fortress raids, but on the same day (16 September), he also sent a message to Air Marshal Evill, who had replaced Harris in Washington. In it he asked Evill to show Harris's minute of 28 June to the President, saying: 'Out of zeal he has no doubt over-stated a good case. None the less the paper is an impressive contribution to thought on the subject.' He also remarked:

> I cannot help feeling some concern at the extent to which the programme for the build-up of American air forces in this country is falling behind expectations, particularly in view of the withdrawal from the UNITED KINGDOM of over 800 British and American aircraft for TORCH.[1]

Indeed, Churchill was now under a constant bombardment from the Air Staff and Harris to raise the priority of the air offensive over Germany, and on 17 September he went so far as to inform Sinclair that Bomber Command must be increased from its existing 32 to 50 front-line squadrons by the end of the year. However, commenting on a paper written by Admiral Tovey, CinC Home Fleet, which pleaded for a high priority in aircraft allocation to the Royal Navy, he saw the issue as being 'not whether we should give everything to Tovey or everything to Harris', but merely in a change of emphasis from time to time. Yet, 'Tovey's paper damns itself by describing our bombing of Germany as "a luxury".'[2] Further encouragement could be drawn from an article in the influential American journal *Time*, which at the beginning of September 1942 carried an article entitled 'The *Real* Bombing of Germany'. Although 'TIME does not know whether Germany can be defeated from the air', this was not the question:

> Air power is no substitute, no panacea for the pangs of war. The question is only whether the US and Britain will elect to concentrate their maximum air strength against Germany this year. Bombing can mutilate Germany's might at home. Bombing, for the present, is the only way of striking the Germans at their sources of power. Bombing, on the grand scale, is the only way to strike a blow which, if it does not defeat Germany, will at least leave Germany crippled for the final blow to come.

Furthermore, it quoted a statement supposedly made by Harris in the previous spring: 'If I could send 20,000 bombers over Germany tonight, Germany would not be in the war tomorrow. If I could send 1,000 bombers over Germany every night, it would end the war by autumn,' and called for a 3,000 bomber force to be set up.[3]

Thus, with Churchill's approval for expansion having been given and definite signs of support from the American public, the Air Staff now began to draw up proposals on how the campaign should be conducted. Harris's own views had been given in a paper dated 3 September, which pressed for a review of air strategy, so as to resolve once and for all whether to concentrate on the bombing of Germany:

> The results secured by less than 30 squadrons at Cologne, Rostock, Lübeck, Emden, Hamburg, etc., (at least twenty German towns), prove beyond the possibility of doubt that given sufficient bomber force it would be possible in the next few months to raze substantially to the ground 30–40 of the principal German cities, and it is suggested that the effect upon German morale and German production of so doing would be fatal to them and decisive as encouragement and direct assistance to Russia.[4]

The Air Staff drew up a draft paper giving the case for a more powerful bomber offensive against Germany. They pointed out that at present only 10 per cent of the RAF's resources were being used in bombing Germany, an argument often used by Harris, and that new equipment and methods had resulted in the 'efficacy of our attacks' being 'more than doubled' during the past six weeks:

> The bomber force is thus poised for the launching of a series of devastating blows at the heart of industrial Germany. The effectiveness of these blows is entirely dependent on the weight behind them. Concentration of large numbers of aircraft against a target not only results in saturation of defences and therefore fewer losses, but it also results in damage which increases more rapidly than the number of aircraft.

There was also a reminder that bombing was, at the time, 'the only means of bringing home directly to the German people the realities of war'. An increased level of bombing would lower German morale, force the enemy to concentrate on fighter rather than bomber production and deploy a 'proportionate defensive organisation' which would reduce his offensive capability.[5]

The Air Staff now believed that it wanted an Allied bombing force rising to 'a peak of between 4,000 and 6,000 heavy bombers in 1944', and Portal stated, at a Chiefs of Staff Committee Meeting on 5 October that with this, he 'could shatter the industrial and economic structure of Germany to a point where an Anglo-American force of reasonable strength could enter the Continent from the West'. Amplifying this in a paper dated 3 November, he foresaw 25,000 tons per month being delivered on Germany by June 1943, rising to 50,000 tons by the end of that year and peaking to 95,000 tons by the end of 1944. 'Under such a plan 1¼ million tons of bombs would be dropped on Germany during 1943 and 1944.' As to the effect of this:

: Vickers Vernon, which Harris converted into a
ıber while in Iraq with 45 Squadron in the
0s. (RAF Museum)

tre: Vickers Virginia, the RAF's standard heavy
ıber between 1924 and 1937, which could fly
miles with a maximum 3,000lb bomb load.
ris, when in command of 58 Squadron during
mid 1920s, established several record
urance flights with the Virginia. (RAF Museum)

ht: Jill, Bert and Addles (full name Adolf) at
ntham in 1940, when Harris was AOC No 5
up. (Michael Tomlinson)

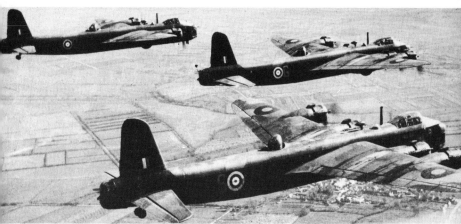

left: A Mk I Manchester of
? Squadron. The Mk IA had the
?tral tail removed, but this
?dification made little difference
?he aircraft's poor performance.
?M)

?ntre left: A Halifax Mk I, Series
?om 10 Squadron. The Halifax,
?r initial problems, became a
?able if unspectacular aircraft.
?M)

?ow left: The slow speed and
? operating altitude of the
?ling had banished it to fringe
?erations by the end of 1943.
?M)

?tom left: The best of them all—
? Lancaster, in this case a Mk I
?3 Squadron, one of the
?ginal Pathfinder Squadrons.
?M)

? right: 'Peter' Portal, AOC-in-
?omber Command and, later,
?m October 1940 to December
?5, Chief of Air Staff. Apart from
? great oil argument of winter
?4/45, the relationship
?ween Portal and Harris was
?se throughout the War, and
?h held the other in high
?ard.

?ow right: A mark of
?reciation to Harry Norman
?o administered the British
?umbia Air Training Programme
? of the Empire Flying
?ining Scheme, which provided
? bulk of Bomber Command
?rews from 1942 onwards. (Brig
?. Frank Norman)

Above: A Junkers Ju88C-6 night fighter with the prominent *Lichtenstein* AI radar aerial array. Although *Lichtenstein* was a very effective radar device, its aerodynamic shape caused a reduction in the aircraft's flying speed. (IWM)

Below: Freya early warning radars along part of the Kammhuber Line. The layout of the German defences, with their combinations of radar, flak, searchlights and ground-controlled night fighters, was a formidable barrier for Bomber Command. (IWM)

Top right: The main weapons i RAF Bomber Command's armoury, c.1944. (IWM)
Below right: Bombing up a Stirling of 7 Squadron at RAF Oakington. (IWM)

12 000 LBS

4000

2000

1000

500

KC 7

YOMG

Above: "Your target for tonight..."; and, **below,** the tensest time of all—before being driven out to board the aircraft, which were kept well dispersed about the airfield in order to present a minimal target. (IWM)

... apart from the direct destruction of industries and public utilities, an attack
on this scale would lead to the destruction of eight million German houses . . .
Civilian casualties are estimated at about 900,000 killed and about 1,000,000
seriously injured. These estimates make no allowance for the fact that the
number of persons per house would tend to increase as the destruction of
dwellings progressed.

With regard to the effect on German industry, Portal listed a total
of 58 towns and cities, with Berlin as the furthest east, and indicated the general industries of each. Using the first 1,000 raid as his
yardstick, and this had resulted in the devastation of a third of the
inner zone of Cologne and 250 factories destroyed or damaged, he
forecast that 'during 1943 and 1944 every industrial town in
Germany with a population exceeding 50,000 could receive, *in
proportion to its size*, ten attacks of "Cologne" intensity'. He
estimated that one-third of Germany's industry would be
destroyed. As for morale, he accepted that the effect was difficult to
quantify in terms of 'a scale of bombardment which would far
transcend anything within human experience. But I have no doubt
whatever against a background of growing casualties, increasing
privations and dying hopes it would be profound indeed.'[6]

Portal had boasted of the number of civilian casualties, but there
was still a sensitivity about admitting that Bomber Command was
purposely inflicting civilian casualties. The Anglo-American
Bombing Policy, which had been drawn-up as a result of the
Combined Chiefs of Staff Meeting in Washington at the beginning
of June, had laid stress on the moral damage to be caused by
bombing centres of population, but an Air Ministry comment on
this stated:

It is unnecessary and undesirable in any document about our bombing policy to
emphasise the aspect, which is contrary to the principles of international law,
such as they are, and also contrary to the statement made some time ago by the
PM, that we should not direct our bombing to terrorise the civilian population,
even in retaliation.

It was recommended that industrial centres be referred to as such,
and not as 'centres of industrial population' or 'centres of population'. The primary objective was the destruction of industry, or
Germany's war potential, and 'the workers who suffer from the
bombing are incidental to that objective'.[7] Yet, on 12 October
ACAS (Policy) had circulated a letter down from Group level,
reminding commanders that 'bombardment should be confined to
military objectives', and that the intentional bombing of civilian
populations was forbidden. Additionally, the target must be identi-
fiable and 'reasonable care' taken to minimise civilian casualties.
However, 'consequent upon the enemy's adoption of a campaign of
unrestricted air warfare, the Cabinet have authorised a bombing

policy which includes the attack of enemy morale. The foregoing rules do not, therefore, apply to our conduct of warfare against German, Italian and Japanese territory.'[8] Thus, civilians were fair game, but this would not be admitted in public, despite growing questioning of it, as we shall see.

Churchill's view on Portal's proposal was, initially:

> The rate of bombing discharge contemplated (about 50,000 tons a month) is at least 5 times greater than we suffered at the height of the blitz. I very much doubt whether Germany could stand it for six months. I am sure she could not stand it for more than a year. As CAS allows two years, and moreover, takes no credit for secondary effects or for the improved accuracy which we should undoubtedly achieve, I consider that this paper errs, if at all, in being too conservative.[9]

Nevertheless, within a few days he was having doubts over the scope of the plan: 'It would be very much better to aim at a smaller target total for 1944 and make sure of hitting it than give way to pleasures of meglomania.'[10] Alanbrooke was even more doubtful. If the Allied air offensive was intended to pave the way for the invasion forces, the latter must also be built up. This, including their close air support, must not be restricted by the growth of the former, which he feared that the Portal plan would produce. He also questioned the assumption that the bombing force would be totally dedicated to bombing Germany. 'We shall have, for example, to meet the claims of Italy, targets in occupied territory, sea-mining, shipping, the Battle of the Atlantic, air transport and airborne forces.' Thus he felt the plan was over-optimistic and indeed out of balance with overall Allied strategy.[11]

AMERICAN BOMBING POLICY QUESTIONED

Yet, within this debate lay another, which caused much confusion between Churchill and the Air Ministry. This was the question of the American approach to strategic bombing. Portal, after the RAF experiences with the B-17 in the summer of 1941, was distinctly disparaging about the US intention to carry out daylight precision bombing, and Churchill agreed with him. As he said in a telegram to Harry Hopkins, Roosevelt's personal aide:

> I must also say to you for your eye alone and only to be used by you in your highest discretion that the very accurate results so far achieved in the daylight bombing of France by your Fortresses under most numerous fighter escort mainly British, does not give our experts as much confidence as yours in the power of the day bomber to operate far into Germany.

Also, several newspaper articles dealing with the Eighth Air Force attacks on Lille in early October, had claimed that the B-17s had shot down 48 German fighters and damaged 38 others and had concluded that 'Flying Fortresses battleship [sic] is making the fighter obsolete'. The Air Ministry dismissed this as spurious, claiming that there were only sixty German fighters operating on that day,[12] and Churchill told Hopkins that he thought that the American claims of fighters shot down were incorrect, and '. . . the dangers of daylight bombing will increase terribly once outside Fighter protection and as the range lengthens'.[13] However, Slessor ACAS (Policy), believed that, given sufficient bombers, the Americans could be successful, and, in any event, '. . . the present time is not the moment for persuading them otherwise especially as elections are pending in America'.[14] Sinclair sided with Portal, believing that the Americans must introduce a night bomber force, but then came a *volte-face*. Churchill now laid down that the Americans must be persuaded to divert their energies to sea operations in support of TORCH. At the same time, Spaatz, Commanding General US Eighth Air Force, and Eaker made clear their concern over Churchill's and the Air Staff's criticism of their policy, not so much that they were offended by it, but because of its implications. As Harris, in another of his impassioned pleas, wrote to Churchill on 23 October:

> My American friends are despondent . . . The US Navy/Army faction are, firstly, determined to stop the bombing of French inland targets by the US Fortresses. If they succeed in this they hope to assert both precedent and pre-occupation to keep the bombers off Germany.
> To that end the US Navy and Army are engaged in pressing that the whole US Bomber resources now in this country should be switched towards the Atlantic War and protection of convoys.[15]

In other words, both US Navy and US Army at this stage were more concerned about the safe passage of troops and *matériel* for the Second Front, as well as the more immediate task of safe-guarding the TORCH convoys. Sinclair also wrote to Churchill on the same day along similar lines. He reminded Churchill of the 4,000–6,000 bomber plan, but said that this could only come about if Churchill declared 'unequivocally' that the heavy bomber was the main instrument of victory, and that the US gave the necessary priorities within its aircraft programme to achieve this size of force. He said that the Air Ministry now believed, with sufficient numbers of bombers and good gunnery training, which echoed Slessor's words, that the daylight policy had 'a chance of success', and painted a picture of RAF attacks on places such as Hamburg by night being followed up the next day by American attacks:

> To ally ourselves with the American Navy against General Spaatz and General Eaker and the United States Air Force in this country, and to force them into diverting their highly trained crews to screening U-boats, instead of the bombing of Germany, would be disastrous.[16]

Churchill, however, in his reply to both, said that it was essential that US Flying Fortresses and Liberators be used to protect the

TORCH convoys, and if they were not used, then Lancaster squadrons would be called upon. Although Sinclair again asked him to reconsider, Churchill continued to have doubts about the US daylight policy and still wanted their priorities to be sea work and night bombing.[17]

As for the Chiefs of Staff, Alanbrooke's arguments on the dangers of committing too much to the air offensive at the expense of the invasion forces caused Portal to amend his views. Whereas the bombing offensive was a necessary preliminary to invasion, as both accepted, Portal predicted that 'the German fighting services will retain their discipline to the last . . .'[18] and realised that the Allied invasion forces would need to be strong, which was a significant move away from the Air Staff's original view that the invasion would be little more than a police action after the bombers had carried out their offensive. Thus, the Chiefs of Staff were able to come up with a common policy, and this was enshrined in a memorandum dated 31 December, which defined the aim of the Allied bombing offensive as 'the progressive destruction and dislocation of the enemy's war industrial and economic system, and the undermining of his morale to a point where his capacity for armed resistance is fatally weakened'. The 4,000–6,000 bomber target was dropped, and in its place was put a target of 3,000 by the end of 1943. It was also emphasised that the new project would not be greatly detrimental to fuel supplies for the invasion forces, a fear which Alanbrooke had expressed with regard to the original plan. It also made the point that: 'It is not claimed that the bomber offensive will at once shatter the enemy's morale. It is claimed that it already has an appreciable, and will have an increasing effect, on the enemy's distributive system and industrial potential – an effect which the German High Command and German people will fear more and more.' Furthermore, as far as the Americans were concerned, they would, if their daylight operations failed, have to be prepared to turn their bomber force into a night one.[19] This was the British view which would be put forward at Casablanca.

Bomber Command, despite its priority of night bombing, had continued to try out daylight operations after Augsburg. In the main, these were carried out by No 2 Group against targets in France and the Low Countries, with escorts from Fighter Command. Lancasters were employed twice more. On 11 July 1942 a force of 44 was sent to attack the U-boat construction yards at Danzig. Although they flew at low level to begin with, they were soon able to gain height and make use of the widespread cloud as cover, even though this made navigation difficult, and a third of the force failed to find the target. The remainder, who were intended, as at Augsburg, to arrive over the target at dusk, were late:

Most of us arrived over Danzig when it was pitch dark. In my aircraft, instead of bombing Danzig at night, where we couldn't even see the docks, let alone the streets, we had bombed a small ship in the outer harbour and missed it by twenty yards from 1,000 feet.[20]

Thus, although two Lancasters were lost from flak, it was hardly a daylight raid, and the only memorable aspect of it was that the round trip of 1,500 miles represented the longest so far attempted by Bomber Command. Another experiment with Lancasters was undertaken on 17 October, when 94 were sent against the Schneider Arsenal at Le Creusot. Here, in order to avoid the German day fighters, they took a long dogleg out into the Atlantic and then came in over the French coast south of Brittany, taking a more direct route home. This involved a total distance of 1,700 miles and was done at low level, with crews practising for some days beforehand, using Fighter Command to make dummy attacks on them. Bombing from between 2,500 and 7,000 feet at dusk, Guy Gibson's official report recorded: 'Huge fires broke out and terrific explosions were seen over a wide area . . .'[21]

However, although few German fighters were met and only one Lancaster failed to return, post-raid photographs revealed disappointing results, with many of the bombs having overshot the target, which was only partially damaged. Bomber Command ORS concluded that much more training would be required to make this type of operation effectual. Furthermore, if Bomber Command were going to take the business of daylight raids by heavies seriously, this training would reduce the power of the night offensive. Also, the aircraft would need to be armoured and carry heavier armament, which would mean a reduction in bomb-load. Indeed, the VCAS, Freeman, had wanted Harris to convert one of his squadrons to specially armoured Lancasters in May 1942, so that they could perfect daylight precision bombing, and informed him that a further one hundred were on order. Harris objected strongly to this, and despite pressure from the Air Staff, which continued throughout the summer, he dug his toes in, complaining that the Air Ministry was interfering in the tactical handling of his forces. With Portal's pessimistic view of American intentions vis-à-vis daylight bombing, Harris, on this occasion, eventually got his way and the matter was dropped,[22] and his part in the strategic bombing campaign was confined to night raids.

U-BOATS AND BALL-BEARINGS

During autumn 1942 there was also another debate on how best to deal with the U-boat threat, which became aggravated during 1942 when the Germans adopted a new Enigma machine, with a fresh code, which meant an uphill struggle for the Ultra codebreakers at Bletchley Park. So concerned was Churchill that he formed a special CID Anti-U-boat Committee in early November. TORCH and American concern to safeguard their transatlantic convoys aggravated the situation, and the Admiralty believed that the best way to reduce the threat would be to bomb the U-boat bases. Consequently, Portal drew up plans for this, proposing that the four main Atlantic bases be attacked by a maximum bomber effort on the first fine night in a full moon period. There was some debate as to whether the French population of the ports concerned should be warned, but it was concluded by Churchill and Eden, then Foreign Secretary, that since the attack would be a precision one, there was no need. Hence on 19 November Harris was issued with an instruction calling for attacks on Lorient, Saint-Nazaire, Brest and La Pallice. 'Need for accuracy is stressed not only to ensure effective attack, but because of desirability on political grounds to avoid undue civilian casualties.' Harris was not happy, however, and replied to Portal on the 21st, saying how 'disheartened' he was by the proposal. He pointed out that the residue of the US bomber force not involved with TORCH had been attacking them by day and was finding that the heavily concreted U-boat pens were impervious to damage. Nevertheless, they were doing sufficient to make 'the Boche very chary of leaving any submarine outside the pens if there is room inside them', and felt that the Fortresses were 'doing more than enough by day'. He then made an interesting admission:

Until we get the Mark XIV Sight* we are virtually unable to do accurate bombing at night. Therefore, as was evidenced in our attacks on Brest, about one bomb in five hundred aimed at the docks might hit a submarine or might hit one of the few workshops engaged in submarine repairs, if we are lucky. All the rest of the bombs would either go in the water or kill Frenchmen in the town.

He argued that GARDENING was much more effective, and claimed that since they had begun laying acoustic mines outside the ports at the beginning of October, two U-boats had been destroyed and five damaged. Even more wounding to the enemy were attacks on U-boat construction, and he gave examples of recent successes against Emden and Wilhelmshaven:

I see therefore that we should press on with this method of dealing with U-boats at the source and not start wasting our substance around the fringes. But I can't do it all myself. The Americans must help and make some worthwhile contribution to the war. Eaker is keen enough but you know his Navy/Army troubles.[23]

Portal accepted Harris's points but, after further lengthy argument with the Admiralty, relented and a number of attacks were

---

*This was a stabilised vector sight, which was introduced into the Pathfinder Force in the late summer of 1942. Having a computer system it allowed gentle evasive tactics without upsetting accuracy, but still required wind velocity over the target to be fed in manually, and thus was not a true precision sight.

launched on Lorient during the second half of January 1943. Although large-scale damage was inflicted, mainly in the dock area, the Air Staff view was that the limited effect on U-boat operations was not commensurate with the diversion from the bombing of the main target, Germany. The Admiralty continued to disagree, but in mid February it was decided to discontinue the attacks until a firm decision could be made by the War Cabinet. During this period, the Admiralty and the Battle of the Atlantic exasperated Harris perhaps more than anything else during his time at High Wycombe. Indeed, at one point in December 1942, he wrote a long minute to Saundby suggesting that:

> Coastal Command should be renamed the High Seas Command and its opera-
> tional control should revert to the Air Ministry. Much of the force in it would
> then become available for the destruction of the centres of U-boat production,
> without in any way jeopardising essential sea routes, and in the knowledge that
> the scale of U-boat attack on these routes would begin thereafter to rapidly
> decline.
>   All vessels engaged in convoy escort duties should be re-constituted into an Air
> Sea Arm and operated in the manner which the old Coastal Command has set as
> a precedent, that is, be provided and manned by the Admiralty and operated in
> retail by them under the overall operational control of the Air Ministry.[24]

Saundby obviously realised that his suggestion that the RAF take over the conduct of the Battle of the Atlantic would have clearly lost Harris what little credibility he had with the Admiralty, and ensured that this view remained firmly inside Bomber Command.

Another call on Bomber Command, and one which would remain a bone of contention throughout the war, was the question of the ball-bearing industry and the MEW view that more than fifty per cent of it was centred on Schweinfurt. Harris had been pressured to attack this town in the spring of 1942, but was concerned about the difficulty in locating it, although he said that he would keep an 'open mind' on it as a target.[25] By August the Air Staff had concluded that it would need an attack by 500 bombers, but required a ground marking system, known as EUREKA, to be emplaced by agents before it could be carried out. There the matter rested until the autumn, when, after a new MEW appreciation, which argued that 'the destruction of this town, and of its factories and the killing and wounding of the greatest possible number of its inhabitants promise to produce such far-reaching effects on the German war effort as to take the project right outside the field of routine bombing operations', Harris was consequently given a directive by Bottomley dated 21 November. He was, in conjunction with Coastal and Fighter Commands, and the Americans, to produce a detailed plan for attack 'on the heaviest scale and in the most effective manner which our total resources in the United Kingdom will permit'. Attached to this letter was a copy of the

MEW appreciation, as was a suggestion that the target was worth a 'maximum effort' on the lines of the 1,000 Raids, with OTU and Conversion Units crews being included as well, and that it would be worth any cost. Harris replied two days later. Although the town could be dealt with by incendiary attack, the factories themselves would require to be taken on at low level in fine weather, or attacked by day. He argued that the target would be too difficult for crews under training and would disrupt the 'fifty squadron' expansion programme. He believed that an attack at low level by night using a total of 455 aircraft, including a Coastal Command contribution, would be the best course, with the best crews going for the factories themselves. If need be, the attack would be repeated until the necessary damage had been done. The Americans could also attack by day, provided the weather was suitable, but this was not essential to the plan. However, he was concerned about the Air Staff's view that 20 per cent or more losses would be acceptable.

Crew losses over a period of a month are replaced gradually and provided the daily rate of loss does not exceed a small percentage, the effects are not serious. On the other hand, the sudden loss of a large number of crews on a single operation has a crippling material effect and moral effect on the squadrons taking part. Squadrons would remain at low strength for a considerable time and new crews could only be fed into them when they became available from OTUs and Conversion Units. The moral effect of concentrated losses and the inability to replace them would be very marked.

He said that he could accept a 10 per cent loss rate for an operation specifically undertaken against a valuable target, but no more. He also considered the MEW assumptions to be 'facile' and felt that further study of the ball-bearing industry not only in Germany, but the Occupied and neutral countries was required, reminding Bottomley of the fact that the year before the authorities had concluded that Germany was suffering from a severe oil shortfall, but that this had not prevented the invasion of Russia. He therefore stated that he would carry out the raid in his own way in the near future and clearly resented the way in which MEW and the Air Ministry were attempting to dictate the method by which he should carry out his operations.[26]

U-boat bases and ball-bearings caused Harris enough trouble at this time, but he might have been further exasperated if he had heard about a request sent by a Member of Parliament, Eric Errington, to the Prime Minister towards the end of September. By this time battle was raging around Stalingrad, and Errington suggested: 'Would it not be possible to send a number of our heavy bombers to bomb the Germans in front of Stalingrad even if it meant loss and failure to return. The uplift to our people and the Russians of Wellingtons bombing Germans in front of Stalingrad would be very great if properly publicised.' Churchill asked Portal to draft a reply, and one can sense the latter's exasperation, although it is not clear as to whether the resultant letter was ever sent:

> I think your idea is simply splendid. I can't think why the Air Staff had not thought of it before. I have told Air Marshal Harris to send 1,000 bombers tonight. As you say, it won't matter at all if they don't return – we've plenty more where they come from. I have also instructed the First Sea Lord to send the Home Fleet up the Volga and all our aircraft carriers to the Sea of Asov to bomb the German L. of C. [Lines of Communication] in the Crimea. If that doesn't uplift our people and the Russians I don't know what will.[27]

Indeed, Churchill and his military leaders were constantly bombarded with suggestions on how the war could be won, as was Harris, and it was hard, given the pressures they were under, to maintain their patience.

Despite Harris's frustrations at attempts to divert Bomber Command from what he saw as its main role in the war, the end of 1942 saw the Command in a much better position than it had been at the end of the previous year. As at 1 January 1943, there were 31 front-line heavy squadrons alone, with 338 heavies available, 292 of them with crews,[28] and on this day No 6 (RCAF) Group was formed. Then on 25 January, at Harris's request, the Pathfinders were grouped into No 8 (PFF) Group under Bennett. The Lancaster had established itself as the backbone of Bomber Command's operations, and of the pre-war types, only the Wellington remained in front-line service. The Manchester, too, to the relief of those who had to fly it, had been removed from the Order of Battle. The new technical aids were now being introduced. H2S had been fitted to Halifaxes of 35 Squadron and Stirlings of 7 Squadron by mid January 1943, and it made its operational début over Hamburg on the night of 30 January but, because of slowness in production, it would not be in universal use until the end of the year. OBOE had already been fitted to the Mosquitoes by December 1942 and was first used against Lutterade on the 20th of that month. The Pathfinders had had the Mark XIV bombsight since the previous summer and were now switching over to the more sophisticated Stabilised Automatic Bombsight Mark II (SABS), while the main force was beginning to receive the Mark XIV. The Pathfinders, too, were now obtaining proper Target Indicators (TI) and these were first used on Berlin on the night of 16/17 January.* The effectiveness of the bombs themselves was also increasing, and by this time there was an 8,000lb High Capacity (HC) bomb in service, which was carried in a modified Lancaster. Thus, Bomber Command was finally

---

*Berlin was attacked again the following night, and Harris sent a personal message to the crews exhorting them to 'Go to it, Chaps, and show them the red rose of the Lancaster in full bloom.'[29]

receiving the means to carry out an effective strategic bombing campaign, and it was now a question as to how it would put these to use. But first, Allied bombing strategy had to be agreed and this was one of the major agenda items at the Allied conference at Casablanca held to decide the overall conduct of the war against the Axis.

CASABLANCA

The historic meeting at Casablanca between Churchill and Roosevelt and their Staffs in January 1943 reaffirmed the policy of 'Germany First' and agreed that the object of this was to obtain her unconditional surrender. In order to bring about her defeat, it was agreed, albeit after some debate, that Sicily (Operation HUSKY) would be the next immediate objective for invasion, with the object of knocking Italy out of the war; that the battle against the U-boat must be won as soon as possible, and that the build up of the Allied forces in Britain (Operation ROUND UP) would continue with a view to invading the Continent of Europe. As far as the strategic bombing campaign went, its aim as drawn up by the British Chiefs of Staff in their 31 December memorandum was agreed almost word for word, and now read, as addressed to 'the appropriate British and United States Commanders, to govern the operation of the British and United States Bomber Commands in the United Kingdom:

> Your primary object will be the progressive destruction and dislocation of the German military, industrial and economic system, and the undermining of morale of the German people to a point where their capacity for armed resistance is fatally weakened.

Within this general aim, primary objectives 'subject to the exigencies of weather and of tactical feasibility' would be in the following order of priority:

(a) German submarine construction yards
(b) The German aircraft industry
(c) Transportation
(d) Oil Plants
(e) Other targets in enemy war industry.

It also stated that other targets of 'great importance either from the political or military point of view' were to be attacked, and mentioned specifically U-boat bases on the Atlantic coast, and the city of Berlin. They were warned to expect to be called upon to attack targets in northern Italy in support of amphibious operations in the Mediterranean theatre, as well as 'fleeting targets' such as German naval ships in harbour or at sea. Every opportunity must be taken to attack Germany by day 'to destroy objectives which are unsuitable for night attack' with the aim of sustaining pressure on German morale and containing her fighter strength. They were also warned that 'when the Allied Armies re-enter the Continent, you will afford them all possible support in the manner most effective'.[30]

This was issued to Harris verbatim, on 4 February 1943, with a covering note from Bottomley stating that it superseded Directive No 22. Harris's interpretation of this was to be crucial to the handling of Bomber Command throughout the rest of the war. His own post-war recollections of it were:

> The subject of morale had been dropped, and I was now required to proceed with the general 'disorganisation' of German industry, giving priority to certain aspects of it such as U-boat building, aircraft production, oil production, transportation and so forth, which gave me a very wide range of choice and allowed me to attack pretty well any German industrial city of 100,000 inhabitants and above.[31]

Yet, it was not until a month after its issue, and then on the eve of the first of his three major offensives of 1943, that he came back to the Air Ministry about it. In a letter dated 6 March he wrote:

> For more than a year the agreed view of the Combined Chiefs of Staff had been that our main enemy, Germany, can be defeated only by increasing the pressure of the combined British and American air attack until internal disintegration is produced and allied invasion of Germany itself is thereby rendered possible, that this view still holds the field is shown by paragraph 1 of the directive . . . which states categorically that the 'primary objective of Bomber Command will be the progressive destruction and dislocation of the German military, industrial and economic system aimed at undermining the morale of the German people to a point where their capacity of armed resistance is fatally weakened'.[32]

Thus, contrary to what he said in his own justification immediately after the war, it was not how he viewed the Directive at the time, in that he had changed the wording of Paragraph 1 to suggest that the ultimate objective was the undermining of German morale. Furthermore, as the Official History points out,[33] he implied that Paragraph 1 in the way that he had amended it was his preserve alone, and that the Americans would be left to deal with the subsidiary targets mentioned in following paragraphs. In this respect, he had a case, in that mention of daylight operations appeared only in Paragraph 5 of a seven-paragraph Directive and everyone was aware of the American intention to pursue the daylight raid policy. On the other hand, Churchill was still convinced that the Americans should bomb by night, which may have accounted for the fact that the American role was not specified at the outset. There was, therefore, room for interpretation, and it is significant that the Air Staff did not come back and correct Harris in his interpretation. Harris, while commenting that it was a 'laudable desire to satisfy everyone and attack all possible targets', also hoped that this would not distract him from his 'primary object'. The Americans, as will be seen in the next chapter, took a very different view.

U-BOATS AGAIN

In the meantime, in spite of the pause called in mid February, Harris was still plagued with demands to bomb the Atlantic ports. Indeed, March 1943 was to be one of the grimmest months in the Battle of the Atlantic, with more than 500,000 tons of shipping being sunk. At a meeting of the Defence Committee on 23 February, Portal stated that the U-boat pens were about to be thickened even further, at which point the First Sea Lord urged that attacks be continued immediately before the concrete was thickened, with the Americans going in by day and the RAF by night. It was agreed that attacks would delay refitting of U-boats, which would be of considerable help, and it was decided that attacks, albeit on a reduced scale, would be carried out on all ports. These went ahead, but Harris maintained that his bombers would be much better used in attacking the sources of supply. In a letter to Portal dated 15 March he employed a different argument, saying that the Admiralty had estimated that the attacks on Lorient had delayed the sailing of nine U-boats by sixty days. Since on Admiralty figures, each U-boat was at sea for two months, this meant that three cruises had been delayed.

> During January and February, as far as I can calculate from the figures in my possession, approximately 395,000 tons of shipping were sunk by U-boats in the Atlantic so that, if we taken an average of 130 U-boats at sea at any given time, the average U-boat sinks 3,000 tons of shipping per cruise. Our attack on Lorient therefore probably saved 9,000 tons, or one fair sized cargo ship. In order to do this, 4,329 tons of bombs were dropped on Lorient, so that it takes over 4,000 tons of bombs on a U-boat base to save one 9,000 tons ship.[34]

Even given that Harris was some 100,000 tons too low in sinkings and that the number of U-boats at sea operating out of Atlantic ports was nearer eighty at this time, there is still an inescapable logic in Harris's assertion. A memorandum by him dated 29 March brought still further arguments into play:

> . . . it is inevitable that at no distant date the Admiralty will recognise that U-boats can be effectively dealt with only by attacking the sources of manufacture but by then much time will have been lost and the whole success of the Bomber Offensive, which may have a decisive influence on the success of Russia and even of her remaining in the war, will have been jeopardised.[35]

But the Royal Navy saw themselves at a crisis point. As the First Lord, A. V. Alexander, had written one week earlier: 'After allowing for the necessary shipping to bring the minimum imports into this country, there is insufficient shipping to allow us to develop the offensives against the enemy which have been decided on. Every ship sunk makes the situation worse.'[36]

Portal, however, came firmly down on Harris's side, especially as he was now well into the Battle of the Ruhr, the first of his offensives of 1943. In a minute also dated 29 March he stated that it was a most unfavourable time to divert bombs from the attack on Germany:

> Our growing strength, so painfully built up during the past winter, coupled with our radio and other aids to accuracy (which the Germans are at present unable to counter) enable us to at least do really heavy damage to transport and morale and therefore afford, substantial support to all other fronts. In my opinion we should make the very most of our opportunity (even if this means the sacrifice of a few extra merchant ships per month) and press home our attack on Germany.[37]

This minute was significant in other ways. First, there was Portal's emphasis on morale, which indicated that he shared the same somewhat twisted interpretation of the Casablanca Directive as Harris, and the only other target mentioned was transportation, which had been laid down at Casablanca as a lower priority than U-boat construction yards and aircraft factories. Yet, the very next day the First Sea Lord came back with a demand that Bordeaux be also placed on the list of Atlantic ports, stressing that attacks must be carried out now on the U-boat bases. Portal apparently got on to Harris immediately, who came back on the same day with a minute detailing the effort required by the Admiralty on the Atlantic ports would mean a diversion of 25 per cent of Bomber Command's effort on Germany for two months. To do the job properly would 'absorb the entire effective effort of Bomber Command for at least two months'.[38] Cherwell, too, launched into the attack on the same day asserting that 'it will surely be held in Russia as well as here that the bomber offensive must have the more immediate effect on the course of the war in 1943'.[39] In the face of all this opposition the Admiralty were forced to climb down, and on 6 April, Bottomley sent Harris an amendment to his directive:

> ... after consideration of the results so far achieved, it has been decided that the employment of your main bomber effort in this form of attack [against U-boat bases] is for the present to be discontinued. The effort thus released is to revert as far as possible to attacks on Germany.

He was, however, to carry out harassing attacks against these bases, and it was thought that they would be suitable targets for Fresher crews. The Americans would also attack them by day, especially Lorient with its U-boat servicing facilities, when weather over Germany was not suitable.[40] Harris had therefore won this round, and was free to devote his attentions to the Ruhr, which had now been under continuous attack for a month.

CHAPTER SIX

THE BATTLE OF THE RUHR

Two years ago we reckoned to get one-fifth within 5 miles of the target. Today we get over two-thirds within 3 miles. – Cherwell

---

'. . . On the night of March 5th–6th, 1943 . . . I was at last able to undertake with real hope of success the task which had been given to me when I first took over the Command a little more than a year before, the task of destroying the main cities of the Ruhr.'[1] On that night, 442 bombers set out for Essen to open what was to be a four-months' battle, the Battle of the Ruhr, or Happy Valley, as it was called by the crews. As usual, in spite of the reasonably clear night and the Met forecast that haze over the target should not present a problem, it did so, and was there, just as thick as ever. This time, however, using tactics perfected during the past ten weeks, eight OBOE-equipped Mosquitoes from 109 Squadron were taking part. At three-minute intervals, beginning at 2100 hours, they dropped red TIs on the Krupp's works, which was the designated aiming-point. To back them up were 22 Pathfinder aircraft, which were to drop green TIs on the reds at one- and two-minute intervals for 38 minutes. The main force attack, which was to be in three waves – Halifaxes, Wellingtons and Stirlings, and finally, Lancasters – was to be compressed into 38 minutes, with the Lancasters completing their attack two minutes after the last green TI had been dropped. The main force crews were briefed to go for the red TIs first, and if they could not identify them, then to go for the greens. In order to help main force navigation, yellow TIs were to be dropped by the marking aircraft and other Pathfinders fifteen miles short of the target. Such then was the plan and, as the Official History pointed out, it was novel in that at no stage did crews have to identify the target visually.[2]

Although OBOE in three of the Mosquitoes failed to function, and 58 (including 14 shot down) other aircraft failed, for one reason or another, to bomb the target, the remainder all claimed to have successfully attacked. A total of 293 photographs were taken, of which 39 showed some detail of the ground – another indication of the haze problem – and of these eighteen were within three miles of the aiming-point. Of the other photographs, from the fire tracks displayed, it was possible to identify another 104 that were within three miles of the aiming-point. From this evidence, Bomber Command ORS concluded that 153 aircraft, or just over 40 per cent of the aircraft which actually attacked, had been within target area, a significant improvement on any previous Essen raid. This demonstrated that OBOE was very effective as a target locator, and Harris determined to capitalise on its success. Because of its limited range, however, the Ruhr was the obvious target to use it on, and his concentration on this area, with the object of reducing 'production in the industries of the Ruhr at least as much by the indirect effect of damage to services, housing, and amenities, as by any direct damage to the factories or railways themselves',[3] was a logical step.

Yet, Harris's next major target was outside OBOE range, and provided an opportunity to use H2S instead. On the night of 8 March a force of 298 heavies, including 157 Lancasters, the largest number of this type so far assembled for an operation, attacked Nuremberg. They were assisted by 36 Pathfinders. The idea was for the latter to use H2S to drop sticks of illuminating flares over the target, and to use them to identify the aiming-point, which was to be marked by green TIs. If the backers-up could not spot the aiming-point from the illumination provided by the original marker aircraft, they were to use their H2S to drop red TIs. The three main force waves were to bomb over a period of thirty minutes and to attack the TIs, be they red or green. However, H2S could give only a general idea of the target area, and accurate target marking was still dependent on good visibility and, like GEE, it was more suitable as a navigation rather than a bombing device.

As it happened, visibility was only moderate over Nuremberg, and the fourteen markers, six of whose H2Ss were inoperable, either dropped red TIs blindly or did their best to drop green TIs through visual identification from their flares. The result was that the TIs were scattered, which meant that the main force attack was scattered too. Even so, post-raid analysis concluded that 142 aircraft had dropped their bombs within three miles of the aiming-point, and photographs taken on the 10th revealed considerable damage to industrial plants, especially in the southern part of the city. Another encouraging aspect was that only seven aircraft were posted missing. Nevertheless, when compared to the Essen raid, where damage was concentrated in a particular area, the results were somewhat disappointing and lacked the punch OBOE could provide.

An important aspect to note, however, was the difficulty of analysing damage from post-raid photographs. In the context of Harris's view that the Admiralty and 'other interested parties' viewed the bomber offensive as 'a futile waste of effort', he felt that Air Intelligence should maintain comprehensive records on its effect, especially on German industry, and produce appreciations on various aspects for general circulation.[4] The ACAS (Intelligence), Inglis, was asked to comment on this, and brought out a very telling and significant point:

> Although we can record the number of hits on plants and the amount of roofing removed, we can seldom record precisely the effect on output, nor do we often receive reliable information with regard to the rate of repair. For instance, within the last 12 months the only definite fact we can record with regard to the effect of bombing on the aircraft industry is that Heinkels at Rostock lost production over a period of 3 or 4 weeks. Yet, without doubt, our bombing of industrial cities must have seriously dislocated production of all types of armament.
>
> We do not know, however, what effect this has had on the general production programme, since the German 'target' figures are not known. Such a review, if based on reliable reports, would therefore fall short of the actual dislocation achieved, while any attempt to give a truer picture would be sheer guess-work.[5]

Thus, without knowing details of German production plans, it was impossible to calculate the delays that bombing had caused on various programmes, and hard to gauge the effect on German industry. Indeed, this would remain a problem throughout the war, and only post-war investigations would reveal the true effect. Nevertheless, Harris himself believed that it was important that the damage being caused should be given wide publicity, and set up what he called 'the blue book'.[6] In this, he was able to display to visitors to High Wycombe the progressive damage to German population centres by marking the areas of devastation with blue paint on air photograph mosaics. This and a display of post-raid photographs viewed in a Victorian stereo lantern projector – a stereoptician – were shown to every visitor of note who came to HQ Bomber Command.

For the next few weeks, in spite of the obvious advantages of OBOE over H2S as a target locating device, there were more attacks on targets beyond the Ruhr than against the latter. Thus Munich, Stuttgart and Berlin (twice) were the subject of major attacks during the remainder of March, as against only two visits to the Ruhr, Essen again and Duisburg. During April, the main attacks were even more varied with three operations against Duisburg, two against Essen, as well as La Spezia and single trips to Kiel, Frankfurt, Stuttgart and Rostock. There was also a double operation mounted against Pilsen and Mannheim on the night of 16/17 April, with 327 aircraft being sent to the former, losing 37 of their number and 18 out of 271 being lost against Mannheim, a combined loss rate of almost 10 per cent. The main reason for this was that it was a bright moonlit night, which made the bombers easy prey to the night fighters. However, towards the end of April, with the nights getting shorter, longer-distance targets became more dangerous to take on, and much greater effort was dedicated to the Ruhr.

May saw a further eight major raids, all of which, apart from another visit to the Skoda works at Pilsen (which had been wrongly identified by the Pathfinders in their previous operation against it), were directed against the Ruhr. A noticeable aspect at this time was the growing number of individual sorties per raid. By 30 June, for the first time, Harris had more than 500 heavies alone available with crews, and with the Wellingtons manfully carrying on, he was able to launch no less than 826 sorties against Dortmund on the night of 23/24 May, the highest number since the 1,000 Raids of the year before. But even on the nights when there were no major operations, other types of sortie were mounted and there was rarely a day or night without some activity. For a start, No 2 Group continued daylight operations, usually against aerodromes in France with their Venturas and Mitchells, and Bostons, which had now taken over from the Blenheim. Their Mosquitoes also carried out precision attacks, often against railway targets in France. By night, too, the Mosquitoes were also active, with pinprick raids against Berlin being a frequent operation, while GARDENING and NICKELS continued unabated. Furthermore, the Whitleys of No 91 Group were used on anti-submarine patrols in support of the Admiralty. Thus, a typical day's operations was that of 19 May. By day, 12 Venturas attacked Ploujean airfield near Morlaix, while No 91 Group mounted five anti-submarine sorties. A No 8 Group Mosquito also undertook a meteorological flight over the Continent to confirm doubts as to the unsuitability of the weather for a major night attack. Then, that night, six Mosquitoes set off for Berlin, with two making successful attacks, while five No 91 Group Wellingtons dropped NICKELS over Orléans. All aircraft returned safely.

So far as the main force was concerned, few crews enjoyed the prospect of trips to Happy Valley. Although the flight time was comparatively short, the ever-increasing strength of the German anti-aircraft defences, both ground and air, made it an unhealthy spot to be in. Always uppermost in their minds was the desire to complete their tour safely, but the growing intensity of the bombing campaign swung the odds against them. Here is how one Lancaster captain felt with only a few more operations to do:

> My crew have the jitters, being now so near the end of their tour and anxious to survive it. I talked to them en route to Base while low over the sea. Told them that as long as they flew with me, we would continue to do our best over every

target. My conscience won't let me do anything else. They agreed to stick to it instead of dropping the load outside the defended areas as we see some planes do. I know how they feel. They're tired. Griffiths is particularly nervous of late. He's only nineteen. So young.[7]

There was, too, the question of what operations counted towards the thirty trips and what did not, and at times some unjust decisions were made. Bottomley, in a letter to Harris dated 20 January 1943, had cited the case of an officer who had been placed in Category 'W'. On one occasion, on the outward flight, his aircraft had been attacked by night fighters over the North Sea and had been forced to jettison its bombs. On another, a GEE failure had necessitated an early return, but his aircraft had then crashed, killing the captain and flight engineer. Since the crew had not reached the target, let alone taken their raid photographs, the squadron commander had ruled that neither of these trips should count towards the tour. With experiences like these, it was understandable that this particular officer should have suffered a loss of nerve. Bottomley felt that, in order to take into consideration cases such as this, if a crew got past a certain meridian east, or penetrated enemy territory to a certain depth; were involved in combat with enemy aircraft which necessitated early return to base; or suffered greater stress than normal, their trip, abortive though it might have been, should be allowed to count. Harris's reply was one of total disagreement:

> I am most unwilling to do anything to foster the idea that our crews are under some description of Trade Union contract to carry out a certain number of carefully defined operations, after which they are free, at any rate for a fixed period, to take no more part in the war.[8]

Nevertheless, at an AOCinCs' conference on tour lengths held on 4 February, Harris did recommend that the second tour be reduced to twenty operations, and that the first tour for Pathfinders be brought down to 45 trips with a second tour liability, crews having the option to withdraw at any time after thirty trips, both of which were agreed. Six weeks later, he was forced to ask the Air Ministry if he could again increase the Pathfinder tour to sixty operations with the guarantee of no second tour for those who volunteered. With the Battle of the Ruhr getting into its stride, the pressure of operations caused problems in the training of sufficient replacement Pathfinder crews.[9]

THE EAKER PLAN

In the meantime, while Bomber Command's attacks on Germany were gathering momentum, the Americans were planning their own version of the Combined Chiefs of Staff Casablanca Directive. At this stage, the Eighth Air Force was still 'nibbling round the edges'.

Part of the reason for this was the need to support the Battle of the Atlantic, which meant attacks not just on the Atlantic U-boat bases, but on German ports as well; but also, as will be seen, because they did not yet consider that they had sufficient bombers in theatre to launch into the Casablanca Directive immediately. On 12 April Eaker presented his 'Combined Bomber Offensive', more familiarly known as the Eaker Plan, and his approach was somewhat different from that of Harris's. His premise was that it was 'better to cause a high degree of destruction in a few really essential industries than to cause a small degree of destruction in many industries', and to this end the American Air Staff had selected six key systems – submarine construction yards and bases, the aircraft industry, ball-bearings, oil production, synthetic rubber and military transport. This faithfully followed the Casablanca Directive, and within these systems the Americans had identified 76 specific targets. In RAF circles, as well as in Churchill's mind, there were gnawing doubts that the Americans could carry this out in daylight, but the experience gained during their first few operations over Germany, which had begun at the end of January, convinced them that they could bomb precision targets from heights of 20,000–30,000 feet, but that for a deep penetration of Germany, they would need a minimum force of 300 bombers, which meant having at least 800 in theatre. To this end, and in pursuance of the joint 3,000 bomber target, the plan called for some 950 heavy bombers to be in the United Kingdom by 1 July 1943; 1,200 by 1 October; 1,750 by 1 January 1944 and 2,700 by 1 April 1944. In addition, US medium bomber strength would rise from 200 to 800 over the same period. Although, unlike Harris, he did not openly claim that the offensive could win the war, Eaker believed that without it a cross-Channel invasion was not possible, and it would work only if he had the required bomber strength.

However, the word 'Combined' had been used in the title of the plan, and Eaker recognised the growing power of Bomber Command; he also realised that its attacks on the morale of the German work force could be harnessed to the American effort:

There is great flexibility in the ability of the RAF to direct its material destruction against these objectives which are closely related to the US bombing effort, which is directed towards the destruction of specific essential industrial targets. It is considered that the most effective results from strategic bombing will be obtained by directing the combined day and night effort of the US and British bomber forces to all-out attacks against targets which are mutually complementary in undermining a limited number of selected objective systems. All-out attacks imply precision bombing of related targets by day and night where tactical conditions permit, and area bombing by night against the cities associated with these targets.

The initial RAF view of this was that it should be supported to the hilt in order to ensure that the Americans contributed maximum weight to the offensive. Thus, Harris told Eaker that he was 'in complete agreement', although he did point out that 'the Plan as it stands may prove somewhat inelastic in the event. In practice, it could and would be modified as necessary to meet developments in the general situation and to accord with new information as to the effects of past attacks on different types of objective.' Portal, too, told Arnold that he considered the plan 'entirely sound' and ordered the RAF Delegation to make the British Air Staff's support for it plain, saying that experience had proved that the Americans could indeed carry out precision attacks by day, and that they had destroyed an 'impressive' number of German fighters.[10]

The opportunity to gain acceptance of the Eaker Plan by the Combined Chiefs of Staff, as well as Churchill and Roosevelt, came at the Washington Conference held in May, and the united front of Arnold and Portal ensured that it was pushed through. However, the document presented at Washington featured some significant changes from Eaker's original plan. For a start, the statement that the preferred principle was to concentrate on a few vital targets was struck out, and, in conjunction with this, Bomber Command was given even more leeway.

> This plan does not attempt to prescribe the major effort of the RAF Bomber Command. It simply recognises the fact that where precision targets are bombed by the Eighth Air Force in daylight, the effort should be completed by RAF bombing attacks against the surrounding industrial area by night.

The document also laid great stress on the German fighter threat:

> If the growth of the German fighter strength is not arrested quickly, it may become literally impossible to carry out the destruction planned and thus create the conditions necessary for ultimate decisive action by our combined forces on the Continent.

The Eighth Air Force therefore proposed to operate its attacks in three parts. First, some fifty heavies with fighter escort would draw the German fighters to a particular area, thereby allowing the 'main striking force' of 200 heavies (minimum) a relatively uninterrupted flight to its target in Germany. Then, as the latter began its return trip, a further diversionary force of the same strength would be sent out. As for the overall conduct of the American part of the offensive, this was to be in four parts. Currently, they were concentrating on targets within fighter range, especially Atlantic Coast U-boat installations. During July–October 1943 they would penetrate to 400 miles depth over Germany, concentrating mainly on fighter factories. During the last three months of 1943, the depletion of German fighters would be maintained and other targets would be attacked. Finally, at the beginning of 1944, steps would be taken to pave the way for 'combined operations on the Continent'. The point was clear, and further, the Washington version of the plan alluded to the possibility that the increase in German fighter strength might hinder night bombing as well, and would have to drastically reduced before the bombing campaign that would pave the way for the invasion got under way.[11]

POINTBLANK (the codename of the combined bombing offensive) was duly approved at Washington. It is important to note, however, that in the 'main objective' statement of POINTBLANK as agreed at Casablanca, the phrase 'fatal weakening' was seen as crucial by the RAF and USAAF, whereas Roosevelt and Churchill, together with various military and naval officers in high command, took it to mean, not in itself decisive in achieving victory in Europe, but to so weaken Germany 'as to permit initiation of final combined operations on the Continent',[12] and this variation in interpretation was to become significant later on.

Bottomley now drafted a fresh directive to reflect the concern over the increasing German fighter threat. 'In these circumstances it has become essential to check the growth and to reduce the strength of the day and night fighter forces which the enemy can concentrate against us in this theatre.' This, including the industry on which they depended, was to be 'first priority' for the combined bomber forces. Although the primary objectives listed in the Casablanca Directive still stood, the Luftwaffe was to be the 'intermediate objective', and it was emphasised that 'the reduction of the German fighter force is essential to our progression to the attack of other sources of the enemy war potential and any delay in its prosecution will make the task progressively more difficult'.[13] When taken in the context of the US four-phase bombing plan, however, it implied that the overall object of the Casablanca Directive could not be properly tackled until the beginning of 1944, but then morale, which Harris saw as the main objective, was not mentioned in this document, only the six specific industrial targets.

Bottomley showed his draft to Harris and Eaker and, as a result of their comments, certain significant changes were made in the final form, which was issued on 10 June. In particular, the main objective of POINTBLANK was reinserted. However, while the Eighth Air Force was given the specific intermediate objective of German fighter strength and the original six industrial objectives, it merely said that 'British Bomber Command will be employed in accordance with the main aim in the general disorganisation of German industry', although 'their action will be designed as far as is practicable to be complementary to the operations of the Eighth Air Force'.[14] Harris had therefore succeeded in avoiding being tied down to the intermediate objective and had, at the same time, retained reasonable latitude to carry out his part in POINTBLANK as he saw fit. The stock of Bomber Command was particularly high at this time, not just because of successes being obtained in the Battle of the Ruhr, but because of a particular 'one off' operation, which had recently been carried out.

THE DAMS RAID

Operation CHASTISE, the Dams Raid of the night 16/17 May 1943, is without doubt, in terms of technical ingenuity, imaginative planning and coldblooded courage, the greatest epic in the annals of RAF Bomber Command. It is not proposed to describe the operation in any detail, since the story is well known, and recently two excellent books[15] have appeared on the subject, which tell the true story in detail, at the same time removing many of the myths that surround it, and an outline will suffice.

The idea of attacking the Ruhr dams was not new; the Air Ministry had been living with the idea since 1937, when their value to German industry was first recognised. Portal, Bottomley and Saundby were all well aware of their importance from personal pre-war considerations, but for long the problem was the lack of a suitable weapon. Unaware of Air Ministry deliberations, Barnes Wallis, designer of the Wellington and the man who made CHASTISE technically possible, had been considering methods of attacking the dams since the outbreak of war, as part of his belief that air bombardment should be concentrated on Germany's sources of energy. His ideas eventually generated sufficient interest for the Ministry of Aircraft Production to set up a special Air Attack on the Dams (AAD) Committee, which met three times during 1942. A number of tests were carried out by Wallis at the National Physical Laboratory at Teddington, and other experiments were carried out at the Road Research Laboratory at Harmondsworth. Through these, Wallis developed his 'bouncing bomb' concept, but for a long time the Air Ministry were sceptical. Indeed, the Admiralty showed somewhat more enthusiasm for it as an anti-ship weapon. Consequently, by the end of 1942, Wallis was working on two versions: HIGHBALL, two of which would be carried by a Mosquito for attacks against ships, and UPKEEP, its big brother, which would be carried in a Lancaster for use against the dams. Trials from a Wellington at Chesil Beach in Dorset at the beginning of 1943 proved the concept, and during the latter half of February won the Air Ministry over. Saundby briefed Harris on it, but the latter, continually bombarded as he was with wild and impractical suggestions on how to win the war from the air, was initially highly sceptical: 'This is tripe of the wildest description. There are so many ifs & ands that there is not the smallest chance of its working.'[16] After further meetings at the Air Ministry, Saundby again briefed his Commander, who then wrote to Portal: '. . . all sorts of enthusiasts and panacaea mongers are now careering round MAP suggesting the taking of about 30 Lancasters off the line to rig them up with this weapon, when the weapon itself exists so far only in the imagination of those who conceived it'.[17] Apart from the fact that he had confused HIGHBALL with UPKEEP, which would have brought suspicions into his mind that this was another Admiralty diversion, he had only recently received the Casablanca Directive and was gearing himself up to launch his attacks on the Ruhr and other targets in Germany, in which the Lancaster was to be his cornerstone. Harris also produced technical arguments as to why the concept would not work, but, with the aid of films of his Chesil Beach trials, Wallis convinced Portal, although Harris, having seen them, still poured scorn on the idea – something which he did not admit in *Bomber Offensive*. Nevertheless, Portal, who had lived with the idea of knocking out the dams since its inception, believed that the idea should be given a try, and three Lancasters were allocated for UPKEEP trials.

By mid March, Harris had been told that the operation was to go ahead, and that twenty Lancasters would be modified to take UPKEEP. It was logical that Harris should choose No 5 Group, now commanded by Cochrane, who had moved from No 3 Group at the end of February, since it was the most experienced on Lancasters. In view of the special nature of the operation, Harris told Cochrane that he must form a special squadron, but that it was not to be to the detriment of the main effort against Germany, and personally selected Wing Commander Guy Gibson, whom Cochrane did not know, but whom Harris did from his No 5 Group days, to command what was then called Squadron 'X', soon to be 617 Squadron.

It is worth looking at the experience of the crews who came together for this raid, as it gives an idea of the general level of operational experience in Bomber Command at this stage in the war. Gibson himself, only one of two pre-war airmen in the squadron, epitomised all that was best in Bomber Command and that gallant band, whom Harris called his 'old lags'. For the first year of the war he had been continuously on operations in Hampdens with 83 Squadron and had won a Distinguished Flying Cross. During 1941 he had had a tour with night fighters, winning a bar to his DFC, and then had been posted in April 1942 to command 106 Squadron, which was equipped with Manchesters, but about to convert to Lancasters. He had, on being posted to Squadron 'X', having been awarded a DSO for his leadership and gallantry, just completed yet another tour with 106, and had carried out no less than 71 operations in bombers alone. His two flight commanders, Maudsley and Young were also experienced. Maudsley had completed a tour in 44 Squadron during 1941, winning a DFC and had just rejoined 50 Squadron for his second tour, while Young, who had joined the RAFVR just before the outbreak of war, had flown one tour with 102 Squadron in 1940, a second tour with 104 Squadron in the Middle East, and had, with two DFCs, just arrived at 57 Squadron for his third tour. Of the other eighteen pilots, one had completed two tours, ten, one tour, and the remainder, contrary to a Bomber Command instruction which called for volunteers from among those who had completed or nearly completed two tours, were still only on their first tour, and five had only begun it in February 1943. As for the remainder of the crews, the same varying pattern of operational experience was reflected and for one or two, especially among the flight engineers, the Dams Raid would be their very first. Those like Gibson, Young and Hopgood, who had theoretically completed their operational flying for the duration, were a breed who were never happy unless they were in the air. Thus, Harris in his introduction to Guy Gibson's *Enemy Coast Ahead* recalls the problems that he had in trying to get Gibson to take a rest:

> In a third and final effort to force him to rest from operations, he was put on his Group's staff. A few days later he was found in his office with – literally – tears in his eyes at being separated from his beloved crews and unable to go on operations. It was in fact breaking his heart.[18]

The difficulty in meeting the Bomber Command directive on crew experience reflects the comparative scarcity of second-tour aircrew at this stage in the war, although clearly there were others flying in No 5 Group at the time who could not be spared from their squadrons. In terms of nationalities, 617 Squadron represented a good cross-section of Bomber Command. Among the pilots alone were twelve RAF, including one Australian, the legendary 'Mickey' Martin, who would finish the war with two DSOs, three DFCs and 83 operations under his belt, three RAAF, five RCAF, including one American, and one RNZAF.

It had originally been planned to launch UPKEEP and HIGHBALL together, with the latter being used against the *Tirpitz*. However, the HIGHBALL trials were unsuccessful and, in view of the favourable weather, which might not recur, the Chiefs of Staff, then in Washington, gave approval on 14 May for UPKEEP to go ahead. The detailed planning was left very much to HQ No 5 Group and Gibson, with Saundby keeping a watching brief and representing the Group's interests at the various Air Ministry conferences on the subject. Harris was now clear as to the vital importance of the raid, and especially the influence its success might bring on the Washington conference. Thus, on the evening of the 16th, he went down to No 5 Group HQ at Grantham and joined Cochrane and Wallis there. The fact that he did so, which was so against his normal practice, shows that he regarded the operation as vital. Nineteen Lancasters took off in three waves. The first, consisting of nine aircraft led by Gibson himself, was to attack the Möhne Dam and then the Eder. Any aircraft with a bomb still on board after these two attacks would tackle the Sorpe. The second group, led by the one American, McCarthy, would take a different route and go for the Sorpe, as well as acting as a diversion for Gibson's group. The third wave were to act as an airborne reserve. At the same time, as a diversion, nine Mosquito sorties were flown against Berlin (3), Düsseldorf (2), Cologne (2) and Munster (2), 54 GARDENING sorties were mounted by Nos 3, 4 and 6 Groups off the Friesian Islands and French U-boat ports, and four Wellingtons from No 92 Group were involved with NICKELS.[19]

Apart from perfecting the technique for actually dropping UPKEEP, 617 Squadron had also spent much time practising low-level flying, since much of the outward and return routes would be flown at a height of 60 feet in order to avoid enemy radar. This was to cause three casualties on the outward trip. One of the second-wave aircraft had to return early when it hit the sea and lost its bomb, while another hit a high tension cable and was destroyed. A third, from the back-up party, crashed when it hit trees while trying to avoid flak. Three more were shot down by flak on the way out, one from each wave, and a further aircraft from the second wave had to abort when flak caused the intercom to become inoperative. Gibson's wave breached the Möhne with the fifth bomb, losing one aircraft in the process, and then went on to attack the Eder which was successfully breached with the third and final bomb. Meanwhile, McCarthy, the only survivor of the second wave, had caused a small breach in the Sorpe Dam, which was later widened, but not decisively, by one of the back-up group aircraft. Tragically, both flight commanders were shot down on their way back, making a total of eight aircraft lost, only three members of the crews of whom survived to become prisoners of war. As the aircraft returned, Harris, Cochrane and Wallis motored over to Scampton to greet them, and one of Harris's first actions was to telephone Washington to inform Portal of the success of CHASTISE.

The Dams Raid undoubtedly produced an enormous fillip not just to British morale, but to that of the Allies and those living in the Occupied Countries. Among the many plaudits was one by Churchill, who used the success of the raid to reiterate the Allied bombing strategy when he addressed the US Congress on 19 May:

The condition to which the great centres of German war industry, and particularly the Ruhr, are being reduced is one of unparalleled devastation. You have just read of the destruction of the great dams which feed the canals and provide power to the enemy's munition works. That was a gallant operation, costing eight out of the nineteen Lancaster bombers employed, but will play a very far-reaching part in reducing the German munition output . . . Wherever their centres [of war industry] exist or are developed, they will be destroyed.[20]

The Americans were clearly impressed, and it certainly helped the Combined Bomber Offensive plan to gain acceptance as official Allied policy. It was also a valuable morale booster to the remainder of Bomber Command, and, as the Dortmund–Ems Canal raid of August 1940 and the Augsburg Raid of April 1942 had previously demonstrated, it showed the skill and determination of which the Command was capable. It was these factors which made the raid so important, and not so much the physical damage caused, which turned out not to be as substantial as first thought or hoped, and which has been the main target for postwar critics of the raid. Nevertheless, the lesson had once more been reinforced that the casualty rate was too high for Bomber Command seriously to contemplate precision operations by day deep into Germany.

THE RUHR – FINAL PHASE

Meanwhile the Battle against the Ruhr continued, although the weather in the early part of June forced a pause. The last raid in May had been against Wuppertal on the night of the 29th/30th when, of 719 bombers which took off, 644 claimed to have attacked, and of these 475 appeared, from post-raid analysis, to have dropped their bombs within three miles of the aiming-point. From this it was deduced that some 110,000 people had probably been made homeless and much of the town's industry destroyed. It was one of the most successful operations to date, despite the loss of 33 aircraft, with another 71 damaged. Yet, it was not until the night of 11/12 June that the next major raid was mounted. In the meantime, conditions were so bad that on three days, 7–9 June, only 'Met' sorties were flown, which prompted a minute from Churchill asking why there had been a lull. On 16 June as a result Harris wrote a letter to Portal explaining his target selection philosophy. In essence, the short nights limited him to an arc Emden – Münster – Dortmund to halfway between Bonn and Coblenz. However, the northern twilight made targets on the German coast dangerous, because it was so easy to pick up the bombers visually. If the night were clear, Harris went for 'the most valuable target on which the heaviest concentration is required', but, when cloudy, which meant air marking being employed, it was better to go for 'a scattered area target or very large town'. He

quoted Gelsenkirchen, Oberhausen and Duisburg as good examples
of the latter, while Dortmund, Bochum, Essen, Düsseldorf and
Cologne required ground marking to reap the best benefit. He was
fully aware that if he merely concentrated on one particular area,
i.e. the Ruhr, he would encourage the Germans to concentrate their
night defences. Hence he used his Lancasters, with their higher
speed and thus increased range, in terms of ability to be able to
operate during the short nights, and Mosquitoes to attack targets
outside the Ruhr. Experience had also shown that OBOE was
'precise' when used in the ground-marking role, but less accurate as
a sky marker. In any event, the size of the main force was limited
by the number of OBOE Mosquitoes available. Thus, one Mosquito
could mark the target for four minutes and the bomber stream
could attack at a rate of ten per minute. Also the higher the top of
the cloud, the fewer types, bearing in mind the lower ceilings of
other bomber types compared to that of the Lancaster, could be
used when sky marking had to be employed. As for H2S, it 'is never
precise, it is only accurate against a compact and *isolated* target'
such as Münster or Osnabrück. Using it against a large city meant
that there was no guarantee of hitting a particular part of it, and
the Ruhr merely showed up as 'a blaze of reaction'. All these factors
limited Harris's options during the midsummer period. Nevertheless:

> As the nights lengthen, we hope to have dealt sufficiently severely with the Ruhr
> to necessitate only an occasional topping up to keep it out of action on the one
> hand, and unwilling to part with any part of its defences on the other. We will
> then go progressively further into Germany in, I hope, sufficient strength to be
> able to leave behind us, as we progress, a state of devastation similar to that now
> obtained in the Ruhr; if the Boche waits for it. We shall then have available to us
> more plums in the way of such as the complete destruction of Hamburg and a
> really hearty hammering of Berlin . . .[21]

The Düsseldorf raid of 11/12 June was the beginning of the final
and most concentrated phase of the Battle of the Ruhr. A total of
783 bombers were launched against it, with a further 72 Pathfinder
Lancasters attacking Münster at the same time. The next night it
was the turn of Bochum, with 503 sorties being mounted. Two
nights later it was Oberhausen, but only Nos 1 and 5 Group
Lancasters were used, 203 in all. On the night of the 16th/17th,
Halifaxes of No 1 Group joined the Lancasters of Nos 5 and 8
Groups in a 212-aircraft attack on Cologne. There was now a short
pause, with operations being mounted against the Schneider Works
at Le Creusot and against Friedrichshafen,* but then on the

---

*This operation mounted by sixty No 5 Group Lancasters on the night of 20/21 June against the Zeppelin works,
where *Würzburg* radars were being made, is significant in two respects. Having attacked, the force flew on to
North Africa – the first of the 'Shuttle' raids. Secondly the 'Master Bomber' technique, as pioneered by Guy
Gibson on CHASTISE, was used to help improve bombing accuracy.

21st/22nd Krefeld was hit, with 705 bombers taking off, Mulheim (557 sorties) on the following night, Wuppertal (630) two nights later, followed immediately by Gelsenkirchen (473) on the night of the 25th/26th. Cologne then came in for punishment with raids on the 28th/29th (608 sorties), 3/4 July (653) and 8/9 July (288). Then it was back to Gelsenkirchen with 422 sorties on the following night, and two nights later, to 'ring the changes', 295 Lancasters set off for Turin, which, apart from nuisance raids by Mosquitoes, would leave the Ruhr in comparative peace for a short time while Harris prepared for the next round in his offensive.

This final phase of the Battle of the Ruhr had not been without cost. Of 6,037 sorties mounted in major raids, 310 bombers and their crews, either killed or captured, had been lost, and the availability of aircraft and crews among the heavies had dropped from 726 on 11 June to 623 on 9 July.[22] This indicated only too clearly that a loss rate of this magnitude could not be borne by Bomber Command for any length of time, and with the realisation that it was the night fighter rather than flak that was wreaking most of the damage, Harris was keen to improve defensive aids and tactics. Previously, the general policy had been for aircraft to make large and frequent changes of course and altitude while over enemy territory. However, Bomber Command ORS found that this made no appreciable difference to aircraft safety, and indeed affected bombing accuracy. Therefore, in mid June, Harris instituted a new policy. From now on aircraft were to 'adhere scrupulously to the ordered route', and only when singled out by flak, searchlights or night fighters were they to take evasive action. When attacked by the latter, they were to employ the diving turn and corkscrew, and it was crucial that the pilot and his gunners perfect proper drills for these.   Gunners must give a clear commentary to the pilot, something which was, at the time, 'a marked weakness', and be able to determine when the fighter was committed to an attack and not merely getting into position. At the same time, there was a commonly held axiom that a bomber was there to bomb and not to fight, and this possibly led to a reluctance among gunners to open fire, although one suspects that another reason was that crews hoped that the fighter would not see them. Nevertheless, gunners were now to be much more aggressive, and must loose off as soon as they spotted a night fighter, but with the caveat that they must take care not to hit fellow bombers.[23]

There were also new technical aids coming into service, which it was hoped would improve the situation. First of all, there were two aerial warning devices, BOOZER and MONICA. BOOZER, which had entered service in spring 1943, was a passive device designed to pick up the transmissions of both the FuG 202/212 aerial radar, with which the German night fighters were equipped and the *Würzburg* ground radar station. Their presence was indicated by a yellow and red lamp respectively. However, the device was not generally popular among crews in that, once over enemy territory, enemy transmissions on the right frequency were so numerous that both lights tended to stay on permanently, which did little for the nerves. MONICA, on the other hand, was an active warning system fitted to the tail of the aircraft. Here again, it had a drawback in that it could not differentiate between friendly and hostile aircraft and when flying in a bomber stream the operator tended to ignore the continuous clicking in his ears, which was the indicator of a contact astern. MONICA made its operational début on the night of 19/20 June.

A third device was SERRATE, which was designed to give bearings on German night fighter radar transmissions, and this was combined with an idea which Harris had had since the previous autumn, of mixing fighters with the bomber stream in order to give more teeth to its defences. He had had the Mosquito in mind for this. Fighter Command, however, appear to have been unenthusiastic and it was not until June 1943 that the idea was tried out, but using the comparatively inferior Beaufighter instead. This was fitted with SERRATE and, to assist navigation, GEE, and was given to 141 Squadron. They were allowed very little time to train and made their début with it on the night of 14/15 June on the Oberhausen raid. It soon became clear that the Beaufighter was no match for the superior speed and manoeuvrability of Ju88, Me110 and Do217, and the idea was temporarily shelved in September. There was also WINDOW, which was finally about to enter service, but more about this in the next chapter.

In spite of the frustrations and concern over casualties, the campaign against the Ruhr had produced some encouraging results. First and foremost, great strides had been made in increasing bombing accuracy. As Cherwell wrote in a minute to Churchill dated 24 June: 'Two years ago we reckoned to get one-fifth within 5 miles of the target. Today we get over two-thirds within 3 miles.'[24] There was, too, no doubt that considerable damage had been done to the towns and cities of the Ruhr. As Harris himself said:

Nothing like the whole succession of catastrophes which overcame the cities of the Ruhr and North-West Germany in the first half of 1943 had ever occurred before, either in Germany or elsewhere. It was an impressive victory . . .[25]

Devastation had been widespread and echoes of German concern over it reached Britain, which perhaps encouraged an over-optimistic tone to the surveys of damage carried out by RE8 at the time. There was, too, as the Official History points out,[26] a tendency to regard Krupp's in Essen as the very core of the German armaments industry, ignoring the fact that it was, although prestigious, only one of a number of armaments firms. That it had suffered extensive damage there was no doubt, but this could not accurately reflect the effect on the armaments industry as a whole. There was, as Inglis had pointed out in April, the problem of gauging loss of production when target figures and plans were not accurately known, and also the fact that because the roofs of factories had been destroyed it was automatically assumed that the plant underneath had been put out of action, something which post-war surveys revealed was often not the case. At the time, however, Harris can scarcely be blamed for accepting the reports as they stood, and the fact that they were so favourable gave him added impetus, now that the nights were beginning to draw out again, to launch the next phase of his campaign, which was to be slightly different and even more awesome in flavour.

CHAPTER SEVEN

GOMORRAH

The English bombers are propagating themselves! – German controller

In his minute to Portal of 16 June Harris had clearly implied that, with the nights becoming longer, Hamburg was to be his next major target. Apart from the need, however, to have a short pause in order to gather Bomber Command's strength for the next blow, the date for opening the attack against Hamburg was also influenced by a technical factor.

WINDOW

As early as 1938, Lord Cherwell, or Professor Lindemann as he then was, had outlined the principle of using 'oscillators', which, when dropped from the air, would cause spurious radar responses. He looked at the idea again in 1940 as a possible means of deflecting the Luftwaffe's bombing beams, but with no successful result and there the matter rested. In September 1941, however, 148 Squadron, which was carrying out wireless trials in the Middle East, noticed that those aircraft carrying the radio equipment appeared to come in for significant attention from German flak, possibly because their aerial arrays produced an enlarged radar echo. It was decided, as a countermeasure, to drop aluminium strips in order to confuse the radar, but this had no apparent effect. Then TRE took up the idea and found that oblong aluminium strips were effective, and in April 1942 Bomber Command's use of WINDOW, as it was codenamed, was officially sanctioned. While preparations for its introduction were being made, however, Fighter Command raised the point that trials had shown that WINDOW interfered with the Mark VIII Airborne Interception (AI) radar used by the night fighters, and should Bomber Command begin to use it, it was natural to expect the Luftwaffe's bombers would follow suit. It was therefore agreed to shelve WINDOW while

Fighter Command investigated ways of guarding against its effects. No further developments occurred until the autumn, when an Air Scientific Intelligence (ASI) Report[1] concluded that the Germans probably had knowledge of the principles involved and knew that the British intended to use it. Tizard, in a paper dated 31 October 1942,[2] concurred with the ASI findings and argued that if this were the case, 'one is logically drawn to support the proposed use of WINDOW on a large scale by Bomber Command'. However, Sholto Douglas, AOCinC Fighter Command, continued to argue that it should not be introduced until he had developed counters to it. The matter was debated at a meeting on 4 November and, with Tizard not present and Saundby, representing Bomber Command, failing to push for it, stating that the concentrated bomber stream was causing sufficient disruption of the German defences, a further postponement was agreed. As the Official History points out, this ran against Harris's claim in *Bomber Offensive* that he had realised the importance of WINDOW in 1942, and his unusual failure to agitate for its introduction is hard to explain.[3]

With the Battle of the Ruhr under way, however, Harris had a change of heart and at a WINDOW Meeting on 2 April 1943, strongly advocated its early introduction. The Air Staff view was that it should be brought in immediately to assist POINTBLANK, especially as they considered that it was likely to prevent the destruction of 35 per cent of the bombers currently being shot down, basing this on the view that 70 per cent of all bombers posted missing were as a result of German night fighter action and that half these were radar-directed attacks.[4] Now the Chiefs of Staff stepped in and asked for it not to be used until after the invasion of Sicily, which was to take place on 10 July. In the meantime, bombers continued to be lost. Then, on 15 July, with the Allies now firmly ashore, yet another meeting was held, which drew the presence of the Prime Minister himself, as well as Herbert Morrison, Minister of Home Security and responsible for civil defence. The latter fought a rearguard action, voicing his concern at what another blitz on England might do to the country, but eventually Churchill gave his personal authorisation for its use, which was to be allowed from 23 July. It had been a long and sorry saga which brought little credit to everyone concerned, especially since its existence had been common knowledge since April 1942, and the *Daily Mirror* had even published a cartoon on it in July of that year.

HAMBURG

The operation order for the attack on Hamburg had already been written and issued to Groups as far back as 27 May. The intention

was simple, 'to destroy Hamburg', which Harris viewed as achieving 'immeasurable results in reducing the industrial capacity of the
enemy's war machine'. Together with the effect on morale, success
'would play a very important part in shortening and winning the
war', but the battle could not be won 'on a single night' and some
10,000 tons of bombs would be needed 'to complete the process of
elimination'.[5] With permission to use WINDOW having been finally
given, Harris planned Operation GOMORRAH, as the offensive
against Hamburg was called, to be launched on the night of 22/23
July, with the first WINDOW being dropped somewhat cheekily at
one minute past midnight. However, the weather was unsuitable
that night, and Harris had to be content with seven No 91 Group
Whitley NICKEL sorties over Paris. Conditions remained unfavourable for the following night, but the next day, with a forecast of
light scattered cloud at worst over Hamburg, Harris at his 0900
hours conference gave the 'green light' for that night.

On the night of 24/25 July, 791 Lancasters, Halifaxes, Stirlings
and Wellingtons took off for Hamburg, while a further 33
Lancasters of No 5 Group attacked Leghorn on the Tuscan coast,
thirteen Mosquito sorties were mounted as diversionary attacks on
Duisburg, Kiel, Lübeck and Bremen, six No 1 Group Wellingtons
went GARDENING and seven from No 92 Group dropped NICKELS
over France. Each aircraft bound for Hamburg carried its own
bundles of WINDOW and the crews were instructed to drop them at
one-minute intervals from the moment that they were within about
sixty miles of the target and to continue doing so until Hamburg
was roughly the same distance behind them. For one wireless
operator the foil strips being unloaded from his aircraft reminded
him of 'a shoal of river fish darting along in the murky water',[6] but
their effect on the German defences was to prove devastating.

Guided and led onto the target by H2S Pathfinder aircraft using
yellow, red and green TIs, the main force attacked the target with a
mixture of HE and incendiaries. In the space of some fifty minutes,
728 aircraft dropped almost 2,400 tons of explosive on the target,
with some 40 per cent getting within three miles of the aiming-
point. Its effect on the ground was that of a firestorm, with the HE
fanning the flames caused by the incendiaries, so that small fires
quickly linked up to become big ones, aided by the fact that the
weather of late had been particularly hot and dry. Such was the
concentration of the attack, that the temperature quickly built up
and fierce hot winds blew. Yet, as those listening in on the German
night fighter nets soon discovered, WINDOW had resulted in a
double blow to the Germans. R. V. Jones recalls:

We heard one German controller get fixed on a packet of this stuff which
obviously was not an aircraft and telling it to waggle its wings and so forth,

without any success. When another controller saw extra aircraft appearing where only one had been before, he burst into indignation over the radio, 'The English bombers are propagating themselves,' and then we heard a quite different voice taking command and I wondered whether it might be Göring himself and it turned out he was.[7]

Indeed, the confusion among the German controllers and night fighter crews was utter; only twelve bombers were posted as missing, and all those from the subsidiary operations also returned safely. It was an auspicious beginning.

The following day, in pursuance of POINTBLANK strategy, the US Eighth Air Force joined in the battle, with 234 Fortresses being sent to the area, 68 of which attacked Hamburg specifically. That night, however, instead of going back to Hamburg, Harris launched a 'maximum effort' on Essen, using OBOE and WINDOW, while three Mosquitoes visited Hamburg to prey on the nerves of the inhabitants and, others mounted diversions on Cologne and Gelsenkirchen. A total of 705 aircraft took off for the main target, with 604 attacking. It was, thanks to OBOE, a remarkably concentrated attack, with 60 per cent of the bombs falling within the target area. In fact it was the most destructive raid on Essen to date; fires were still burning two days later, and heavy damage was done to the Krupp's works. Losses, too, thanks to WINDOW, were comparatively light for Essen, with only 26 aircraft being shot down. This was to be the last visit to this target for some time, and indeed such was the supposed damage that there was a rumour among crews at OTUs that it was one place to which they would not be required to go. Furthermore, there was no doubt that the crews were impressed by WINDOW and their added confidence gave rise to the suggestion that its use had contributed to the high standard of accuracy achieved on the Essen raid.[8]

Two nights' operations in a row was as much as could be expected from the crews, so the night of the 26th/27th was a stand down for the majority. During the day, however, the Americans had paid another visit to Hamburg with 54 Fortresses attacking and two only being lost. Also five Mosquitoes attacked the city by night. The following night, a second major attack was launched against Hamburg. This time 787 bombers took off, and the effect was much more concentrated than the previous effort. WINDOW again proved effective, but the Germans, who had recognised what it was as a result of the Essen raid, now adopted a new system with the controllers concentrating on giving a running commentary on the height and position of the bomber stream rather than trying to acquire individual targets for the night fighters. Nevertheless, only seventeen bombers were lost. Once again the firestorm raged, and the four Mosquitoes which returned the following night reported extensive fires still blazing.

The third visit by the main force to the city took place on the night of 29/30 July, with 777 sorties being flown against it, including Mosquitoes combining with the heavies for the first time, but accuracy was not so good; only one-third of the attacking crews dropped their bombs within the target area. Also, 28 aircraft were shot down, which indicated that the running commentary technique was beginning to regain the ground which the Germans had lost with the introduction of WINDOW. Nevertheless, with the fires once again stoked up, Harris left Hamburg entirely alone the following night and went for the Ruhr, with an attack by 273 aircraft on Remscheid. Here, using OBOE Mosquitoes once more, no fewer than 191 crews were reckoned to have got their bombs within the target area, and indeed, post-raid photographs showed the centre of the town to be virtually gutted. Of the fifteen bombers shot down, no less than eight were Stirlings, part of a force of 87 of this type put up by No 3 Group. Much of their problem lay in that they were slower than other types and fell behind, making them easier targets for the night fighters. As a consequence, the Stirling was now to be gradually withdrawn from attacks on Germany *per se* and retained for fringe operations only.

The final attack on Hamburg came on the night of 2/3 August and was marked by appalling weather, with much dense cloud, which resulted in only 425 of the 740 crews dispatched, claiming to have attacked the target. Even then, the H2s-laid markers were almost impossible to see and most aircraft had to bomb blind. Thirty aircraft failed to return and another 51 were damaged, but the city was devastated by the four raids, and it seemed that Bomber Command was now finally capable of inflicting decisive punishment and, thanks to WINDOW, with a significantly lower casualty rate than hitherto. Hamburg had been selected as a target not just because it was the second most important city in Germany, but also because, being near the coast it was easy to find, and showed up clearly on H2s. Whether the same results could be achieved against targets deeper into Germany remained to be seen.

The remainder of the first half of August was taken up with raids on Mannheim and Nuremberg and a number of attacks against targets in northern Italy. However, 17 August 1943 was to prove a noteworthy date in the history of the strategic bombing campaign for two reasons, Schweinfurt and Peenemunde.

THE SCHWEINFURT – REGENSBURG RAID

The US Eighth Air Force attack on the twin targets of Regensburg and Schweinfurt was the first American deep penetration raid on Germany, and the anniversary of the operational début of the US strategic bombing force over Europe. The importance of Schweinfurt's ball-bearing industry has already been stressed, and Regensburg, too, was on the American target list as a centre of Me109 manufacture. Both targets had originally been tied in with attacks on Wiener Neustadt, which also produced Me109s, and the oil refineries at Ploesti, and the attacks on all four were to be co-ordinated between the Eighth Air Force in England and the Ninth in North Africa. In the event, the Ninth attacked the latter two, and, after several modifications, it was decided that the Eighth Air Force should launch simultaneous attacks on the first two. The 4th Bombardment Wing would take on Regensburg and fly on to North Africa, while the 1st was given Schweinfurt and would return to its bases in England. Fighter cover for both would be provided as far as the German border (the maximum range of the P-47, although RAF Spitfire squadrons would also be used as fighter cover) and again on 1st Bombardment Group's return flight. This, however, left the bombers on their own for some 300 miles until they reached their targets. Although the Americans still believed in the ability of the B-17 to ward off fighters, the fact that they had suffered a loss rate of 6.8 per cent during 'Blitz Week' at the end of July, when they had launched their attacks in support of GOMORRAH and on other targets in northern Germany, and that the Ploesti raid of 1 August had seen 54 of 177 B-24s shot down, warned them that they could expect heavy casualties. Nevertheless, a number of 'milk runs' against airfields in France in the days preceding the raids gave them hope that they had weakened the German fighter strength. As it was, no less than sixty of the 376 bombers dispatched were shot down and many others were damaged. The Regensburg aircraft factory appeared to have been severely damaged, but, like Bomber Command, the Americans fell into the trap of believing that because the roofs of factory buildings had been destroyed, the machinery beneath them must have been put out of action. The bombing on Schweinfurt, on the other hand, was scattered and inaccurate.

The result of this day's operations was that the Americans began to waver for the first time in their conviction that daylight raids were the answer. Indeed, Brigadier-General Anderson, commanding VIIIth Bomber Command (the operational element of Eighth Air Force), who had secretly flown on two RAF night raids a few weeks before, arranged for one of his squadrons, the 422nd, to fly with the RAF during September, in order to evolve tactics, should he be forced to join the RAF in attacks by night. In the event, the Americans persevered, perhaps the major reason being that otherwise they would find themselves forced to play 'second fiddle' to the British. Nevertheless, until the P-51B Mustang made its appearance in early 1944, the American bombing effort would be severely hampered.

As part of the 'round the clock' policy, it had originally been planned that RAF Bomber Command should visit Schweinfurt on the night of the American attack against it,* but, apart from Harris's continued reluctance to divert his main effort to such 'panacea targets', the night of 17/18 August found him involved in an entirely different, but vital operation.

PEENEMÜNDE

Information that the Germans were developing long-range rockets had been first acquired by the British in November 1939, when an anonymous informant passed the British Naval Attaché in Oslo a report on activities at Peenemünde, on the Baltic Coast, where the Germans had set up a secret experimental base two years before. At that time the report was considered to be a German 'spoof', and it was not until December 1942 that more concrete information was received from a Danish chemical engineer who had been working in Berlin, and this was followed up by a report of an overheard conversation between two German Generals captured in North Africa, Cruewell and von Thoma. It was only this last piece of evidence which persuaded the Intelligence services to take the matter seriously, and this culminated in a decision by the War Cabinet in mid April 1943 to appoint a team headed by Duncan Sandys to investigate the whole matter. Piecing together all the evidence, and making much use of RAF reconnaissance photographs, Sandys submitted his report to the War Cabinet on 29 June. He stated that the Germans were producing a v-2 rocket at Peenemünde and that it had a range of up to 130 miles (its true range was nearer 200). The War Cabinet quickly saw the grave potential threat to the United Kingdom and decided that Peenemünde should be attacked by the RAF as soon as possible.

In order to knock out Peenemünde, a heavy bomb tonnage would be required, so a daylight Mosquito raid was rejected, even though accuracy would have been guaranteed. The other force available was the Eighth US Air Force, but this option was never considered. The only alternative was a Bomber Command main force attack by night. However, with the nights still very short, Harris asked for a six weeks' delay until there would be sufficient darkness to cover both outward and inward trips over enemy territory. This was agreed; Harris could get on with the planning.

---

*One of the lessons from Hamburg was that the Americans could not bomb accurately, attacking as they did after Bomber Command, because of the pall of smoke. It was therefore decided that in future the B-17s would attack first by day, with the RAF following them by night.

What set this operation apart from the normal pattern of Bomber Command operations was that, for the first time, the main force was being asked to carry out a precision, as opposed to area, attack and the main problem was how to ensure the highest possible accuracy. Interestingly enough, Harris, instead of first consulting Bennett about this, called in Ralph Cochrane, AOC No 5 Group. The reason for this was because of the new techniques which Cochrane had used in his attack on Friedrichshafen on the night of 20/21 June. Apart from the use of a Master Bomber, as pioneered by Guy Gibson on the Dams Raid, there was the employment of 'offset marking' combined with 'time-and-distance' bombing. Offset marking was a means of marking an obscured target by placing markers at an easily visible point away from it. The bomb aimers merely adjusted their sights so that aiming at the markers would ensure that the bombs hit the target. 'Time-and-distance' had been used against Friedrichshafen when a wind change flawed the former method, but use was made of three visible reference points which were in line with the target. The time taken to cover the distance between the first two was used to calculate the time from the third reference point to the aiming-point. Thus the bomb aimer did not need artificial indicators and merely released the bombs according to the navigator's stop-watch. In this way, provided that the reference points were visible, the target could be accurately bombed, however poor the visibility above it. Initially though, Harris preferred to use his Pathfinders, but he did borrow the Master Bomber idea from Cochrane, stipulating that he come from No 8 Group, who chose the very experienced Group Captain Searby, then commanding 83 Squadron. Searby was allowed one rehearsal, during the raid by Nos 1 and 8 Groups on Turin on the night of 7/8 August, but, such was the secrecy surrounding the Peenemünde operation, was not told the purpose. The main force was to use the new standard Pathfinder marking techniques, although at a later stage Harris did agree to allow No 5 Group to use their 'time-and-distance' method. Yet, when Cochrane saw the results of daylight practice runs, which he instituted for his crews during the days leading up to the raid, he was appalled at the lack of accuracy and the failure of the crews to time their runs properly, and could only hope that it would go better on the night.

As another means of ensuring accuracy, Harris had to go against his normal practice and choose a full moon period, and to select a night when the weather over the target would be clear. These, of course, were ideal conditions for the night fighters, and it was a question of how they could be put off the scent. For a start, he decided on a northern route, which would avoid the German mainland. Hence the bomber stream was to overfly Denmark, and then pass over the Baltic before turning south-east to the target. More important was a diversionary raid on Berlin by eight Mosquitoes. These were to follow roughly the same route as the main force. As a further refinement, Mosquito attacks, also using this route, were carried out against Berlin on three of the four nights preceding the main attack. The purpose of this was twofold – first, to get the inhabitants of Peenemünde used to the air raid sirens, which would presumably sound when enemy aircraft were in the area, and secondly to make the Germans believe that Berlin was to be the next major target. Harris had made very public his intention to go for Berlin after Hamburg, and a bomber stream approaching the German coast in the same direction as the Mosquitoes would make the Germans believe that it was heading for the capital, and hence they would hold their night fighters back until it came within closer range. It was an ingenious ploy, and illustrates just how imaginative operational planning had become by this stage of the war.

The full moon period began on 11 August, but not until the 17th was the weather favourable. Harris gave orders for the operation to be mounted that night under the codename Operation HYDRA. The attack was to be in three waves, with No 3 Group's vulnerable Stirlings in the leading wave so as to avoid their straggling. However, they were initially beset by problems in that many of them had been involved in a raid on Turin the previous night when fog prevented some of them from landing on their own airfields. This fog persisted during the day and struck some sixty aircraft off the availability total for the night. Nevertheless, they began to take off at just before 2030 hours, and soon 596 bombers were on their way. Although much of the outward flight was without incident, the fact that they were flying on a clear moonlit night gave the crews a feeling of unease. At least it made navigation easier, although two bombers paid the penalty for wandering off course, being brought down by flak over Flensburg. In the meantime, the eight Mosquitoes from 139 Squadron arrived over Berlin at 2300 hours and dropped 500lb bombs, target indicators, a further measure to make the Germans believe that a major attack was on its way, and WINDOW. They succeeded in making 150 night fighters scramble, who remained aloft waiting for the main force, and then turned for home, one of them being shot down by a night fighter. The first Pathfinder aircraft released their markers shortly after midnight. Using H2S, sixteen aircraft were to mark the northern end of Ruden Island, seven miles from the target, with what were called 'Red Spot Fires', a new marking device consisting of impregnated cotton wool, which ignited at 3,000 feet and then burned on the ground for ten minutes. Then red TIs were to be dropped blind on the aiming-points (there were three of these), together with flares. Finally yellow TIs were to be dropped visually on the exact aiming-point. Unfortunately, Ruden Island did not show up too well on H2S, despite expert opinion to the contrary, and the majority of Red Spot Fires were dropped too late, which meant that most of the aiming-point TIs went down south of where they should have been. Thus, the first of the main force Stirlings bombed the wrong target, but now the value of the Master Bomber was demonstrated in that he was able to correct the later No 3 Group aircraft onto the right target, assisted by the Pathfinders Backers-Up. However, as the second wave (Nos 1 and 3 Groups' Lancasters) came in, there was another problem with the marking, this time because of a wind change, which sent the TIs drifting out over the sea, and again Searby had to intervene. Finally, in came Nos 5 and 6 Groups. The former, however, had been told that while they were to use 'time-and-distance', they were only to bomb automatically at the end of their timed run if they could not see any markers. Otherwise they were to aim for the TIs and disregard their own calculations as to when they should bomb. Unfortunately, at this stage, Searby did not notice that the markers on the third aiming-point, the experimental works, were inaccurate, and so many of No 5 Group's bomb-loads went adrift.

Flak was very light and indeed was virtually suppressed by the first wave, and the first two waves suffered little from night fighters because Harris's diversionary tactics worked very successfully. The controllers' running commentaries kept the bulk of the night fighters hanging about over Berlin. Then they thought that the bomber stream might be heading for Rostock, then Swinemunde, and then Stettin. Only when the attack actually started were they directed to the correct area, but by then many had been forced to land through lack of fuel. Nevertheless, sufficient reached the area in time to be able to inflict punishment on the last wave. Thus, while Nos 1, 3 and 4 Groups lost only three aircraft each, No 5 Group lost seventeen of its 117 Lancasters and No 6 Group, twelve of its 61 Lancasters and Halifaxes.

Post-raid photographs revealed considerable damage, although, if there had not been problems and more of the 3,422,480 pounds of HE and 598,300 pounds of incendiaries had fallen on target, the results might have been far-reaching.[9] Nevertheless, it was sufficient to cause some delay in V-2 production, and to this end it was successful. It also demonstrated that it was possible to bomb accurately by night, and that, with further perfection of the techniques used against Peenemünde, RAF Bomber Command could switch to precision bombing. To Harris, however, with the successes against the Ruhr and Hamburg foremost in his mind,

Peenemünde was, albeit successful, a 'one off' operation, and he was determined to get on with the next phase of his overall plan. The Master Bomber technique, however, would now become a standard bombing technique.

POINTBLANK REAFFIRMED

In August 1943 the Allied leaders met in Quebec under the code-name of QUADRANT and confirmed that the prime event of 1944 was to be the long-awaited invasion of the Continent of Europe (OVERLORD), and the Combined Chiefs of Staff further agreed that:

> The progressive destruction and dislocation of the German military industrial and economic system, the destruction of vital elements of lines of communication, and the material reduction of the German air combat strength by the successful prosecution of the Combined Bomber Offensive from all convenient bases is a pre-requisite to 'Overlord' (barring an independent and complete Russian victory before 'Overlord' can be mounted). This operation must therefore continue to have the highest strategic priority.[10]

This was repeated verbatim to Harris in a directive sent to him by Bottomley on 3 September.[11] POINTBLANK was therefore reaffirmed, but it is significant that although the primary object as agreed at Casablanca was exactly the same, with the additions of communications and German air combat strength, all mention of morale had been omitted. Nevertheless, the Air Ministry, in a telegram to QUADRANT dated 29 August stated that Harris was going to initiate operations on Berlin with the waning of the moon. He considered that it would need some 40,000 tons of bombs if destruction on the Hamburg scale was to be achieved, and that the battle would be long, not just because of the bomb weight required, but also because of the need to shift attacks intermittently to other towns.[12] Although Berlin, with its comparative lack of industry, did not fit easily into the military, industrial and economic categories, it appears to have been accepted by the Combined Chiefs of Staff without dissent, probably in view of RAF Bomber Command's successes during recent months. Thus, Harris was to continue to be allowed a very free rein.

In fact, Bomber Command's main force had already visited Berlin on the night of 23 August, when 719 aircraft had taken off for the city. Although, 625 claimed to have attacked, few got within three miles of the aiming-point, and the reason for this was mainly that the city showed up too indistinctly on H2S, being merely a blaze of light. A further worrying aspect was that no less than 57 aircraft failed to return. The Germans were now recovering fast from their setback over WINDOW, and with their controllers early identifying Berlin as the target, the fighters had a good night.

Visits to Nuremberg on the 27th/28th (33 lost from 674) and München-Gladbach on the 30th/31st (25 missing from 660), although not as bad as Berlin, also served to confirm that the loss rate was on the increase. Indeed, the previous high morale of the crews was beginning to fall. Thus, a letter written from RAF Syerston, home of 61 and 106 Squadrons, dated 30 August, to SASO No 5 Group, reflected the crews' concern over the increasing success of the night fighters. They believed that much of this was attributable to 'cat's eye', as opposed to radar-controlled, fighters, that were helped by aircraft marking the bomber path with flares. They believed that waves should be spaced wider apart or that each wave should follow a different path. In conclusion, the letter said:

> Many people seem to be of the opinion that methods now being followed by Bomber Command have become somewhat stereotyped and that we should do every possible thing to invent and make use of fresh tactics, even if only to try them out.[13]

As if to emphasise the point, the next visit to Berlin on the last night of August resulted in 47 of 612 aircraft failing to return. Then, on the night of the 3rd/4th, Harris tried using Lancasters only, but even then 22 aircraft were lost out of 316. It was obvious, that with this sort of loss rate, Bomber Command could not afford to mount a prolonged offensive on Berlin at this juncture, and Harris was forced to call off his attacks and concentrate on other targets while ways and means were worked out for a more effective and less costly course. It would be almost three months before the main force returned to the capital once more.

The remainder of September was taken up with raids on Mannheim and Munich, followed by three on French targets, which resulted in minimum loss rates, and then heavier attacks on Hannover (twice), Mannheim again, and Bochum. The first of the two Hannover raids, on the night of 22/23 September, was not successful, with the markers being poorly placed, and this provoked Bennett to write to Harris. He complained that the overall standard of the crews coming to his group was falling – in February 1943 Pathfinder captains had an average of 32 operations under their belts, but this was now down to twenty, and that one-third of his crews came as complete freshers. Furthermore, he did not consider that he had sufficient time in which to properly train the crews, especially when it came to conversion to other aircraft types, and in H2S. In terms of equipment, Bennett also felt that No 8 Group should have more control over its development and introduction and pointed to the delays in obtaining the improved Mark III H2S, which operated on a 3cm as opposed to 9cm wavelength, and incorporated a modification involving a stabilised scanner. He also thought that too much effort was being put into the development of the OBOE Mark I Repeater, which was designed to extend the range of OBOE using airborne repeating stations, at the expense of the centimetric Mark II Repeater.[14] This illustrates the dilemma of having what might be regarded as a *corps d'élite* within the Command, but Harris was sympathetic in his reply, and said that he would write to the main force Groups to stress the importance of high-quality crews being selected for the Pathfinders. As for training, he pointed out to Bennett that, in fact, his group flew fewer operations than the main force, since for targets within range, OBOE-fitted Mosquitoes were used.[15]

Although Pathfinder results were disappointing at this time, two other techniques were introduced in an endeavour to keep down casualty rates. First, from the end of September onwards Harris introduced 'spoof' raids (known as BULL'S EYES) or feints in order to disperse the night fighters. Thus, for the second attack on Hannover on 27/28 September, while 678 aircraft were put up against this target, 27 Mosquitoes and Lancasters from No 8 Group attacked Brunswick, and the next time the town was attacked, on 8/9 October, no less than 119 aircraft were sent on a diversion to Bremen, while 504 attacked Hannover. Indeed, during these two months Hannover seems to have become a fixation with Harris, with four main attacks on it, but again, like Berlin, the town did not show up well on H2S. The other innovation consisted of a much more concentrated streaming than hitherto. This was advocated by the Bomber Command ORS, whose studies had concluded that the loss rate showed a significant increase if attacks lasted longer than 35 minutes. Therefore, the standard ten bombers per minute stream was increased to thirty per minute, which had the added advantage of greater accuracy in that there was less drift away from the aiming-point. During October no raid was planned to last for more than 26 minutes and the loss rate for September and October was kept at just below 3.5 per cent as compared to 7 per cent in August. The introduction of additional radio-countermeasures (RCM) devices also helped. Among these were TINSEL, a means of jamming the frequencies used by the German controllers; AIRBORNE CIGAR (ABC) which interfered with night fighter radio communications; and CORONA, another ground-based system, also designed to jam night fighter transmissions and to give the pilots false information. However, such was the wide range of RCM devices now in existence that they were becoming difficult to control and in November, on Bomber Command's recommendation, it was decided to bring them all under one umbrella, No 100 (Special Duties) Group, Bomber Command under Air Vice-Marshal Addison.

While RAF Bomber Command strove to prepare itself for the main assault on Berlin, the US Eighth Air Force was also going through a recovery phase after its reverses over Regensburg and Schweinfurt. Once again, operations were restricted to the fringes, with particular concentration on French airfields. Only once in September did they venture into the German heartland again when Stuttgart and other targets were attacked on the 6th for the loss of 45 bombers. However, the increasing of the range of the P-38 to 450 miles and the arrival of the B-17G, with its nose turret which enabled gunners to confront head-on attacks, a favourite German tactic until now, encouraged Eaker to become more adventurous during October. On the 9th, 215 bombers attacked the Focke-Wulf plants at Anklam and Marienburg and lost 20 aircraft. Nevertheless, both raids were very successful, and Portal, commenting on the Marienburg attack, wrote to Churchill: 'This is the best high-altitude bombing we have seen in this war. All but one building of the factory was destroyed, and that was damaged. It was a magnificent attack.'[16] On the same day, 51 aircraft were sent to Danzig and 112 to Gdynia, both on the Baltic Coast, and these raids marked the longest flights made until now by the Americans. Next day, 274 bombers were earmarked for an attack on Munster, but only half claimed to have attacked, and the leading Group, 100th, suffered very severely at the hands of the fighters, who broke up its formation and sent all but one of its aircraft down in flames. A fighter pilot described what it was like to meet the returning B-17s:

Here and there in the Fortress formations there were gaps. From close to you could see machines with one, sometimes two stationary engines and feathered propellers. Others had lacerated tail-planes, gaping holes in the fuselages, wings tarnished by fire or glistening with black oil oozing from gutted engines.

Behind the formations were the stragglers, making for the coast, for the haven of a refuge of an advanced air base on the other side of the Channel, flying only by a sublime effort of will. You could imagine the blood pouring over the heaps of empty cartridges, the pilot nursing his remaining engines and anxiously eyeing the long white trail of petrol escaping from his riddled tanks. These isolated Fortresses were the Focke-Wulf's favourite prey. Therefore the squadrons detached two or three pairs of Spitfires, charged with bringing each one back safe: an exhausting task as these damaged Fortresses often dragged along on a third of their total power, stretching the endurance of their escort to the limit.[17]

Then, on the 14th, came a second attempt on Schweinfurt, but the results were even worse than before with sixty out of 291 being posted as missing. Although since the first Schweinfurt raid Eaker had been badgering 'Hap' Arnold for P-51 long-range fighters to be sent to England, it was not until after this second raid that Arnold recognised the urgency and took steps for this to be done. In the meantime, the Eighth Air Force withdrew once more to the fringes.

At this time there was a major reorganisation of the US Air Forces in Europe. In October Arnold came up with a plan for dividing the Twelfth Air Force in the Mediterranean, making one part a strategic force, and the other devoting itself to tactical support of the ground forces. He proposed to form a Fifteenth Air Force and base it in Italy in order to fulfil the first role, arguing that targets beyond the range of the United Kingdom could be taken on, and German defences in the West would have to be weakened in order to meet this new threat. Furthermore, Arnold wanted to bring the operations of all three air forces under the umbrella of a new command, US Strategic Air Forces in Europe (USSTAFE). Eaker, for one, objected to this plan, especially since he discovered that, in order to form Fifteenth Air Force, several units earmarked for him were to be diverted. In any event, he suspected that suitable airfields would take time to find in Italy and that the weather would not be so suitable for strategic bomber operations. All this led him to conclude that the plan would act as a brake on POINTBLANK. Harris, too, agreed with this, and wrote an impassioned plea to Lovett, the US Assistant Secretary for Air. He pointed out that the main POINTBLANK targets lay out of range of Italy, in north and north-west Germany. He was also concerned that there would be too much centralised control of the bombing offensive, and warned that 'blind following up of day with night attacks on the same objective would, if adopted as a matter of routine make the task of the defences easy'. He also asserted that diversions from the Eighth Air Force's strength had been one reason for its high casualties in recent months.[18] Portal, too, after initial acceptance of the idea went against it, but when the matter was discussed at the Cairo Conference in November (SEXTANT), Arnold had his way and General Spaatz was appointed to command USSTAFE, with Doolittle, who had won a Medal of Honor for leading the first raid over Japan in June 1942, being appointed to the Fifteenth Air Force.

By mid November, however, Harris had other matters on his mind, for he now felt ready to launch his long-awaited offensive on Berlin.

CHAPTER EIGHT

THE BATTLE OF BERLIN

There was no glamour in this winter Battle of Berlin . . . – Pathfinder navigator

On 3 November 1943 Harris sent a minute to Churchill with some details of what POINTBLANK had achieved so far. He listed nineteen towns and cities in Germany, which he claimed were 'virtually destroyed' and these included Hamburg, Cologne, Essen and the majority of the Ruhr towns. Under 'seriously damaged' were a further nineteen population centres, including Munich, Nuremberg and Berlin, while a further nine were considered 'damaged'. He said, 'we can only claim what can be seen in the photographs. What actually occurs is much more than can be seen in any photograph.' As for future plans, he listed target areas in order of priority, with Berlin at the top. 'I await promised USAAF help in this the greatest of air battles. But I would not propose to wait for ever, or for long if opportunity serves.' Next on the list came 'The Central Complex', which included Schweinfurt, which Harris claimed as being 'seriously damaged', followed by the 'Berlin Road', the Upper Rhine, the South-East Complex, the East, the Baltic, the Saar and finally the Ruhr.* In conclusion, he wrote:

> I feel certain that Germany must collapse before this programme which is more than half completed already, has proceeded much further. We have not got far to go. We must get the USAAF to wade in in greater force. If they will only get going according to plan and avoid such disastrous diversions as Ploesti, and getting 'nearer' to Germany from the plains of Lombardy (which are further from 9/10ths of Germany than is Norfolk), we can get through with it very quickly. We can wreck Berlin from end to end if the USAAF will come in on it. It will cost between us 400–500 aircraft. It will cost Germany the war.[1]

---

*Harris defined these areas more specifically as follows. CENTRAL COMPLEX: Leipzig, Chemnitz, Dresden, and the 'Little Ruhr', Eisenach, Gotha, Erfurt, Weimar, Schweinfurt. THE BERLIN ROAD: Bremen, Hannover, Brunswick, Magdeburg, Osnabruck. THE UPPER RHINE: Frankfurt, Ludwigshaven, Karlsruhe, Darmstadt, Stuttgart. THE SOUTH-EAST COMPLEX: Friedrichshafen, Augsburg, Munich, Nuremberg. THE EAST: Pilsen, Posen, Breslau, Vienna, Wiener Neustadt. THE BALTIC: Kiel, Wismar, Stettin. THE SAAR: the small steel and coal towns in that region. THE RUHR: he wished to concentrate on Solingen, Witten and Leverkusen and 'tidy up all round when occasion serves'.

This may seem to be a typical Harris boast, but reports and Intelligence estimates of the time did add weight to his beliefs. Thus, an MEW and Air Intelligence report dated 4 November stated:

> The maintenance of morale is the gravest single problem confronting the home authorities. The full effects of air attack since the devastation of Hamburg have become known in all parts of the country. The increasing death toll is an important factor and coupled with military failures the general attitude is approaching one of peace at any price, and the avoidance of wholesale destruction of further cities in Germany.[2]

Three days later a further Air Intelligence report drawn up in consultation with the Political Warfare Executive concluded:

> 1. Fear of air attack has been the dominating preoccupation of a large part of the German civilian population and contributes to a situation in which fear of consequences of continuing the war is greater than fear of consequences of defeat.
> 2. Air attack on Germany has resulted in social disruption on a scale which has greatly impaired the German ability to prosecute the war . . .
> 3. Through forces of repression, hopes of a compromise with one or other of the belligerents and the favourable climatic conditions of the past three months have so far prevented a general break in morale, it is not reasonable to infer that no such break in morale can occur, and we do not exclude the possibility that in conjunction with further large scale military reverses and the advent of winter, air operations can exercise *decisive influence** on conditions inside Germany.[3]

The view was that it was Harris's attacks on morale, rather than the effects on German industry and physical capacity to wage war, which were causing the damage. This, combined with the fact that, despite objections to the contrary, Fifteenth Air Force was being activated, which meant that the Eighth would be starved of aircraft for some time to come, made Harris conclude that he should begin his attack on Berlin, or the 'Big City' as the aircrews called it, sooner rather than later.

On the night of 18 November 1943, 444 Mosquitoes and Lancasters set out to bomb the city. Simultaneously, another force of 395 Lancasters, Halifaxes and Stirlings visited Mannheim and Ludwigshafen, twin towns separated from each other only by the Rhine. These had been attacked the night before by No 8 Group as an experiment in blind bombing with H2S. Nine were lost in the Berlin attack and 23 aircraft against Mannheim/Ludwigshafen, and it is likely that the Berlin attack got off so lightly because many of the night fighters were diverted to Mannheim. An attack against Leverkusen took place the following night, and then on the night of the 22nd Berlin was visited again, with Mosquitoes carrying out a diversion against the former. The second trip to Berlin marked the last main force raid by the Stirling, which from now on would be used on periphery operations only, especially GARDENING and

*Author's italics.

dropping supplies to Resistance groups. Once again, the casualty rate was encouragingly low, with only 26 being lost out of 764 aircraft dispatched. Berlin was attacked twice more before the month was out, with a large diversion going to Stuttgart on the second occasion. In all, 2,040 sorties were put up against the city in these four raids, with 84 aircraft failing to return. This was encouraging compared to the loss rate for the attacks in the late summer, but there was much frustration because of the weather. Harris himself wrote:

> Scarcely a single crew caught a single glimpse of the objective they were attacking and for long periods we were wholly ignorant except from such admissions as the enemy made from time to time, of how the battle was going. Thousands upon thousands of tons of bombs were aimed at the Pathfinders' pyrotechnic sky-markers and fell through unbroken cloud which concealed everything below it except the confused glare of fires. Scarcely any photographs taken during the bombing showed anything except clouds, and day after day reconnaissance aircraft flew over the capital to return with no information.[4]

As for the aircrews, a Pathfinder navigator wrote:

> There was no glamour in this winter Battle of Berlin, and the crews got no kick out of it apart from the fact that it was the capital of the Reich that they were attacking. The trips were long, dull, and dangerous. Lining the route, we would see strings of fighter flares, generally in threes, and every now and then the gunners would report an aircraft falling in flames. You just sat there and awaited for your time to come. At the target, the concentration of bombers was such that the aircraft would bucket in the slipstream of others ahead, and every now and then you would see the black shape of another Lancaster or Halifax on his bombing run.[5]

Because of the appalling prevailing weather, evidence of damage, as Harris said, was hard to obtain, but a report at the beginning of December concluded that a minimum of 800,000 Berliners had been made homeless, although casualties were not expected to be so high as in Hamburg because of the wider streets in Berlin which gave people more chance of escaping even though the buildings on either side were on fire.[6] This, combined with the comparatively low casualty rate for the bombers, led Portal to comment that it was 'particularly encouraging', and Churchill to say that it was 'all very good'.[7] Others, however, were concerned for different reasons.

QUESTIONS OF MORALITY

On 26 November the Marquess of Salisbury wrote to Sinclair:

> Forgive a somewhat critical note. Your praise of the valour and skill of the air force in their attack on Berlin is abundantly deserved. They are splendid. But Sir Arthur Harris's reply gives one a shake. These attacks are to go on 'until the heart of Nazi Germany ceases to beat'. This would seem to bring us up short against the repeated Government declarations that we are bombing only military

and industrial targets. Perhaps this is all that Harris contemplates, and I shall be delighted if you tell me so. But there is a great deal of evidence that makes some of us afraid that we are losing moral superiority to the Germans . . .

Having sought Bottomley's advice, Sinclair replied:

> There has been no change in the Government's bombing policy. Our aim is the progressive dislocation and destruction of the German military, industrial and economic system.* I have never pretended in the House of Commons or else-where that it is possible to pursue this aim without inflicting terrible casualties on the civilian population of Germany. But neither I, nor any responsible speaker on behalf of the Government, has ever gloated over the destruction of German homes . . .
>
> You told me that it is Sir Arthur Harris's answer to my message which has shaken you, and in particular, his reference to the heart of Germany ceasing to beat; and you interpret this as meaning 'that the residential heart of Berlin is to cease to beat'. But, Harris is an airman, and thinks of Germany in terms of war. He thinks of Berlin as the heart of the German war organism.[8]

There was also much discussion about the preservation of historic buildings. Lord Esher, Chairman of the Society for Protection of Ancient Buildings, had written to Sinclair towards the end of September urging a more cautious approach to the bombing of museum towns, and enclosed a list of eight such which should be avoided, and one of nine which should only be attacked in daylight. As a result, Harris was told that he must not attack any towns on the first list without reference to the Air Ministry, while Esher was told that Bomber Command could not guarantee to avoid such targets if they were of military value. It was then suggested that connoisseurs should be attached to HQ Bomber Command to advise on historic buildings and monuments in Italy. The Air Staff comment to Sinclair on this was:

> The area bombing which we are generally obliged to practice would not probably allow for the deliberate avoidance by our air crews of these monuments . . .
>
> I can well imagine the feelings of one of our aircrew on being asked perhaps to add to the risk of his life and to the loss of the crew and aircraft in avoiding some ancient monument . . . Anyway, I would advise against sending an expert any-where near Bomber Command HQ except in one of those new suits of body armour and a crash helmet![9]

Nevertheless, Esher persisted and, after a debate in the House of Lords, it was eventually agreed to set up a committee under Harold Macmillan, which the War Office and Air Ministry could consult when they needed.

THE OFFENSIVE CONTINUES

On 2/3 December Berlin was visited yet again, but there was a sharp rise in aircraft lost, with forty out of 458 posted as missing.

*In his minute to Sinclair, Bottomley advised leaving out the part of the POINTBLANK aim which covered under-mining morale. 'There is no need to inform Lord Salisbury . . . since it will follow on success of the first part of the stated aim'.

Leipzig was attacked on the following night, but then the weather forced a pause until the 16th/17th, when 497 Mosquitoes and Lancasters attacked Berlin once more, with another 25 aircraft being shot down. Two further attacks were carried out against it before December was over, preceded by a visit to Frankfurt. Although the heavy cloud made life difficult for the night fighters as well as the bombers, the Germans continued to perfect their counter-WINDOW tactics and had also concentrated more fighter units around Berlin. Indeed, Bomber Command ORS reviewing the casualties for December noted that enemy 'freelance' fighters were now increasingly efficient and were intercepting the bomber stream before it reached the target.[10] The frustrations of not being able to use H2S, even the 3cm Mark III which the Pathfinders now had, were growing. No 100 Group, too, was still not yet operational, although it did begin SERRATE operations in support of the main force in the middle of the month, and claimed two successes against German night fighters over Berlin for the loss of one of its own aircraft.

In addition to the main attacks, other operational sorties such as Mosquito pinpoint raids on factories, GARDENING, NICKELS and Met flights continued to be carried out. December, however, also saw a new type of target, CROSSBOW. After 617 Squadron's success against the Dams in May, Harris decided to keep the squadron in being for special tasks, after it had been refurbished. However, its next precision operation, an attempt to breach the banks of the Dortmund–Ems Canal on the night of 15 September ended in disaster with five of the eight aircraft, including that flown by Gibson's successor in command, Squadron Leader Holden, being shot down. The Squadron then took part in two further unsuccessful operations to destroy the Anthéor viaduct in the South of France. By the end of November, however, V-weapon launch sites had been identified as springing up in northern France. They were small and well protected and obviously not suited to area attack. At the same time, Barnes Wallis had invented a new bomb, the 12,000lb TALLBOY, which was designed to detonate underground, and could be the ideal means of dealing with them. Consequently, 617 Squadron, now commanded by Leonard Cheshire, carried out two operations, known as CROSSBOW, against these targets during December. For marking, they relied on Pathfinder OBOE Mosquitoes using target indicator bombs, and they also had the new stabilised automatic bombsight (SABS). The Lancasters, too, had to be modified in order to take TALLBOY. Unfortunately, the markers were slightly inaccurately placed on the first attack on the night of 16 December, and on the second, two weeks later, the Lancasters were unable to bomb because the markers were hidden by cloud. From this, Cheshire concluded that 617 Squadron would have to develop its own marking techniques, which involved marking at low level using Mosquitoes.

PANACEA TARGETS

Nevertheless, in spite of all these frustrations, Harris remained optimistic. On 7 December he wrote a formal letter to Sinclair and the Air Staff. He began by asserting that during the first ten months of 1943 Bomber Command had destroyed 25 per cent of the acreage of the 38 principal towns attacked, and believed that the enemy would 'capitulate' when 40–45 per cent destruction of his principal towns had been achieved. So long as he was able to maintain the same tempo of attack, he calculated that 40 per cent would have been achieved by 1 April, the closing date for POINTBLANK. Based on a forecast loss rate of 5 per cent and the planned production of 212 Lancasters per month:

> . . . it appears that the Lancaster force alone should be sufficient but only just sufficient to produce in Germany by April 1st 1944, a state of devastation in which surrender is inevitable. This, however, is a reasonable expectation only if the assumptions made are actually fulfilled.

He emphasised that Lancaster production must be increased over the next four months, and that the equipping of No 100 Group should be given top priority. Finally, he stressed that:

> Time is an essential factor and if we are to fulfill our task by the 1st April 1944, or indeed at all, any delay in taking all measures possible to ensure the delivery of sufficient aircraft suitably equipped for their difficult task and adequately protected against the ever-increasing defences of the enemy is likely to prove fatal.[11]

As the Official History points out,[12] Harris clearly believed that Bomber Command, given the necessary tools, could finish the war on its own. The Americans were not mentioned, contrary to his minute to Churchill of 3 November, and neither, for that matter, was OVERLORD, the invasion of the Continent, which was scheduled to take place on 1 May 1944, a month after the end of POINTBLANK. Yet in concentrating on the principal German population centres, Harris was doing nothing more than follow the official Air Staff policy, which had been extant since mid 1941, and confirmed by the POINTBLANK Directive. Both Portal and Bottomley had become increasingly concerned over the need to reduce German fighter strength and there was nothing in Harris's letter to indicate that he had this in mind, other than in the context of defending the bombers. Even so, Bottomley's reply was surprising. He pointed out that Harris's 38 principal cities contained only 11 per cent of the German population, and those de-housed could always be accom-

modated in towns in the Occupied countries. He then reminded
Harris that the Eighth Air Force's priorities were the wearing down
of German fighter strength and the destruction of the German ball-
bearing industry as a prerequisite to OVERLORD, and that the terms
of POINTBLANK were that 'as far as is practicable your efforts should
be co-ordinated with and complementary to those of the Eighth Air
Force'. He went on to tell Harris that 'your night bombers would
make the greatest contribution by completely destroying those vital
industries which can be reached by day only at heavy cost;
examples are Schweinfurt, Leipzig and centres of twin-engined
aircraft'. He also believed that Hitler could control German
morale, but feared precision day attacks on vital industries.[13] In
other words, Harris was being told that he must alter his complete
policy. The suggestion of Schweinfurt as a target had already been
put by Bottomley to Harris on 17 December. Harris had replied on
the 23rd, and used much the same arguments as he had in 1942 (see
page 103), pointing out that 'the claims as to the actual percentage
of Germany's ball-bearing supply manufactured in Schweinfurt
have always been exaggerated and have been progressively reduced,
even by their authors'. He was quite certain that the Germans
would have now dispersed this particular industry. He cited other
past appreciations:

> For years we have been told that the destruction of the Moehne Dam alone
> would be a vital blow to Germany. Both the Moehne and Eder Dams were
> destroyed and I have seen nothing, either in the present circumstances in
> Germany or in MEW reports, to show that the effort was worthwhile except as a
> spectacular operation.

After quoting further examples, including molybdenum and
synthetic petrol, he went on to say:

> In the light of the above examples of the infallible fallibility of Panacea mongers
> and parochial experts, you must excuse me if I have become cynical with regard
> to the continual diversions of the bomber effort from its legitimate effort in
> which, as we all know, it has inflicted the most grievous and intolerable damage
> to Germany.

If Schweinfurt were a vital target, the Eighth Air Force should be
invited to carry out another attack on it, and 'if they can set the
place alight in daylight, then we may have some reasonable chance
of hitting it in the dark on the same night.[14]

Not unnaturally, Harris also took exception to Bottomley's letter
replying to his of 7 December. He considered that his devastation
calculations were reasonable and added:

> It is surely impossible to believe that an increase by more than one half of
> existing devastation within four months could be sustained by Germany without
> total loss.

He did not agree that 'de-housing' was 'an end in itself', but had for its main effect the devastation of economic life. He also bridled at being reminded that his efforts should be complementary to those of the Eighth Air Force, when Bomber Command had dropped ten times the bomb-load of the latter on Germany during 1943 and, in any event, the American effort had been mainly against fringe targets.[15] Bottomley did not reply to either letter until 14 January 1944 and his letter was framed as a Directive. Harris was to 'adhere to the spirit' of the 10 June Directive and was to attack 'as far as practicable, those industrial centres associated with German fighter airframe factories and ball-bearing industry'. In particular he was to attack Schweinfurt and destroy it and the ball-bearing industry there 'at as early a date as possible'. Although it was appreciated that there were 'tactical difficulties involved', 'it is believed that the task is not beyond the present operational capabilities of your Command with the navigational aids now available, and in any case it is impossible to accept that the successful bombing of any German town within range is impracticable until it has been tried, if necessary several times'. In addition to Schweinfurt, Leipzig, Brunswick, Gotha and Augsburg, being aircraft-manufacturing centres, were specified as priority targets.[16] In other words, with Berlin not mentioned, Harris was being brought to heel.

Nevertheless, during the first part of January 1944, attacks on Berlin were continued, despite the appalling weather. On the night of the 1st/2nd, 421 Lancasters were sent against it and 28 failed to return. The following night 383 Lancasters, Halifaxes and Mosquitoes attacked and a further 27 were shot down. Stettin was visited on the night of the 5th, with a slightly lower loss rate of fifteen, brought about by a Mosquito diversion on Berlin. The weather prevented any further major operations until the night of the 14th when, in response to Bottomley's Schweinfurt Directive, 498 bombers attacked Brunswick, losing 38 in the process. A third attack on Berlin, the largest yet, was mounted on 20/21 January, with 769 aircraft taking off, and 35 being shot down. The next night Magdeburg was attacked, with another Mosquito diversion on Berlin, but this time the night fighters were not taken in, and 55 bombers failed to return. This brought a sharp response in the shape of a minute to Bottomley from Air Commodore Bufton, now Director of Bombing Operations at the Air Ministry. He wondered why Harris had not chosen Brunswick or Leipzig:

As conditions at these targets were equally favourable last night it now appears that the Command is operating to a policy of its own and is disregarding both the policy and the precise instructions for its implementation which have been laid down by the Air Staff. It is realised that this is a most serious statement to make, but following so closely upon recent correspondence and discussions in which the Command have criticised the policy of the Air Staff and in the light of the directive of the 14th January 1944, I am forced to the conclusion that the selection of Magdeburg demonstrated clearly that Bomber Command does not intend to comply with the instruction of the Air Staff. This state of affairs cannot be allowed to continue during the critical months ahead, when it is essential that the closest co-operation should be maintained.[17]

It was probably this which sparked off a fresh and more specific Directive from Bottomley, which was issued on 28 January. Addressed to Harris, Spaatz and Leigh-Mallory, whose appointment as CinC Allied Expeditionary Air Force (AEAF) had been agreed at QUADRANT, it reiterated the priority as lying with attacks on the fighter aircraft and ball-bearing industries, and then listed the specific associated targets that the USAAF were to attack by day. Bomber Command was 'to accord first priority in its operations' to the attack of (1) Schweinfurt, (2) Leipzig, (3) Brunswick, (4) Regensburg, (5) Augsburg, (6) Gotha. The Jaeger ball-bearing factory at Wuppertal was to be given top priority for OBOE and G-H* attacks, and CROSSBOW targets were to be engaged when conditions were unsuitable for POINTBLANK. As for Berlin, the only other Bomber Command target mentioned, 'when conditions are not suitable' for the six top priority targets 'RAF Bomber Command and Eighth Air Force are to attack Berlin when weather and tactical conditions are suitable for such attacks.'[18] Harris, therefore, was being allowed very little leeway.

He mounted three more attacks on Berlin before January was out, involving a total of 1,759 sorties, but with a lower casualty bill of 102 bombers missing. However, although his sortie rate for the month was almost up to the figure he had calculated in his letter of 7 December, the overall loss rate in January against major targets in Germany was more than 6 per cent, well above his allowable figure of 5 per cent. Furthermore, No 100 Group was still not operational, and the SERRATE Mosquitoes, although they had four more successes against night fighters during the month, were suffering from the fact that they were elderly in terms of flying hours and therefore mechanically unreliable. Thus, Harris was hardly fulfilling the conditions which he had laid down for himself for decisive success by 1 April. In addition, the Eighth Air Force, though it was now beginning to receive sufficient bombers to be able to take a more active part in POINTBLANK, and its total sorties had risen from 3,900 in November to 6,073 in December, was only cautiously beginning to penetrate deep into Germany again. Three

*G-H was a combined navigation/blind-bombing system and incorporated GEE and H, an airborne transmitter and receiver by which an aircraft could measure its distance from two ground stations. This limited its range, but its accuracy did not decrease with distance. 139 Squadron carried out operational trials over Germany in October 1943, and the first attack by G-H Lancasters was against a factory at Düsseldorf on the night of 3 November, but not until the autumn of 1944 was it widely installed.

such attacks were made in January, against aircraft plants in the Brunswick area (633 sorties), Frankfurt (863) and Brunswick again (777), but losses for these attacks were kept to below 4 per cent. It is, however, important to note that close liaison was maintained between HQ Bomber Command and VIII Bomber Command, the operational element of the US Eighth Air Force, and General Anderson attended Harris's daily 0900 hours conference.

The weather during the first part of February prevented any major operations, and it was not until the night of the 15th that the main force was able to launch another attack, again on Berlin, with 42 out of 891 aircraft failing to return. On the night of 19/20 February Leipzig was attacked in accordance with the January Directives. On this occasion, however, no less than 78 of the 823 bombers dispatched failed to return, and it became clear that German defences on the northern route had grown very strong, and Harris was forced to switch to targets in the south of the country. Indeed, there was only one more major Bomber Command attack on Berlin, on 24 March, and, as the Official History observes, because this was so and the city had not been destroyed meant that 'the Germans had already won the Battle of Berlin'.[19] Different tactics were now adopted by Bomber Command. Flares put out by the Pathfinders to mark the course for the main force were clearly helping the night fighters as well, so these were reduced, and 'spoof' courses were laid. Even more emphasis was placed on diversionary attacks, and main attacks were often divided into two waves, which would approach the target from different directions.

Thus, on the night following the Leipzig raid, Stuttgart was attacked, with the very low loss rate of only nine bombers out of 598 dispatched. Then, on the 24th/25th Schweinfurt was finally attacked by Bomber Command. During the day the Americans had attacked with 266 bombers for the loss of only eleven shot down, while other groups of B-17s went for Gotha and Rostock. That night, Harris put up 734 aircraft against the town, which they bombed using the fires started by the Americans. Although the accuracy was not as good as the last American visit in October, three of the four ball-bearing plants were seriously damaged. The same pattern of the Americans going in by day and Bomber Command following up by night was repeated the next night against Augsburg, which was the last Bomber Command raid of the month.

March, the final month of POINTBLANK, continued to be depressing for Harris, although the Eighth Air Force, which at last had received the P-51 Mustang, now began daylight attacks on Berlin. Significantly he did not attack any of the towns listed in the Directive of 28 January. Stuttgart and Frankfurt were each attacked twice, and then the final visit was made to Berlin on the night of 24 March, and it turned out to be a costly one, with 73 aircraft (9.1 per cent of the force) failing to return. On this occasion, however, it was not the night fighters that caused the losses but strong winds which took the bomber stream over the formidable Ruhr defences. Two nights later, only nine of 705 aircraft were lost over Essen. Then, on the night of 30 March came the last RAF Bomber Command POINTBLANK operation.

NUREMBERG

Harris selected a target which had been little visited of late, but which was important both politically and economically. This was Nuremberg. Much has been written about this raid:[20] suffice it to say that it was the worst night of the war for Bomber Command with 96 aircraft out of 795 being posted missing. Apart from the fact that Harris took a gamble on the weather, most of the losses were caused by a new tactic developed by the Germans to combat diversionary raids. This had been first noticed during the Stuttgart attack on 15/16 March, when the night fighters had been divided into two forces. While one harried the bomber stream, the other was held back to deploy over the target, once identified, where they took advantage of the fact that the bomber formations were at their most concentrated during this phase of the operation. Nuremberg confirmed that the only answer to this was to divide the bomber force, and on 1 April Harris laid down that from now on the main force would attack at least two targets each time it operated. Otherwise, it was clearly a night that Harris wished to forget and there is no mention of it in his book. He has been faulted for using tactics which played into the hands of the German defences, but some 27 years after the event he stated in justification:

> . . . when you're fighting 1,000 offensive battles in the course of the longest continuous battle of the war, it is difficult to find the changes of tactics every time that will fox the enemy; and one of the changes you have to include occasionally is to do what the enemy thinks you would not dare to do – avoid extensive diversionary operations for once and take a fairly direct route to the target, as with Nuremberg.[21]

As for the crews themselves, when they heard of the total casualty bill, there was perhaps more relief at having survived than any despondency over the missing. As one of them later said:

> Although shaken by the losses, I don't remember anyone quitting nor do I remember any blame being laid on 'Butch' or, as we called him, 'Chopper' Harris. In fact, rather a feeling of pity for him and his burden of responsibility. Our crews did what we always did at those times. We got drunk.[22]

Thus, Harris had failed in his attempt to bring Germany to her knees by 1 April 1944. In all, during the five months from

November to March, he had dispatched 28,903 sorties by night, from which 1,128 aircraft had failed to return, and another 2,034 had been damaged. As for his own review on the success against his main target during this period:

> Judging by the standards of our attacks on Hamburg, the Battle of Berlin did not appear to be an overwhelming success. With many times more sorties, a far greater bomb load, and ten times as many casualties, we appeared to have succeeded in destroying about a third of the acreage destroyed in the attack on Hamburg . . .[23]

Yet, he had no time to bewail his failure or mourn his losses, for the Allies were about to embark on another phase of the war, the planning of which had been increasingly drawing his attention during the past few months.

CHAPTER NINE

THE OVERLORD DEBATE

This is the greatest morale booster we have experienced, and it shows our complete mastery of the air to perfection. – British tank officer

As early as 26 April 1943 a directive had been issued to General Sir Frederick Morgan, newly appointed as Chief of Staff to the Supreme Allied Commander (COSSAC), ordering him to draw up plans whose object would be 'to defeat the German fighting forces in north-west Europe'.[1] It would be some time before the British and American air staffs were drawn into the planning, mainly because they were too engrossed in the prosecution of POINTBLANK, but some of the air elements to support the invasion were organised at a very early stage. Thus, on 1 June was formed the 2nd Tactical Air Force, which consisted of No 2 Group (transferred from Bomber Command), Nos 83 and 84 Fighter Groups and, a little later, Nos 38 and 46 Transport Groups. Then, in August, it was agreed at QUADRANT to appoint Air Chief Marshal Sir Trafford Leigh-Mallory as CinC Allied Expeditionary Air Force (AEAF), and Ninth US Air Force was brought under his command in October. The main significance of Leigh-Mallory's appointment was that he had extensive fighter experience and had controlled the air cover for the Dieppe operation in 1942. As AEAF would deploy fighters, medium bombers and transports, and was designed to gain cover over the beachhead, it seemed an ideal appointment, but a growing body of opinion advocated that the strategic air forces should also be brought in to give direct support to OVERLORD.

By the end of October Churchill was writing to Portal to ask for his views on the subject, and Portal suggested that the strategic forces based in the United Kingdom might not be involved until fourteen days before D-Day, when 50 per cent of their effort should be switched to the support of OVERLORD, while the whole of the strategic force in the Mediterranean would be dedicated to this task over the period D minus 14 to D-Day. The United Kingdom forces would then devote 100 per cent effort to the invasion during the landings, 75 per cent on D-Day and the 21 days following it, then 50 per cent until D-Day plus 50, and after that it was impossible to estimate. He also expressed concern over an American idea to use heavy bombers to help with the airlift on D-Day, and even more so that the 'OVERLORD Supreme Commander shall command the whole of the Strategic bomber forces, British and American, probably from an early date after his appointment and certainly from D minus 14'.[2] The actual proposal put forward by the Americans was even more far-reaching than this, in that the Supreme Allied Commander should actually command *all* United Nations forces in Europe and the Mediterranean. The British objected strenuously, however, and the matter was dropped. Nevertheless, Portal's estimates did accord closely with what the air planners under COSSAC were thinking. They recognised POINT-BLANK as being an essential preliminary to OVERLORD and certainly saw no diversions until D minus 34, with strategic air support building up rapidly from D minus 14 onwards, with 'probably only an occasional attack against Germany until at least D plus 14'.[3]

However, not until the Allied conference at Teheran was it formally agreed by the Combined Chiefs of Staff that 'in the preparatory phase immediately preceding the invasion, the whole of the available air power in the United Kingdom, tactical and strategic, will be employed in a concentrated effort to create the conditions essential to assault'.[4]

On 23 December 1943 Portal wrote to Harris saying that, as 'we are now committed for good or ill to OVERLORD', it was necessary to examine the tasks that might be given to Bomber Command and to work out how they might be carried out, while the Supreme Commander, recently nominated as Eisenhower, and Leigh-Mallory should be clear on 'the capabilities and limitations of your command'. He stressed, however, that the British Chiefs of Staff view was that Harris and Eaker were to be placed 'at the disposal' of Eisenhower and not 'under the control of him'.[5] Harris replied to this on the 27th. He accepted the commitment to OVERLORD and expressed himself 'most ready' to discuss the matter with the AEAF Commanders with the object of rendering 'the execution of it [OVERLORD] as inexpensive as may be in lives which we can ill afford to lose'. He did, however, want Portal's support on two major points. First, he wanted confirmation that the overall aim of POINT-BLANK still held good, and that in order to prevent 'the whole of the German fighter force from falling on "Overlord" the bomber offensive must be maintained against "Germany proper".' Any failure of the Combined Bomber Offensive to restrict German fighter production 'would, in any case, rule out Overlord altogether'. Secondly, while there 'should be no difficulty in

reaching agreement' on heavy bomber targets prior to the operation, tactical bombing during the landings and beyond was only
feasible if the weather was right.[6] Portal reassured Harris on the
second point, but needed to clear his own mind on how best the
strategic bombing forces could support OVERLORD during the
preparatory phase. Nevertheless, he warned Harris that as far as
attacks on Germany were concerned 'the criterion by which they
will be judged will then be the extent to which they assist
"Overlord" and not as at present the extent to which they weaken
Germany's general power to make war'.[7]

The original AEAF plan envisaged the sealing off of the
Normandy battlefield through attacks on railway lines in order to
force the enemy reserves to detrain a considerable distance away
from the coast, but this would need a sustained offensive prior to
D–Day in order to achieve a significant result. Portal's own confusion as to the right balance between this and attacks on Germany
is revealed in a minute he wrote to Air Vice-Marshal Medhurst,
ACAS (Policy), on 5 January. While he accepted the sense of the
AEAF plan, he felt that to halt all bombing of Germany during the
preparatory period would not be right. However, in order to continue these attacks 'up to the last possible moment' the Air Staff
would 'have to produce arguments to establish the case that this will
help OVERLORD greatly'. He, therefore asked Medhurst to see (if
necessary in consultation with Harris) if he could 'produce a really
strong case for the continued bombing of Germany with a large
part of the strategic bomber force, especially the night bombers'.[8]

Harris, however, now waded in with a paper on his views on the
use of Bomber Command in support of OVERLORD, which was
submitted to both AEAF and the Air Staff. The overall theme was
the apparent inflexibility of the heavy bomber force, whose task, in
Harris's words, was 'the destruction of the enemy's industrial
centres', to which end it was equipped with 'highly specialised
aircraft'. The AEAF comment on this was that they were not clear
as to why targets in France should be any less suitable than
industrial centres in Germany, while the Air Staff remarked that it
was not the specialised aircraft which restricted the choice of target,
but the inability to bomb accurately. Both, however, agreed with
Harris's statement that his force was totally unsuited to operations
by day, but that in any case it was unlikely that he would be called
upon to carry out this type of attack. Harris then discussed the
problems of bombing accurately by night, outlining the limitations
of his technical aids, the problems over weather, the fact that the
Pathfinder Force could not mark more than two targets in one
night and that if used more than two nights in a row its efficiency
would be impaired. He stated that the maximum monthly effort of

his Command was 5,000 sorties provided that the operational loss rate was not more than 4 per cent. This equated to some eight major operations. His Command was not suited to attacks on 'Fleeting Targets' because of the long preparation time required for an operation, and that 'Programme Bombing', whereby particular targets were attacked on specific dates as part of a long-term plan, was also impracticable. He warned that any cessation of attacks against Germany would lead to a resurgence of German strength and morale. In conclusion, he wrote:

> It is thus clear that the best and indeed the only efficient support which Bomber Command can give to 'OVERLORD' is the intensification of attacks on suitable industrial centres in Germany as and when the opportunity offers. If we attempt to substitute for this process attacks on gun emplacements, beach defences, communications or dumps in occupied territory we shall commit the irremediable [sic] error of diverting our best weapons from the military function, for which it has been equipped and trained, to tasks which it cannot effectively carry out. Though this might give a specious appearance of 'supporting' the Army, in reality it would be the greatest disservice we could do them. It would lead directly to disaster.

Both AEAF and the Air Staff pinpointed the flaw in Harris's argument in that it was based entirely on his experience of tackling deep penetration targets in Germany. He ignored the fact that the much shorter range of the targets he would be called upon to attack in support of OVERLORD would mean that his technical aids would be that much more effective, he would be able to mount more sorties, and that weather forecasting would be much more accurate. Both also dismissed the assertion that attacks on Fleeting Targets were impossible, and the Air Staff pointed out that, using the marker bombing technique, targets could be changed at short notice. As for halting attacks on Germany, Harris had based his arguments on a six-month phase, while support for OVERLORD was being considered merely in terms of weeks. In any event, as the Air Staff pointed out, it should still be possible to carry out some attacks on Germany during this time. The AEAF view on this was that failure of OVERLORD would create far greater repercussions than a temporary halt to attacks on Germany, but, in any event, diversions from the latter would be considered and decisions to do so taken at the 'highest level'.[9] One cannot help but suspect that Harris, while overtly willing to support OVERLORD, secretly still believed that air attack could defeat Germany before any invasion had to be launched. Indeed, he wrote this paper only a month after his 7 December letter to Sinclair in which he claimed that he could, if conditions were right, do just this by 1 April 1944. Thus his heart was not in OVERLORD and he had purposely 'situated his appreciation' in order to prove that Bomber Command should not be diverted from its main task as he saw it. Portal, too, obviously had a similar suspicion of the way that Harris's mind was working, for in his covering letter to Harris on the AEAF and Air Staffs' comments he said:

> I agree generally with the views of the Staff as set out in the enclosed paper. The United Nations are irrevocably committed to 'OVERLORD' and I am sure that both before and during that operation, Bomber Command will wish to help to the utmost, even if this means trying out new techniques and tactics against the kind of targets which you rightly consider to be outside the scope of normal night operations.[10]

One of the other flaws in Harris's paper was that he made no consideration of the types of targets, i.e. communications, which AEAF were expecting him to undertake, merely restricting his remarks to defences actually on the beaches. It is most unlikely that he would not have had some idea of the plan by this stage, and one can only assume that he omitted mention of it because it did not suit his overall argument. However, just over a week after Harris had written his paper, AEAF came out with a fresh plan.

COMMUNICATIONS VERSUS OIL

A planning paper put out on 22 January 1944 and entitled *Delay and Disorganization of Enemy Movement by Rail* proposed that an attack on the 76 most important railway servicing and repair facilities in North-West Europe would 'paralyse movement in the whole region they serve and render almost impossible the subsequent movement by rail of major reserves into France'.[11] The chief author of this plan was Solly Zuckerman, who had been scientific adviser to Arthur Tedder when he was Allied Air Commander in the Mediterranean; on 21 January Tedder had been appointed Deputy Supreme Allied Commander. It was during the planning for the invasion of Sicily (HUSKY) that Zuckerman had concluded that attacks on enemy road and rail communications would make the best use of strategic air support to the invasion, and, as a result of post-HUSKY investigations, he produced a report, dated 28 December 1943, which recommended that attacks on railway communications were best served by going for large centres rather than particular points in the system such as bridges and tunnels. The main reason was that the target in the former case was less precise and hence less bombing accuracy was needed to cause decisive results. Now that Zuckerman had been appointed to advise Leigh-Mallory, it is not surprising that Tedder, from his new position of influence, should back Zuckerman's plan, and it quickly became the accepted AEAF policy. Others, however, were not so convinced. Spaatz and the US Strategic Bombing Force were against the plan because they, like Harris, wanted to continue attacks against

Germany after 1 April. Indeed, Spaatz, as a result of an analysis completed during February by the Economic Objectives Unit (EOU) of the Economic War Division of the US Embassy in London, wanted now to make oil the prime objective. Lack of oil resources would damage the German war machine more quickly than the Transportation Plan, and in any event it would certainly force the German fighter force into the air, whereas attacks on communications targets in Occupied countries would not provoke such an intense reaction. However, the British Air Staff, while viewing oil as a good secondary target system, did not see it as relevant to the prime strategic bombing aim of destroying the Luftwaffe. Harris, too, was against it as it meant too many precision targets, which he saw as being beyond his capabilities. There were also deep reservations from Churchill and the War Cabinet in that the Transportation Plan would cause the deaths of many French civilians, something which went against a long-standing War Cabinet ruling that this type of attack was unacceptable.

Furthermore, there was the whole question of command and control of the strategic air element of OVERLORD. A draft of the Air Plan put out for comment on 12 February placed both Harris and Spaatz firmly under Supreme Headquarters Allied Expeditionary Force (SHAEF). This was unacceptable not just to them, but to Churchill and the Combined Chiefs of Staff as well. Much of the problem lay in the fact that Spaatz and Harris saw themselves taking orders from Leigh-Mallory, who, apart from having a reputation of being aggressive and dogmatic, had no experience of strategic bombing operations. Churchill, too, was concerned about the latter point. Tedder, however, was deeply concerned about the effect of prolonged disagreement on this aspect:

> As I see it, one of the main lessons of the Mediterranean campaign was not merely the advisability of, but the necessity for, unified command of the Air Force . . . I think everybody in authority, both British and American, realises that this is going to be hard work . . . to maintain harmonious co-operation during this next job. A split on the question of the control of air forces might well . . . precipitate a quite irremedial cleavage.[12]

In early March, however, there was a hopeful glimmer on the horizon so far as the AEAF planners and SHAEF were concerned. Portal felt that the least Harris could do was to carry out experiments in attacking precision transportation targets. During February, as part of the plan to destroy German air strength, a series of attacks had been launched to prevent the Germans using French aircraft factories. Twelve such targets were identified and the task of destroying them was entrusted to 617 Squadron, using a 12,000lb blast bomb. The low-level marking techniques developed by Leonard Cheshire during this short and very successful campaign resulted in high bombing accuracy. Consequently, in a directive dated 4 March, Harris was ordered to attack six marshalling yards in France by way of an experiment, on nights when 'POINTBLANK night operations were not practicable'.[13] The first of these operations took place on the night of 6/7 March against Trappes, and proved to be very successful, with civilian casualties few and the yards being out of commission for a month.

EISENHOWER DECIDES

Nevertheless, by the middle of March the arguments were coming to a head, and so desperate was the question of command of the strategic air forces that Eisenhower recorded on 22 March: 'If a satisfactory answer is not reached I am going to take drastic action and inform the Chiefs of Staff that unless the matter is settled at once I will request relief from this Command'.[14] Then, Leigh-Mallory removed the Ninth Air Force P-47s from their escort role with the Eighth Air Force and began to deploy them on railway targets. Spaatz complained bitterly, and Eisenhower called both into his office, adjudicating in favour of Spaatz in that the time to put the Transportation Plan into action had not yet arrived. Eisenhower now called a meeting for 25 March to thrash out the problem of the strategic bombing forces' role in OVERLORD and invited Portal to chair it. Harris, who had been invited to attend, wrote to Portal on the eve of the meeting. His letter indicated that he believed that Portal, despite his comments on Harris's 13 January paper, still considered that the prime role of RAF Bomber Command in the OVERLORD preparatory phase would be against targets in Germany, and that Spaatz's would be the same. He thus argued that his Command should not be tied to attacking aircraft-production targets which the Americans had taken on by day, and invoked the weather in support of his argument. Instead, as he had always maintained, he should be allowed a free hand in target selection. However, he did, in his final paragraph, state that, because his Stirlings and Halifax II and V Squadrons were 'normally incapable of operating over Germany', they 'are normally allocated' to 'Sea-mining, SOE work and possibly railway targets'. The limited range of the Halifax III, which prevented them being used on very deep penetration raids into Germany, 'would enable me to occasionally use them to supplement such effort'. Thus, provided that the backbone of his force, the Lancaster squadrons, would not be deflected from attacking Germany, he was happy to allocate the remainder of his aircraft to targets as dictated by SHAEF.[15]

ove: Over the target, in this case Hanau on the night 18/19 March 1945. Of the 285 Lancasters and
squitoes of Nos 1 and 8 Groups involved, 280 attacked and two failed to return. (Chaz Bowyer)

ve left: Another 'op' completed. Relief plainly
vs on the faces of these Lancaster crewmen
44 Squadron on their return from Berlin in the
y hours of 2 March 1943. (Chaz Bowyer)
w left: Debriefing on return from Stuttgart. (Chaz
yer)
ve: Harris's Rolls-Bentley staff car, of which he
very proud. He obtained the 'priority' sign from

Portal, and used it as an excuse to disregard speed
limits and, on occasion, traffic lights. (Peter
Tomlinson)
Below: Crew morale was very dependent on good
leadership at Squadron level. Guy Gibson
(foreground centre) with crews from 106 Squadron
on the day after the first 1,000 bomber raid, May
1942. (IWM)

Above left: The American 'Bomber Barons', Ira C. Eaker and Carl 'Tooey' Spaatz in 1944. Harris formed a close relationship with both men during the formation of POINTBLANK, but Spaatz fell in his estimation towards the end of the war. (Brig. Gen. Frank Norman)

Below left: B-17Fs of 569th Bomber Squadron, 390th Bomber Group of US Eighth Air Force, based at Framlingham. Note the box formation, designed to give maximum protection against fighters. (Chaz Bowyer)

Above: HM King George VI visits RAF Scampton after the Dams Raid of 16/17 May 1943; left to right, Cochrane, Gibson, The King, Whitworth (station commander), unknown. (RAF Museum)

Below right: Zuckerman's Communications Plan—Vaires marshalling yard outside Paris. (Chaz Bowyer)

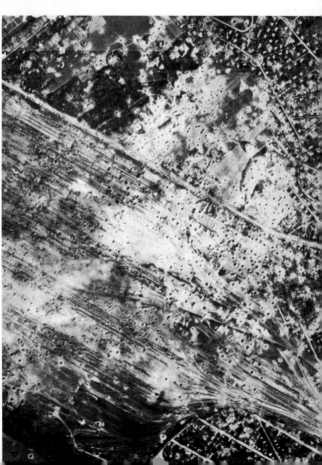

Right: The Air Council, July 1944; left to right, Howitt (Additional Member), Courtney (Air Member for Supply and Organisation), Sutton (Air Member for Personnel), Sherwood (Joint Parliamentary Under-Secretary for Air), Balfour (Joint Parliamentary Under-Secretary for Air), Sinclair (Secretary of State for Air), Portal (CAS), Street (Permanent Under-Secretary for Air), Evill (VCAS), Sorley (Additional Member), Drummond (Air Member for Training). (Brig. Gen. Frank Norman)
Below left: Area bombing—Cologne in April 1945. The Cathedral can be seen in the top right-hand corner. (Chaz Bowyer)
Below right: A 'daylight' over Calais, flown by Halifaxes in support of Allied ground forces, 25 September 1944. (Chaz Bowyer)

Above: 'Bloody Hell, look at that!' Dresden on the night of 13/14 February 1945. (Chaz Bowyer)
Below: Harris signs dollar bills in Brazil during a goodwill visit with three Lancasters at the end of 1945. S/L Peter Tomlinson, his personal assistan stands behind. (Peter Tomlinson)

The main figures attending the meeting on the 25th were Eisenhower, Portal, Tedder, Leigh-Mallory, Harris and Spaatz. Tedder began by outlining the Transportation Plan, but emphasised that Luftwaffe targets should 'remain on highest priority'. The object of the meeting was therefore 'to consider what target system ought to be attacked with the effort remaining after what was necessary had been allocated to the attack of GAF [German Air Force] targets'. He also emphasised that the latter included ball-bearing factories. The War Office was doubtful as to whether the plan would be decisive, but Eisenhower was convinced that it would be. Spaatz then brought up his Oil Plan, and recommended that the priorities should be (1) GAF (2) Oil (3) direct assistance to the land battle. The MEW representative, however, did not believe that the Germans in the West would begin to feel the effects of the Oil Plan until 'four or five months after the plan began to be put into effect'. Portal then observed that this would not help OVERLORD during the first critical weeks after the landing, but felt that it should be seriously considered after the initial crises in Normandy had passed. It was now Harris's turn to speak.

He believed that Bomber Command could contribute in two ways. First, he could attack railway centres within OBOE range during the moon periods. However, in view of the fact that he had now been given a list of 26 such targets and had only dealt with three or four, he was concerned as to his ability to get through the list by June. In any event, he was also doubtful as to the effectiveness of the Transportation Plan. He was also not enamoured with the War Office proposal that strictly military targets such as depots and motor transport parks should be attacked, in that these were likely to be precise and numerous and beyond the capabilities of his Command. He went on to state that continuing attacks on German cities would, however, help, and was anxious to continue his attacks on eastern Germany so long as the hours of darkness made this possible. He could guide his attacks onto transportation targets in this context, and Tedder agreed that there were good rail targets in eastern Germany, but warned Eisenhower that the effect would be 'largely fortuitous'. The latter concluded, though, that the Transportation Plan meant 'very little change' to Harris's programme and turned his attention to Spaatz, who said that half the Eighth and Fifteenth Air Force effort would be required on GAF targets, but wanted the other target systems to be such as to produce at least some fighter reaction, and was very doubtful that the Transportation Plan would fulfil this condition. Tedder, however, said that there were four marshalling yards on the east side of the Ruhr and that the 28 targets allotted to USSTAFE should provide what Spaatz required. Portal once more expressed concern over French civilian casualties. Finally, it was agreed that Spaatz would confirm that he could carry out his share of the Transportation programme and that a draft directive would be drawn up by Tedder.[16] Thus, transportation had won the day, but it seemed that Harris was still to be allowed a measure of independence. Furthermore, Eisenhower managed to get round the business of the command problem, by placing ultimate control of the air operations in Tedder's rather than Leigh-Mallory's hands.

The Supreme Commander's Directive was finally issued on 17 April 1944. The overall mission remained as for POINTBLANK, but in execution of this '. . . the immediate objective is first the destruction of the German air combat strength, by the successful prosecution of the Combined Bomber Offensive'. Also, with OVERLORD as 'the supreme operation for 1944', 'all possible support must . . . be afforded to the Allied armies by our Air Forces to assist them in establishing themselves in the lodgement area'. While a further directive would be issued to cover the period after the landings, the particular missions for the strategic air forces prior to them were depletion of the Luftwaffe and transportation. USSTAFE were given these targets as first and second priorities, with precise subcategories of target for the first priority, and were also told that 'whenever weather or tactical conditions were unsuitable for attack of the primary objectives, attacks will be delivered by blind-bombing technique on BERLIN, or other important industrial targets. Targets will be selected so as to further the aim of attrition of the German Air Force, and the dislocation of the enemy's transport system.' The paragraph dealing with RAF Bomber Command was, however, very much more vague:

> In view of the tactical difficulties of destroying precise targets by night, RAF Bomber Command will continue to be employed in accordance with their main aim of disorganising German industry. Their operations will, however, be designed as far as practicable to be complementary to the operations of the USSTAFE. In particular, where tactical conditions allow, their targets will be selected so as to give the maximum assistance in the aims of reducing the strength of the German Air Force, and destroying and disrupting enemy rail communications.

A list of targets would be issued separately. As for other categories, the strategic bombing forces might be called upon to tackle 'objectives of great or fleeting importance' and CROSSBOW targets. In the case of the latter, this was the responsibility of Leigh-Mallory, but should he require strategic bomber assistance he would have to go through Tedder.[17]

The precision attacks against French marshalling yards, which had begun at the beginning of March, belied acceptance of the fact that Bomber Command was incapable of tackling this type of target. Indeed, all six of the initial targets had been successfully bombed by the end of the month, mainly using the Halifaxes of Nos 4 and 6 Groups. The aiming-points were chosen so as to keep civilian casualties to a minimum, and the crews were given strict instructions not to bomb if they could not identify the OBOE-Mosquito markers. As for the bomb tonnages required to knock out each target, these were worked out by the Bomber Command ORS. Indeed, it was Dr. Dickins who first persuaded Harris that it was possible to carry out this form of precision attack using OBOE,[18] and Harris, as he later admitted,[19] was surprised by the good results obtained.

OVERLORD SUPPORT

On 14 April direction of Bomber Command was formally passed to the Supreme Allied Commander, who exercised this through his Deputy, Tedder. At the same time, Harris, in order to take advantage of the expertise which existed in the Command, and in pursuit of his post-Nuremberg policy of taking on more than one major target per night in his attacks on Germany, decided to divorce No 5 Group from the main force, and gave it its own Pathfinder Squadrons – 83 and 97 Lancaster Squadrons and 627 Mosquito Squadron, the latter being specialists in low marking.* Together with 617 Squadron and Guy Gibson's other former command, 106 Squadron, these formed what was known as No 54 Base, and were to become a very highly-specialised marking and precision bombing organisation. Furthermore, No 1 Group was also getting into the target-marking business, and had developed its own variation on OBOE marking. This had first been used on the night of 10/11 April in an attack on the marshalling yards at Aulnoye, when two No 1 Group Master Bombers, having assessed the inaccuracy of the OBOE green TIs, used these as a reference to drop more accurate red markers and ordered the crews to aim for them. This technique became known as 'Controlled OBOE'. As Harris himself wrote '. . . we were getting towards that state of affairs which I had recommended when the formation of the Pathfinder Force was first under discussion, for we now had the benefit of several different techniques developed by different Groups, which were suitable for a variety of targets or conditions of weather'.[21] Yet, this was not to denigrate the work of No 8 Group, who continued to play a vitally important role.

---

*According to Bennett, the idea of low marking originated with Cochrane, who had suggested it as a method for increasing the accuracy of the attacks on Berlin. Bennett told Harris that he did believe it was possible over a densely built-up area. Harris did not accept this and forcibly removed the squadrons, much to Bennett's chagrin.[20]

Thus, Harris now whole-heartedly began work to implement the Transportation Plan, and appears to have taken little advantage of the woolly wording of the 17 April Directive by Tedder, which implied that his first priority was still attacks on German industry. Nevertheless, doubts about the Transportation Plan still existed, particularly in Churchill's mind. RE8's original estimate had been that the Plan might cause 80,000–160,000 casualties to French and Belgian civilians, and the Defence Committee had on 6 April invited Tedder to modify the plan in order to remove targets situated in densely-populated areas. As a result of these amendments to the target list, Portal estimated that the casualty level would now be 10,500 killed and a further 5,500 seriously injured. This was discussed at a War Cabinet meeting on 14 April, but Churchill was evidently still doubtful:

> This slaughter was likely to put the French against us and he was doubtful if the results achieved by the plan would justify this. There was a limit to the slaughter and the resulting anger and resentment which it would arouse among the French, beyond which we could not go.

Cherwell, too, was against the plan, but Sinclair pointed out that, when the French had felt that unjustifiable civilian casualties had been caused in the past, the Free French authorities had made complaints which had not happened so far with the execution of the Transportation Plan.[22] Still, the Germans, through their own media and those in Occupied Belgium and France, were capitalising on the propaganda value to be gained, calling the operations 'terror attacks'. There was, however, relief in the Allied camp that the enemy had clearly failed to connect these attacks with OVERLORD preparations. Nevertheless, it was decided that it was only fair that the French and Belgian populations be warned, and Bomber Command put out a broadcast on the evening of 18 April:

> Air Attacks against factories and railways in France and Belgium will be intensified in the coming weeks. The means by which the enemy concentrates troops and material must be disrupted . . . With a heavy heart we have taken this decision. Our pilots realise perfectly that the lives and homes of their friends are involved and they will thus take every possible precaution . . . but inevitably the extent of these attacks must increase the suffering which you, our loyal friends have borne with so much courage during this war.[23]

Churchill, however, remained unhappy and on 29 April the War Cabinet agreed that transportation targets should be restricted to those where the casualty estimates would not exceed 100–150, and Eisenhower was forced to drop 27 targets in the more populated areas. A week later, though, this was rescinded. Churchill then, on 7 May, sent a personal telegram to President Roosevelt warning him that the Cabinet feared that civilian casualties might 'easily bring about a great revulsion in French feeling towards their approaching United States and British liberators',[24] but Roosevelt replied that the decision was a military and not a political one.

On 15 May, there was a gathering of Allied commanders at Saint Paul's School in London, where much of the OVERLORD planning had been carried out. It provided the opportunity for each commander to brief the others on his role in the forthcoming operations and among those who spoke was Harris. Although he had been conscientiously operating to the dictates of the Transportation Plan, he could not resist the opportunity to point out his reservations. He warned that if the bombing of Germany dropped below 10,000 tons per month, her industry would recuperate, and that if it ceased she would be back to normal production in five months.[25] His speech did not go down well. Alanbrooke noted in his diary that: 'Bert Harris told us how well he might have won the war if it had not been for the handicap imposed by the other two Services.'[26] General George Patton considered his arguments in favour of 'bombardment instead of attack' . . . 'very ill-timed'.[27] Churchill, however, made it plain that he had dropped his opposition to the Transportation Plan, stating: 'Gentlemen, I am hardening to this enterprise.'[28] Next day he instructed the War Cabinet not to press the matter of civilian casualties further.

Meanwhile, the air campaign in support of OVERLORD continued, but in May conditions became noticeably more difficult. By this time Harris was keeping his nightly operations well dispersed, in order to dilute the night fighters. Thus, on 3 May, Mailly-le-Camp, Montdidier, Châteaudun and Ludwigshafen were attacked, together with GARDENING off the Friesians and French Atlantic ports, and NICKELS over northern France. However, of the 362 bombers sent to the first-named target, 42 failed to return, and the same happened a week later when twelve out of 89 were posted as missing from an attack on the marshalling yards at Lille. It was clear that the Germans had radically increased their night fighter strength over northern France. It was also noted that they were carrying out many of their attacks unseen by the bombers, and in particular making their approach from below and firing upwards into the belly. Indeed, Bomber Command losses over north-west France and Belgium jumped from 1.9 per cent in April to 4.3 per cent in May,[29] and the crews were relieved when the value of these operations was raised from one-third to a full operation in terms of counting towards the end of their tours. Much of the problem lay in the fact that since they were precision targets, the bombers had to spend more time over the target waiting until the Master Bombers were satisfied that the markers were in the right place. It was a very worrying time for Harris and there was little he could do about it apart from continuing to disperse his forces to attack as many different simultaneous targets as possible. In spite of this, Bomber Command's contribution to the Plan was spectacular. A high standard of accuracy was achieved and it succeeded in knocking out all 37 targets assigned to it.

Bomber Command also made a significant contribution during the night prior to D-Day itself. While the three jamming squadrons of No 100 Group, which included one American squadron, worked above the invasion fleet itself, a force of 111 aircraft armed with WINDOW flew diversions over the Pas de Calais to simulate an invasion in the Boulogne area, and a bomber stream flew over the area of the River Somme to create another invasion scare in the area of Le Havre.* In addition, 1,136 Halifaxes, Lancasters and Mosquitoes attacked coastal batteries.

As for the Americans, although Spaatz had lost his battle for oil in support of OVERLORD, he managed to get agreement for the Fifteenth Air Force to attack oil targets in Roumania, and three such attacks were made on Ploesti during April. Furthermore, using the argument of attracting the Luftwaffe into the air, he also got Eisenhower's acquiescence for two attacks on German oil installations during the same month, but because of the weather and diversions to CROSSBOW targets, he did not actually carry out the attacks until 12 May. By the end of that month Portal was also becoming more certain that Bomber Command, once the situation in Normandy was secure, should concentrate part of its effort on this target, and on 3 June Bottomley wrote to Harris asking for his views on attacking ten such targets in the Ruhr. The latter thought that it was possible, but, assuming a 2,000-yard margin of error, considered that it would take over 30,000 tons of bombs to knock them out. He also pointed out that he was now under SHAEF Command and not that of the Air Staff, but that he had already agreed with Tedder to take on some of these targets.[31] Indeed, the Air Staff now found themselves in a frustrating position at having no operational control over Bomber Command, and Harris even went to the stage of objecting to being sent copies of requests from the Air Ministry to SHAEF for him to take on CROSSBOW targets.[32] Nevertheless, in June Harris did carry out four oil attacks. Although all these used OBOE-marking Mosquitoes, only one of them, that against the Nordstern plant at Gelsenkirchen on the night of 12 June could be said to have been successful, and of a total of 832 heavy bombers sent against the four, 93 failed to return. However, five further attacks in July produced better results, with improved accuracy, and these combined with area

---

*These two operations, codenamed GLIMMER and TAXABLE, were devised by TRE and required very precise navigation and timings as to when to drop WINDOW in order to make the German radars believe that these really were invasion fleets. They were assisted by naval launches in the Channel using loud hailers to simulate the noises of a large invasion fleet.[30]

attacks on Kiel, Hamburg and Stuttgart resulted in only 132 aircraft being lost from 3,419 sorties. Much of this can be attributed to the increasing effectiveness of No 100 Group.

With the armies now ashore in Normandy, Harris had to devote attention to close support of their operations. While many attacks continued to be made on railway centres, there were other targets to be taken on as well. Thus, on the night of 7/8 June 212 aircraft took off to attack a troop concentration in the Forêt de Cerisy and 617 Squadron, using TALLBOY, successfully demolished a railway tunnel at Saumur on the following night. Then, on the 14th and 15th there was a noticeable change in Bomber Command tactics when attacks were made on shipping at Le Havre and Boulogne by daylight. On the first, 234 aircraft were involved and against Boulogne 297, but in neither case was a single casualty suffered. Indeed, the Air Staff had been trying to persuade Harris to undertake daylight operations since early April, believing that a strong fighter escort combined with the deterioration in Luftwaffe day fighter strength, would reap much benefit. Harris, however, had resisted the idea on the grounds that there was no guarantee that fighter escort would be available the whole time; that the 0.303in-based defensive armaments of the bombers would be ineffectual against day fighters; that it was dependent on clear weather, and that it would detract from his night operations.[33] However, the sharp rise in his losses by night over France persuaded him to try it out, and it was very successful, with only 0.4 per cent of the 9,563 daylight sorties dispatched in June and July failing to return. Of course, there was no time to train the crews in the formation and bombing tactics used by the Americans, and attacks were carried out using night marking techniques with an ungainly gaggle of aircraft, each aiming individually, which made it difficult for the escorting fighters. Yet, with the Luftwaffe day opposition having been decimated by POINTBLANK, this was not a serious problem, and in view of this success it was not unexpected that daylight operations would be extended to targets within Germany, albeit within fighter escort range. Consequently, on 27 August a force of 216 No 4 Group Halifaxes, together with 27 Pathfinder Mosquitoes and Lancasters, were sent to attack an oil plant at Homberg in the Ruhr. During the next three weeks another four such operations were mounted, and there were some impressive results, with only ten bombers out of 803 failing to return. Indeed, Harris was sufficiently enthusiastic about the success of these operations to wish to have escort fighters placed under his command, although this was turned down. He did, however, order that No 3 Group be turned into a specialist daylight precision blind-bombing formation, using G-H when poor visibility prevailed.

Two other types of target are worthy of mention during this phase. First, Bomber Command was used to great effect on the German garrisons in the Channel ports, which Hitler had ordered to be turned into fortresses, and the bombing effort undoubtedly contributed much to their eventual reduction. Attacks were also made in direct support of other ground operations, notably around Caen. As to what these daylight operations by Bomber Command looked like from the ground, a tank officer describes such an attack on Caen:

> Then, just as the evening shadows are beginning to dim the skies of a lovely evening, there is a great droning in the air and out of the haze from the north a few tiny specks appear – our bombers . . . The first Lancasters are over the target, only a mile or two from where we are, and masses of red glittering flames are put down to guide the others. Now, literally as far as the range of my binoculars, the sky is filled with bombers, coming on in a slow relentless stream like something out of a Wellsian dream, or one of the early war films of the sky filled with the Luftwaffe, but now there is not a single German plane in sight. High above our bombers, Spitfires and Lightnings are weaving about like little silver minnows in a great inverted fish bowl, with the bombers moving like trout near the surface of a pool. Still the stream of bombers comes on and great vibrations shake the ground as their loads of bombs crash down. A vast red glow shows that fires have been started, and one by one they wheel over and stream northwards for England again.
>
> Then a second wave comes in, this time at a higher altitude. By this time the flak has almost faded out, but there are still occasional puffs of black smoke quite close to our planes, but they fly steadily on and once again there is the crump-crump of heavy bombs going down. One only of this massive air fleet is shot down, and as the darkness closes in, the last attackers become tiny specks in the sky. This is the greatest morale booster we have experienced, and it shows our complete mastery of the air to perfection.*[34]

There was also the question of CROSSBOW targets. On the night of the 12th/13th the Germans began their v-1 offensive on England, and within a few days a significant part of the Bomber Command effort had been diverted to deal with this menace. Indeed, no less than one-third of Bomber Command's strength was concentrated on CROSSBOW during the period 7 June–15 September,[35] and its part in reducing the intensity of the v-1 attacks was significant. Despite all these efforts, Harris did not feel that his crews were reaping the credit due to them. On 1 July he wrote to Portal:

> I think you should be aware of the full depth of feeling that is being aroused by the lack of adequate or even reasonable credit to the RAF in particular and the air forces as a whole, for their efforts in the invasion. I have no personal ambition that has not years ago been satisfied in full, but I for one cannot forbear a most emphatic protest against the grave injustice which is being done to my crews. There are over 10,500 aircrew in my operational squadrons. In

---

*This particular raid took place on 7 July, with 467 aircraft of Nos 1, 4, 6 and 8 Groups being dispatched, 457 attacking and two being lost.

three months we have lost over half that number.* They have a right that their story be adequately told, and it is a military necessity that it should be.[36]

It had always been intended that the strategic bomber forces should revert to the Combined Chiefs of Staff once the ground situation on the Continent was secure. But, even after the break-out from Normandy and the subsequent spectacular dash across France by both British and American troops, Eisenhower wished to retain control, arguing that lack of airfields in France and the fact that the front line had moved so far east meant that only heavy bombers could give worthwhile support. The Combined Chiefs of Staff meeting in Quebec at the beginning of September refused to accede to his request, and on 14 September 1944 Eisenhower surrendered control over them, USSTAFE reverting to Arnold, with Spaatz as his executive officer, and Bomber Command to Portal and Bottomley. However, the agreement remained that Eisenhower could still bid for their support if he so required. Harris wrote to Eisenhower: 'I wish personally and on behalf of my Command to proffer you my thanks and gratitude for your unvarying helpfulness, encouragement and support which has never failed us throughout the good fortunes and occasional emergencies of the campaign . . .' Eisenhower was clearly touched by this, especially in view of the difficulties which he had feared he might have with Harris, and kept the letter as a treasured momento.[37] Indeed, Harris had given Eisenhower unstinted support. Another who also appreciated Bomber Command's efforts was Montgomery, who wrote to Harris after the air attacks on enemy concentrations around Caen:

> Again the Allied Armies in France would like to thank you personally and Bomber Command for your magnificent co-operation last night. We know well that your main work was further afield and we applaud your continuous and sustained bombing of German war industries and the effect this has on the German war effort. But we also know well that you are always ready to bring your mighty effort closer in when such action is really needed and to co-operate in our tactical battle.[38]

However, although Harris might now appear to be willingly following directives sent to him, the last phase of the war against Germany was to see sharp divergence of views between him and the Air Staff.

---

*In a minute to Churchill dated 3 July, Harris gave Bomber Command casualties over the period 1 April 1944–28 June 1944 as 285 killed and 5,804 missing. He compared this to those killed in the Allied armies in Normandy, giving a figure of 7,704. (PRO AIR 14/3507).

CHAPTER TEN

THE LAST ROUND

. . . the history of bombing throughout this war will, when it is summed up, show repeated lapses from that essential principle of war, the maintenance of the objective. – Harris

On 14 September Portal and Arnold issued a directive to Spaatz and Bottomley laying down the overall mission of the strategic bomber forces as 'the progressive destruction and dislocation of the German military, industrial and economic systems and the direct support of land and naval forces'. Then, in turn, on the 25th Spaatz and Bottomley drew up their joint directive, a copy of which was sent with a covering letter to Harris. Oil was now given top priority, and transportation, tank production and ordnance depots, together with MT production and depots were grouped together as the next most important target category. The German Air Force was given no specific priority in view of the fact that 'its fighting effectiveness has been substantially reduced', and operations against the GAF were to be 'regulated by the tactical situation existing'. As for industrial areas:

> When weather or tactical conditions are unsuitable for operations against specific primary objectives, attacks should be delivered on important industrial areas, using blind bombing technique as necessary.[1]

Furthermore, in his covering letter Bottomley reminded Harris that he would be expected to comply with Eisenhower's requirements for direct support of the land battle and to co-operate with AOCinC Coastal Command in support of naval operations.*[2] Thus, precision bombing was now to be the prime technique used, and area targets were very much in a subsidiary position.

Harris raised no objection to this directive and during the early part of October it seemed as though he were carrying it out. The first two days of the month saw little else but No 8 Group

---

*This reflected the Allies' realisation that the Germans had developed the schnorkel, which enabled their U-boats to remain under the surface for considerable periods, thereby making them more difficult to attack, especially from the air.

Mosquito operations against a whole range of targets, including oil and transportation, and the first heavy bomber raid was on the night of the 3rd on the Westkapelle dyke in support of the ground forces, while next day Nos 6 and 8 Groups carried out an attack on the U-boat pens at Bergen in Norway. A further daylight raid on the 5th, when No 5 Group attacked Wilhelmshaven, could also be construed as a naval target. That night 551 bombers from Nos 1 and 3 Groups attacked Saarbrucken, with a third of the force concentrating on the marshalling yards. On the 6th, it was No 4 Group's turn and they attacked the synthetic oil plants at Sterkrade and Gelsenkirchen. Dortmund was attacked by 523 aircraft that night, and Cleve, another military target, the following day. A force of 435 aircraft visited Bochum on the night of the 9th/10th, but further ground force support attacks were made in the Walcheren area on the 11th, and the Wanne-Eickel oil refinery was visited on the 12th. Suddenly, on 14 October, Harris altered his tactics. For the first time since June 1942, he sent 1,000 bombers against a single target, when 1,013 aircraft of Nos 1, 3, 4, 6 and 8 Groups attacked Duisburg by day, with a further fifty No 1 Group Lancasters attacking the blast-furnaces and rolling-mills in the Hamborn suburb of the town. But this was not all, for that night 1,008 bombers returned to Duisburg, while No 5 Group, with 240 aircraft, attacked Brunswick. Mosquitoes, too, were busy over Berlin, Mannheim railway centre and the airfield at Düsseldorf, and 120 No 100 Group RCM sorties were put up. Furthermore, all Groups, including the three OTU Groups, mounted 141 sorties in the form of diversionary sweeps. No 3 Group also sent eight aircraft to drop supplies to the Resistance and No 100 Group conducted twelve signals and patrol sorties. If one bears in mind that the Bomber Command strength of operational heavies with crews was 1,317 as at 12 October, this was undoubtedly the busiest 24 hours experienced by the Command to date. Significantly, too, only fifteen aircraft were lost over Duisburg by day, and six by night. One Lancaster failed to return from Brunswick and one Mosquito from Berlin. Even so, after 9 Squadron of No 5 Group had attempted to breach the Sorpe Dam by day with TALLBOYS, Harris was still able to muster 506 aircraft to attack Wilhelmshaven again the following night.

There was now an understandable lull, but No 3 Group did send 128 Lancasters against Bonn by day on the 18th, and then Stuttgart and Nuremberg were attacked respectively by 583 and 270 Lancasters and Mosquitoes on the 19th/20th, and, two nights later, Hannover was hit by 263 aircraft. On the night of the 23rd/24th, Harris sent 1,055 bombers against Essen, of which only eight failed to return, and this target was visited again two nights later by 771 aircraft, while simultaneously 243 bombers attacked one of the refineries at Homberg. On the same night also, 327 bombers attacked military targets in the Walcheren area. Bergen was bombed again by 244 aircraft of No 5 Group on the following night, and the next day 9 and 617 Squadrons, led by Wing Commander Tait, who had succeeded Cheshire in command of 617, attacked the *Tirpitz* without success, although they returned on 12 November and caused her to capsize. By day on the 30th, 102 bombers attacked the refinery at Wesseling and 110 returned for another attempt on the batteries on Walcheren. That night 905 bombers went to Cologne, and on the last day of the month the refinery at Bottrop was hit by day by 101 bombers and Cologne was attacked again by night with 493 aircraft.

The first striking aspect is the significant increase in the tempo of Bomber Command operations compared to POINTBLANK in the later months of 1943 and early 1944. During this period, the peak had been reached in March 1944 with 9,031 sorties by night and eighteen by day. Now, in October, 10,183 were dispatched by night and 6,713 by day. Admittedly, during the summer the total monthly sortie rate had exceeded this, but the emphasis then was on short-range targets. Even more marked was the very low casualty rate, less than 1 per cent both by day and night. Overwhelming Allied air superiority kept the losses from flak above those from night fighters. The overrunning of the German early warning system after the break-out from Normandy, and the converse that it was now possible to deploy GEE, H2S and G-H ground stations to the Continent, the increasingly effective jamming of German ground radars by No 100 Group, and the fact that a Ju88 equipped with SN2, the latest German AI radar, had fortuitously mistaken England for Germany on 13 July, enabling WINDOW to be adapted to jam it, were other reasons why casualties were kept so low.

As for the pattern of Harris's operations during the month, he tried to satisfy closely all the demands being made on him, but there was a significant emphasis on area targets, which seemed to indicate that he was veering back towards his long-held belief in this. On 13 October, however, Bottomley had sent Harris an additional directive, which at least gave him some justification for continuing to pursue area attacks.

While the strategic air forces, after they had been formally disengaged from support of the land battle, wished to concentrate on oil, Tedder still believed that communications should remain the prime target in order to assist the advance into Germany. Eisenhower saw the Ruhr as his intermediate objective, and he and Tedder believed that weighty attacks here would be of much help to the ground forces. Consequently, as a compromise, Bottomley's new directive, although stressing that the priorities as laid down in his previous directive remained, ordered Harris to undertake special operations for the following purposes:

(i)   In order to concentrate bombing effort on the vital areas of the Ruhr. Outside the question of the great concentration of enemy economic and military resources in the Ruhr, the Supreme Commander has stated that our best opportunity of defeating the enemy in the West lies in the Ruhr and Saar.

(ii) In order to demonstrate to the enemy in Germany generally the overwhelming superiority of the Allied Air Forces in this theatre.

In order to achieve this, two plans had been drawn up, HURRICANE 1 and 2. The former gave VIII Bomber Command oil targets in the Ruhr, while RAF Bomber Command was to attack 'areas selected from the undamaged parts of the major industrial cities'. Furthermore, 'the maximum tonnage' was to be used on these areas 'in order to achieve a virtual destruction of the areas attacked'. The initial stage of the operation might require 'two days' visual effort for its completion' and was aimed at 'the maximum disorganisation of the Ruhr and the denial to the enemy of essential facilities and particularly its communications'. In addition, it was thought that the sight of so many bombers overhead would affect morale, and the 'unprecedented impact of this new form of attack coupled with the belief that it will be repeated, may well cause a panic evacuation'. This, then, was the rationale behind Harris's Duisburg attacks. The pressure on the Ruhr was also to be maintained after the initial phase, albeit not 'to the prejudice of any operations which can be delivered on oil targets in Germany generally'. HURRICANE 2, on the other hand, was designed to fulfil the second requirement, and the effort here was to be concentrated on oil targets when the weather permitted, with Bomber Command attacking those in the Ruhr and Rhineland.[3]

It would thus seem that Harris by his attacks in October had been closely following this directive, but the Air Staff were not so sure. The nature of Harris's attacks demonstrated to them that not only was there a fundamental conflict between oil and communications, but also that he was trying to switch his emphasis back to area bombing. Indeed, he had made his views clear in a letter to Churchill on 30 September when asked by him to comment on an ULTRA intercept from the Japanese Military Attaché in Berlin to Tokyo stating that the main German aim was to regain air supremacy. Harris made it plain that he believed air power had been the main ingredient of success in Normandy. He also warned that:

. . . no matter how well the Bosche has fought outside his own frontiers, we should see him for the first time really fight his damndest when driven back on his own frontiers, with his rifle in one hand, his essential personal properties in the

other, and an awful fear of the wrath and retribution of his victims spurring his
final endeavour.

He pointed out that the armies in France had not yet suffered the
casualties incurred on the first day of the Battle of the Somme in
July 1916, but implied that they were in danger of heavy casualties
once they crossed the German border. Therefore, the Allies should
'now get on and knock Germany flat', while they still had overwhelming air superiority. He also warned that, although the
bombing of Germany had not stopped over the past six months, its
easing had given her 'considerable breathers'. Furthermore, the
advent of the jet and rocket-propelled fighter and other possible
measures would result in the bomber, 'like the U-boat', meeting its
'counter in the end'. The final air strike against Germany should
therefore take place 'while the going is good'. Churchill's private
comment was that it was 'a characteristic letter . . . I am sure that he
is right in a great deal of what he says, though I do not rate the
share of the Air Force as high as he does', and, in his reply to
Harris, he expressed the same view. 'I recognise, however, this is a
becoming view for you to take. I am all for cracking everything
now on Germany that can be spared from the battlefields.'[4]

THE OIL DEBATE

Harris thus had reason to believe that he had at least a measure of
support from the Prime Minister. Portal, however, having received
a minute from Tedder dated 25 October advocating communications as the prime target, felt that he would sound Harris out by
sending him a copy of it. Harris, in his reply, thought that there
was too much of the element of programme bombing about it and
that it ignored the exigencies of the weather and tactical factors. He
emphasised the need to divide and dilute the enemy's defences, but
ignored the decline of the Luftwaffe. He believed that attacks
against precision targets should be accompanied by diversions on
area ones, but also complained that there were too many 'panacea
merchants' now engaged in 'stirring the broth', including the
Admiralty and The Special Operations Executive (SOE). He then
pointed out that Bomber Command had now destroyed some 45 of
sixty cities in Germany, including a rate of two and half per month
during the OVERLORD diversions. 'Are we now to abandon this task
just as it nears completion?' Once more he reiterated that, although
he could finish his programme of the destruction of the cities
without detracting from his support of the ground armies, he
believed that his policy would bring about the defeat of Germany
more quickly than the land forces 'have yet done – or will do'.
Before Portal had replied to this, however, Harris had been issued

with another directive dated 1 November, with a covering letter from Bottomley making it quite clear that oil was the first priority and transportation the second, and that HURRICANE operations should be launched only in consultation with Tedder. Harris's comment in the margin to Saundby was 'here we go round the mulberry bush',[5] but there is no doubt that the Air Staff were now trying to rein him in.

Portal replied to Harris on the 5th, 'At the risk of you dubbing me "another panacea merchant", I believe the air offensive against oil gives us by far the best hope of complete victory in the next few months.' The correspondence continued during the first half of November, with Harris assuring Portal that he fully appreciated the importance of oil, although he voiced his doubts on his ability to be effective against it.[6] Indeed, the weather had now worsened, with much cloud, which meant that not only was bombing accuracy affected, but also that there was a problem in obtaining clear post-raid photographs to check on the damage done and whether the target needed to be attacked again. Portal relied on Harris's determination to overcome these problems, and indeed the latter did markedly increase his attacks on oil that month, with 20 per cent of his sorties being involved against it, as opposed to only 5 per cent in October.[7]

As far as Harris's 'cities plan' was concerned, he started November off with raids on Oberhausen, Düsseldorf, which was, with 992 sorties put up, just short of another 1,000 Raid, Bochum and Gelsenkirchen during the first week of the month. Then his efforts became less concentrated as he devoted more time to oil, although Dortmund, Munster, Munich, Freiburg, Neuss, Essen, Duisburg and Dortmund again were visited before the month was over, though the average number of sorties for each of these attacks was less than 400. He also continued to be called upon to support the land battle, and on 16 November launched his heaviest attacks when 1,188 bombers attacked Duren, Julich and Heinsburg by day in support of Operation QUEEN, the US First and Ninth Armies' attack towards the River Roer and the Rhineland. This offensive became bogged down, but then attention was drawn to the seven dams on the Roer and its tributaries. It was realised that the Germans could, by demolishing some of these, flood not only the Roer valley, but the area as far as the Meuse and into Holland. This obviously would seriously impede future Allied operations. General Hodges, commanding the US First Army, initially recommended that two of these dams be destroyed by air action, the resultant floods having time to recede before the next push forward began. His request was passed to SHAEF, who, remembering RAF Bomber Command's success against the Ruhr Dams eighteen months before, passed it to Harris on 29 November. Harris looked at the prospect, but recognised that the two dams in question were similar to the Sorpe, which although hit by UPKEEP, had not broken because the retaining earth had proved impervious to it.

> As with the Sorpe dam, there was just a chance that an explosion or series of explosions on the Urft and Schwammenauel Dams would cause seepage and eventually lead to the complete disintegration of the structure, but I did not think much of this chance and, moreover, the enemy was in a position to adjust the water level so as to avoid erosion of the dam.[8]

Harris warned SHAEF that he thought it unlikely that he would have any success. Furthermore, because the dams were so near the Allied forward positions, he could not risk blind bombing. In the event, it was not until 3 December that the visibility was good enough, but two hundred No 1 Group Lancasters with Pathfinder Mosquitoes were still unable to identify the target. On the 4th, he sent thirty Lancasters and Mosquitoes of No 8 Group against the Urft but, although they hit both ends of it, no damage was done. The defences were very strong, which ruled out low-level attack as suicidal, and Harris wanted to cancel any further attempts, considering them a waste of time, but Eisenhower insisted that they be made. An attempt by No 3 Group Lancasters on the 5th against the Schwammenauel also failed because they could not identify it with any certainty, and although 129 of 205 Lancaster sorties from No 5 Group attacked the Urft on the 8th, again there was no damage. In desperation No 5 Group tried once more on the night of the 9th/10th, when they attempted to bomb using a searchlight put up over Aachen to provide artificial illumination, but this did not work, and the 230 aircraft returned home with their bombs still on board. Finally, No 5 Group returned again to the Urft by day on the 11th, and succeeded in dropping their bombs, but again with no positive result. Harris, now sent a signal on the 12th suggesting that he bomb the spillway on the Urft, hoping that the head of water would erode out the hillside, although he suspected that the hill was solid rock, in which case this would not work. Tedder, obviously realising that Harris had given of his best, ordered that the idea be dropped, despite a further request by Bradley's US Twelfth Army Group Headquarters.[9] The German counter-offensive in the Ardennes then broke, and Harris heard nothing more of it. The saga does, however, illustrate two points. Such was the successful propaganda campaign in the aftermath of CHASTISE, that the Americans refused to believe that Bomber Command could not tackle this target, and also that Harris was prepared to persevere with an operation which he knew was not feasible and was to the detriment of other targets closer to his heart, because it was in support of the ground forces.

If Harris co-operated with Tedder with little complaint, this does not indicate that he was prepared to drag his feet less over directives from Air Staff. On 12 December, he wrote to Portal saying that his ORS had just completed a study 'into the feasibility of the oil plan', reminding him that past estimates by Bomber Command ORS had always been reliable, giving as an example their statement that 'it would take three times the effort estimated by the "expert", Mr Solly Zuckerman, to knock out the French marshalling yards and that was precisely what happened'. Their calculations showed that Bomber Command would require 9,000 sorties per month to knock out and keep out of action the 42 synthetic oil and benzol plants in the Western theatre of operations. He could cope with those in the west of the country, which could be attacked by day, but the fifteen targets in central Germany, which required 6,400 sorties per month were more difficult, especially as they would have to be tackled by night. Also, there was the uncertain weather – statistical records showed that there were likely to be only 3–4 suitable nights per month. He therefore argued that the Americans would have to take on the bulk of those targets. He concluded with a scathing attack on MEW, whom he accused of failing to identify all the sources of supply, which made a mockery of their original calculations.

Ten days later, Portal replied. Harris had based his argument on a false premise that the Americans would not be attacking these targets as well. Thus it was fallacious to view the calculations as applying to Bomber Command only. Furthermore, the priority was on the synthetic oil plants, whose output was ten times that of the benzol plants. He reminded Harris that 'the essence of the immediate task before the Allied bomber forces is *to put out and keep out of action the 11 synthetic plants in Central Germany*'. He stressed that:

> It is not expected by anyone that your command can do the job by itself; neither can the Eighth Air Force by itself. Over the Winter months, it is essential, however, that no single opportunity is lost, whether by day or by night. With this provision I believe that the task is within the capability of the three strategic bomber forces if they put their hearts into it. If they do, and the job can be done this winter, strategic bombing will go down to history as a decisive factor in winning this war.

He was 'profoundly' disappointed that Harris regarded oil as just another 'panacea', and that he appeared to be 'reluctantly' prepared to attack only two plants in central Germany, Politz and Leuna, but was glad that the initial attacks on these two had been carried out with only light losses,* in spite of Harris's forebodings. He found it difficult 'to feel that your staff can be devoting its

---

*Politz was attacked on the night of 21/22 December by 207 aircraft of No 5 Group. Three aircraft only were lost, but Leuna had not yet been dealt with.

maximum thought and energies to the accomplishment of your first priority if you yourself are not wholeheartedly in support of it'. He also resented Harris's attack on MEW. To this, Harris replied on 28 December that:

> . . . the history of bombing throughout this war will, when it is summed up, show repeated lapses from that essential principle of war, the maintenance of the objective. Three years of bitter struggle have gone on in our area blitzing. All Germany openly bemoans it as their worst trial. We know that on more than one occasion they have nearly collapsed under it. As the programme nears completion we chuck it all up – for a panacea.

He was doubtful about the oil plan because 'I put no reliance whatever on any estimate by the Ministry of Economic Warfare.' As for the Bomber Command Staff not devoting enough attention to oil, 'I do not give my staff views. I give them orders. They do and always have done exactly what I tell them to. I have told them to miss no opportunity to prosecute the oil plan and they have missed no worthwhile opportunity.' Portal had, in his letter of the 22nd, stated that he was prepared to accept 5 per cent or 10 per cent losses in knocking out Politz and Leuna, but Harris now seized on this as applying to the complete oil offensive, and wrote that it reminded him of 'a statement I once received from the Air Ministry that it was worth the virtual destruction of my force over a period of months if we could knock out Schweinfurt. Where should we be if I had agreed to that?' Finally, he reminded Portal of what he, Harris, had said about the dangers of reducing the attack on Germany during OVERLORD at the 15 May Conference at Saint Paul's: 'We need look no further for the cause of what has happened in this last fortnight', which referred to the German offensive in the Ardennes.

An analysis of Bomber Command's sorties during December shows that Harris devoted no less than 30 per cent of his effort on area attacks, 25 per cent on transportation (railway targets) and slightly less than 8 per cent on oil. Indeed, the 1,119 oil sorties were well below his ORS's calculations of what was required even to deal with the oil targets in western Germany.[10] Yet, Bomber Command had attacked 2½ times as many oil targets as the Eighth Air Force during the month, with over twice the total bomb tonnage, and only the Fifteenth Air Force, with 33 attacks and a bomb tonnage slightly in excess of that of Bomber Command had made an extensive effort. However, the weather, in terms of visibility over western Germany, had been bad during the month, which inhibited the Eighth Air Force, and during the last part of the month they were mainly engaged in supporting the ground forces in the Ardennes. Thus, it was clear that Portal did have a strong case that Harris was not putting the effort that he should into oil.

Portal asked Bufton to comment on Harris's latest outburst, which he did on 3 January. He pointed out that the measures to which the Germans were resorting to protect their oil installations indicated how seriously they viewed the attacks on them, and that the offensive was beginning to bite in that the German fighters were already short of fuel. As for area attacks, he knew of:

> . . . no evidence to support CinC's statement that on more than one occasion Germany has nearly collapsed under our area blitzkrieg. We know she was seriously alarmed by Hamburg and the early Berlin attacks, but this condition was far from collapse.

In any event, it was difficult to establish the extent to which area attacks had to be carried out to be decisive, and it was much better to use the bomber forces against a target, the effects of damage on which could be calculated. Furthermore, although area bombing might eventually force a German capitulation, precision attacks would have to be maintained to keep the strength of the Luftwaffe down. 'I do not know whether the CinC is susceptible to conversion but the evidence available may help to strengthen his determination to attack oil.' Portal now wrote to Harris again (8 January), once more marshalling all the arguments in favour of oil. However, he did express concern at the way Harris conducted his operations:

> I must confess it is difficult for me to see how the whole bomber offensive can be run single-handed without a constant interplay of ideas and suggestions between you and your staff. If you really do not believe in the attack of oil I should have thought it would be difficult for them to spend much time or take much thought over it. And if they do not, they will be less likely to think out new methods, and thus create additional opportunities to attack oil targets. I can never feel entirely satisfied that the oil offensive is being conducted with maximum effectiveness by Bomber Command until I feel sure that you and your staff have really come to believe in it.

He took Harris to task for stating that the recent resurgence of the German Air Force* demonstrated the futility of precision bombing, making it quite clear that if the Americans had not concentrated on aircraft factories and ball-bearings, to the extent that they had, the air superiority enjoyed from D-Day onwards would never have been achieved. The latest rise in Luftwaffe activity could be smothered by attacking oil, which would prevent its aircraft taking to the air in sufficient numbers to degrade Allied operations. 'This is the defensive argument'. As for the offensive view:

> The completion of the plan lies so well within our capabilities that it can be pressed to a point at which the operational effectiveness of the German armies and air forces on all fronts will be decisively restricted; but to do this it is essential to hold firmly to this aim.

---

*This was demonstrated by Operation BODENPLATTE on New Year's Day 1945 when 800 German fighters attacked Allied airfields in France and Belgium, destroying or damaging 465 aircraft, but losing 400 of their own.

In conclusion, Portal wrote: 'The energy, resource and determination displayed by the enemy in his efforts to maintain his oil production must be more than matched by our own determination to destroy it; and *your* determination matters more than that of all the rest of us put together!'

Portal's letter had been more than reasonable in tone, and yet Harris would not accept his argument and his next letter, written on 18 January, was in places vitriolic. For a start, he resented Portal's accusation that he ran his Command 'single-handed'. He pointed out that on policy and strategy he took his instructions from Bottomley, and discussed them only with Saundby. As for his Staff: 'Their hearts are . . . in the job of engineering the tactical and technical battle against the targets, whatever and wherever these targets may be'. He then turned Portal's accusation back on him. 'I note no inclination on your part, or anywhere else in the Air Ministry for that matter, to discuss with me, or even to consult me beforehand upon such matters as the strategic policy applicable to my force, or to take me into confidence or consultation thereafter.' He clearly resented being sent targets by the Air Ministry which emanated from 'a committee presided over, where the RAF is concerned, by an ex-Station Commander of my Command [Bufton], who has always been persona non grata to me and my staff, as I also understand to my late commander, Tedder'. He bewailed the fact that Portal no longer held his AOCinC's meetings, and pointed out that when he was under command of SHAEF he had made some 85 journeys to France to 'obtain their views, requirements and instructions'.

> When you placed me under executive control of Air Marshal Bottomley (who is, incidentally, my junior in the Service) I lost no time in getting into contact with him personally, or opportunity of keeping in contact and on the best of terms with him, and of seeking his orders and instructions; in spite of so unusual an arrangement and so many and somewhat confusing channels and disorganising changes in command; yet little I now do appears to meet with approval.

He then went on to list 'panacea' targets which he had been ordered to attack over the years, but whose destruction had not resulted in the decisive effects prophesied. Included among these was CHASTISE once more, which 'achieved nothing compared with the effort and loss'. He then pointed out that these targets were dependent 'on the assumption that the enemy has been fool enough to allow vital bottlenecks to persist even at this stage of the war' and had not dispersed his industries. Furthermore, to fight a defensive war, the enemy needed 'so very little in the way of oil'. Hence, 'it is no good knocking out 75% of something if 25% suffices for essentials'. He pleaded that the next three months 'will be our *last* opportunity for knocking out the central and eastern industrial areas in Germany' and that, anyway, 'it is quite true the Germans are short of oil. What are they not short of? and why?' Finally, he came back to the conduct of bomber operations, accusing Portal of intimating that he had not carried out directives to the best of his ability in the past.

> I will not willingly lay myself open to the charge that the lack of success of a policy, which I have declared at the outset, or when it first came to my knowledge, not to contain the seeds of success is, after the event, due to my personal failure in not having really tried. That situation is simply one of heads I lose tails you win, and is an intolerable situation.
> I therefore ask you to consider whether it is best for the prosecution of the war and the success of our arms, which alone matters, that I should remain in this situation.

Although it is surprising, in view of his character and style that Harris did not express it in more forthright terms, it is quite clear that he was now offering to resign from his post. Portal's reply of the 20th also indicates that he believed the same. He explained that the command organisation was necessarily complicated by the span of Harris's operations, which encompassed 'an infinite variety of targets in an area stretching from northern Norway to Austria, and where the choice of the policy for its [Bomber Command's] employment has a direct bearing on operations of the other Services and the Allies on every front . . .' He was more than happy to resume their weekly meetings, but pointed out that it was Harris who had ceased them when he came under SHAEF control. Likewise, he would gladly accept more senior Bomber Command representatives on the various committees involved with bombing. However, he 'could not accept' any objection to 'my choice of officers for my own staff'. He conceded that he could not convince Harris of the soundness of the Oil Plan, but hoped that Harris would 'have enough effort left after doing your best on oil to enable you to flatten out' some of the cities in eastern Germany. Finally:

> I willingly accept your assurance that you will continue to do your utmost to ensure the successful execution of the policy laid down. I am very sorry that you do not believe in it but it is no use my craving for what is evidently unattainable. We must wait until after the end of the war to see who was right and I sincerely hope that until then you will continue in the command of the force which has done so much towards defeating the enemy and has brought such credit and renown to yourself and the Air Force.

Harris replied to this on the 24th in a much more conciliatory tone. He reassured Portal that he had no quarrel with Bottomley for whom he had 'the greatest personal regard and admiration', but that it was Bufton whom he resented in that he appeared to ignore a 'major and essential part of his job, namely, to press forward the interests, urgent requirements and doctrines of Bomber Command . . . while spending much of his time trying to run my command'.

He accepted that it might be a personality clash, which is probably what it was, for Bufton's position as Director of Bomber Operations meant that he was there to represent the Air Staff's views and not to be in Bomber Command's pocket. Nevertheless, in spite of his obvious capabilities, it was perhaps unfortunate that Portal should have placed him in this position if he was clearly held in such low regard by HQ Bomber Command. Harris then went on to suggest a weekly meeting with Spaatz and Eaker so that 'the repercussions in our Commands of any changes of policy that appeared likely or desirable' could be discussed. He said that he was often confused over what was 'brewing or occasionally even what is intended', especially in the context of Spaatz, whom he described as a 'weather cock'. 'He tends to ride a new hobby horse or to have a new and brighter idea almost every time I meet him'. He also pointed out that Spaatz, with his Headquarters alongside SHAEF, and his personality 'tend to produce a *de facto* state of affairs wherein he himself . . . imagines that he is running the show as a one-man band, except insofar as the British occasionally make a few noises off'. Finally, he believed that sight was being lost of the fact that the bomber was a 'prime offensive weapon'. 'We have ample proof that, used offensively, it has all along been the thing which the Germans have feared most, while at the same time its reactions on the enemy forces, land, sea and air, have been and still are extremely severe.' It was a source of 'very great personal regret' that Harris had had this disagreement with Portal and he pledged himself to do his 'utmost to carry out the policy which has been decided upon'.

Portal's letter of 25 January was the last in this series of correspondence. He felt that Harris had had plenty of opportunity in the past to be consulted, and reminded him of the Air Ministry letter of 7 November which invited him to send representatives to advise on the feasibility of proposals under consideration. Nevertheless, he agreed with Harris's idea of a Commanders' conference, but pointed out that, because of his position of joint command with Arnold, it would not be appropriate for him to attend, but that Bottomley would arrange it with Spaatz. Nevertheless, he welcomed the opportunity to resume his weekly meetings with Harris.[11]

This profound disagreement between Portal and Harris was an unhappy state of affairs, particularly at this late stage in the war. The fact, too, as Portal's biographer pointed out:

> That two such extremely hard-pressed men, only 25 miles apart and with 'scrambler' telephones on their desks, should have favoured this method of discussion seems surprising; but clearly each wished his views to be impressed on the other with the clarity and durability of the written word.[12]

It was in such marked contrast to Harris's dealings with SHAEF, but, although he held Tedder in high regard, he had no less respect for Portal. Yet, whereas he could see the necessity of lending support to the ground forces, past experience had made him fight shy of anything other than the destruction of cities and, even

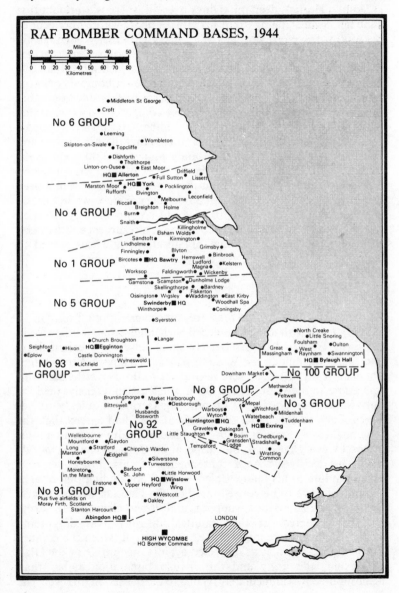

RAF BOMBER COMMAND BASES, 1944

though his Command was now infinitely better equipped to carry out precision attacks, it was still very dependent on the vagaries of the weather. Thus, if the bombs missed a precision target, they were as often as not wasted, while with area attacks, at least every bomb was of some value.

Despite Harris's deep misgivings over oil, there is no doubt that January saw a stepping up of his attacks on it, with 20 per cent of his total sortie effort devoted to it. Admittedly, 'city blitzing' still accounted for more than 30 per cent, but only on seven occasions during the month did he attack these targets with more than 300 bombers, while oil attacks, which required fewer bombers over the target, exceeded 100 bombers on eight occasions, besides a number of Mosquito attacks. His oil efforts also compared very favourably with those of the Americans. While Bomber Command dropped a total bomb-load of over 10,000 tons, Eighth Air Force and Fifteenth Air Force respectively only managed 3,500 and 2,000 tons.[13] Thus, he could hardly be accused of dragging his feet. However, it must be pointed out that a further directive had been issued to Spaatz and Harris on 15 January which, while oil and communications retained both first and second priority, stressed the importance of attacking the Luftwaffe's resurgence in fighters, especially jet, and the U-boat organisation, and this served to deflect attention from oil, especially by the Americans.

DRESDEN

At the end of January the pressure came even more off oil. On 12 January the Russians had launched their long-awaited offensive in the East. They had been relatively static since the previous July, and there was among the Western Allies a feeling that they might not achieve all that they were setting out to do. Nevertheless, with operations in the West bogged down, the Russian offensive held the only immediate possibility of bringing Germany quickly to her knees. Back in July 1944, the Chiefs of Staff had agreed that 'the time might well come in the not too distant future when an all-out attack by every means at our disposal on German civilian morale might be decisive'.[14] As a consequence of this, Portal wrote a memorandum to his fellow Chiefs of Staff concluding that attacks should continue to be concentrated on the German war economy, the army and its essential supplies, until it was clear that the army was facing defeat or that 'political disunity' was developing 'critically'. Yet, there might come 'a moment at which the balance can be tipped by an attack directed against the morale of the High Command, the army and the civilian population rather than against objectives immediately related to the battle'. In this event, he suggested an all-out attack on Berlin, and the Chiefs of Staff agreed that such a plan be prepared, concentrating on SS and Nazi Party centres.[15]

Now, towards the end of January 1945, the Joint Intelligence Sub-Committee produced a report, in which they concluded that, although they did not believe that 'the devastation of Berlin itself would break Germany's will to resist, shatter the control of the Nazi regimen, or lead to a plea for an armistice', and hence was not worth the diversions from oil and tank factories, such attacks could help the Russian offensive. They envisaged some 25,000 tons of bombs being dropped by the Allied air forces over four days and nights, and thought that the resultant flood of refugees from Berlin clashing with those fleeing from the east 'would be bound to create great confusion, interfere with the orderly movement of troops to the front and hamper the German military and administrative machine'.[16] Independently, three days earlier, Bufton had reached the same conclusion, and saw THUNDERCLAP, as this scheme was called, as a means of decreasing the enemy's morale in that the operation might be seen by the Germans to be closely coordinated between the Russians and the Western Allies.[17] Churchill now stepped in, and on the night of 25 January asked Sinclair what plans the RAF had for 'basting the Germans in their retreat from Breslau'.[18] Portal's view was that, in any event Spaatz, Tedder and the Combined Chiefs of Staff would need to be consulted, but:

> Subject to the overriding claims of oil and such other agreed targets as the rocket and jet engine factories, submarine-building yards for marginal effort etc, we should use every available effort in one big attack on Berlin and attacks on Dresden, Leipzig, Chemnitz, or any other cities where a severe blitz will not only cause confusion in the evacuation from the East, but will also hamper movement from the West.[19]

Sinclair replied to Churchill that operations on these lines were being considered, but this was not enough for the Prime Minister, who wished to be able to demonstrate to Stalin at Yalta that his offensive was being materially assisted by the Allies, which would counteract Stalin's likely claim that the British and Americans had become bogged down and were leaving everything to him. Consequently, Harris was instructed by Bottomley on 27 January to put THUNDERCLAP into effect. Harris wanted to wait until the moon had waned, and did not see the operation taking place before 4 February. Portal, *en route* to Yalta, discussed the matter with the Combined Chiefs of Staff, and they agreed that while oil was to continue as top priority, THUNDERCLAP would be second followed by communications and then jet aircraft plants. At Yalta the Russians came up with a request for Allied air assistance, and specifically mentioned the bombing of Berlin and Leipzig.[20] Thus, although it had not been through his own attempts to influence the situation, Harris had finally achieved what he wanted in that, albeit with the restriction that oil was still his prime target, he could wage an area bombing campaign in the East.

In fact, it was the Americans who launched THUNDERCLAP first, when Spaatz made heavy attacks on Berlin and Magdeburg. Harris, meanwhile was waiting for the right conditions. Of the eighteen attacks with over one hundred sorties, which he made during the first twelve days of the month, eight were on oil targets, seven area, two in support of the ground forces and one against communications. Then, on the night of 13/14 February he unleashed what has become probably the most controversial Allied bombing attack of the war, that against Dresden.

Dresden was seen as an important communications centre, and apart from the fact that it was relatively unscathed, except from a light attack by the US Eighth Air Force in October 1944, it was known to be filled with refugees. Therefore, in the light of the THUNDERCLAP concept, it was a logical and indeed listed target. Originally, the plan was for the Americans to strike first in daylight on the 13th, and the 1st Air Division did set off to attack the city, but bad weather diverted its groups to attacks on Münster, Brux and Pilsen. Therefore, contrary to standard practice in 'round the clock' bombing, the RAF went in first, with 805 Lancasters and Mosquitoes from all Groups except No 4. This was by no means the only Bomber Command operation that night. A force of 368 aircraft from Nos 4, 6 and 8 Groups attacked the oil refinery at Böhlen, and No 8 Group Mosquitoes were active over Magdeburg, Dortmund, Bonn and Misburg (another oil target), while 117 aircraft including INTRUDERS, WINDOW and RCM, were put up by No 100 Group.

The Bomber Command attack on Dresden was carried out by two waves, each with its own Master Bomber in a Mosquito. The forecast was for 10/10ths cloud, but that the skies would clear over the city at about 2200 hours for a short while. At 2205 hours the Master Bomber and his eight marker Mosquitoes arrived over the target and came down below the cloud at 2,500 feet and laid red TIs accurately on the aiming-point, which was in the centre of the town. These were thickened up by the No 5 Group Pathfinders and then the Group's main force bombed, coming down to 10,000 feet to do so. The second wave, with 529 aircraft, did not begin its attack until almost 0130 hours in order to cause maximum disorganisation of the rescue services on the ground. As one who took part in the second wave remembers it:

We could see the light on the clouds. We didn't come into clear air until over the target. So there was first a glow through cloud, and then clarity over the target.

Then a cry from the crew: 'Bloody hell, look at that!'
Below us was a town well ablaze, giving the impression of flying over a town in peacetime – lights all over the place. But there was only a quick, snatched glimpse for gunners – then you had to go back on sky search . . .
The master bomber was on the air, calling instructions where to bomb. The bomb aimer made his usual run-up. 'Bomb-doors open – left – left – steady – bombs away.' Having delivered the bombs, we only had one thought in mind: 'Let's go home and get the hell out of it.'
We knew the town had really taken a pounding, but I can't remember flak over the target . . .
The glare followed us back 100 miles or more.[21]

In all, 772 aircraft claimed to have attacked the target, and raid and post-raid photographs made it clear that this had been one of Bomber Command's most successful attacks. Apart from the weather being just as forecast, which kept the night fighters virtually grounded, the flak was very limited, most having been sent to the Eastern Front, and there were little more than 20mm guns, which were ineffectual above 8,000 feet, to defend the city. Hence the bombers were able to bomb much lower than normal. The fact, too, that the town was old, with many wooden buildings, meant that fires quickly raged, especially with the preponderance of incendiaries dropped, although this was more because Bomber Command was running short of HE bombs rather than through any specific intent.

Next day, just after noon, it was the turn of the Americans, with 400 aircraft attacking, and they would return the following day, and again on 2 March. In the meantime, on the night of the 15th/16th Bomber Command attacked Chemnitz, although cloud caused a mere shadow of the results on Dresden.

On 16 February Air Commodore Grierson of the SHAEF Air Staff briefed war correspondents on what had happened. He explained in some 'off the record' remarks that the aim of THUNDERCLAP was to bomb large population centres and prevent relief supplies from getting through. A dispatch was then filed by an Associated Press correspondent, which stated that the 'Allied Air Chiefs' had made the 'long awaited decision to adopt deliberate terror bombing of German population centres as a ruthless expedient to hastening Hitler's doom'. Although five hours later Reuters issued a denial, it was too late, for the story broke in the American evening papers.[22] This caused much embarrassment on both sides of the Atlantic, and during the debate on the Air Estimates in the House of Commons, Richard Stokes, MP, another long-standing opponent of area bombing, rose and asked:

What are you going to find, with all the cities blasted to pieces, and with disease rampant? May not the disease, filth and poverty which will arise be almost impossible to arrest or to overcome? I wonder very much whether it is realised at this stage. When I heard the Minister speak of the 'crescendo of destruction', I thought: What a magnificent expression for a Cabinet Minister of Great Britain at this stage of the war.[23]

His words were shortly to be heeded, especially as Dresden, much more than any other target, made people, including some of the aircrews, question whether what the strategic bombing forces was doing was morally right. Harris, however, suffered no such pangs:

The feeling such as there is . . . could be easily explained by any psychiatrist. It is connected with German bands and Dresden shepherdesses. Actually Dresden was a mass of munitions works, an intact government centre and key transportation centre to the east. It is now none of these things.[24]

THE FINAL WEEKS

Yet, after the Chemnitz raid, Bomber Command did not return to the population centres in the East. Harris continued to put much emphasis on attacks on oil, but was also drawn into supporting a new plan drawn up by Eisenhower for sealing off the Ruhr, which meant the destruction of eighteen bridges, five of which were earmarked for the strategic bombing forces. This was the type of task for which No 5 Group was particularly suited, especially 617 Squadron. Armed with Barnes Wallis's latest weapon, a TALLBOY derivative known as GRAND SLAM, weighing 22,000lb, they had some impressive successes against viaducts, notably that at Bielefeld. Another plan, CLARION, which had been a brainchild of the Americans, called for attacks on smaller towns which had not previously been bombed, as another means of attacking civilian morale, and Bomber Command was also involved in some of these, including Pforzheim and Wörms. Harris, with the Allies now closing up to the Rhine, also devoted attention to his favourite 'stamping-ground', the Ruhr, and added to the damage already inflicted, in order to make life as difficult as possible for the German armies in the West.

Once the Allies had crossed the Rhine it was clear that the sands of time were rapidly running out for Germany, and it was perhaps then that Richard Stokes's outburst in the House of Commons struck home. For on 28 March, Churchill addressed a minute to the Chiefs of Staff:

It seems to me that the moment has come when the question of bombing of German cities simply for the sake of increasing the terror, though under other pretexts, should be reviewed. Otherwise we shall come into control of an utterly ruined land. We shall not, for instance be able to get housing materials out of Germany for our own needs because some temporary provision would have to be made for the Germans themselves. The destruction of Dresden remains a serious query against the conduct of Allied bombing. I am of the opinion that military objectives must henceforth be more strictly studied in our own interests rather than that of the enemy.[25]

While the point of the danger of taking over a completely devastated country was sound, the comment about Dresden was somewhat unfair in that it was Churchill who, in January, had agitated for such an offensive on the cities in the east, and, as the Official History points out, the situation was now very different from what it had been six weeks earlier, with the Western Allies moving from stalemate to break out in Germany. Bottomley showed Harris a copy, to which the latter reacted in characteristic tone:

> To suggest that we have bombed German cities 'simply for the sake of increasing the terror though under other pretexts' and to speak of our offensive as including 'mere acts of terror and wanton destruction' is an insult both to the bombing policy of the Air Ministry and to the manner in which that policy has been executed by Bomber Command . . . we have never gone in for terror bombing and in the attacks which we have made in accordance with my Directive have in fact produced the strategic consequences for which they were designed and from which the armies now profit . . .
> Attacks on cities, like any other act of war, are intolerable unless they are strategically justified. But they are strategically justified in so far as they tend to shorten the war and so preserve the lives of Allied soldiers. To my mind we have absolutely no right to give them up unless it is certain that they will not have this effect. I do not personally regard the whole of the remaining cities of Germany as worth the bones of one British Grenadier . . .[26]

Portal clearly agreed with Harris's sentiments and the Prime Minister was persuaded to water-down his minute, which was presented to the Chiefs of Staff on 1 April, with 'area bombing' substituted for 'terror attacks', and with the suggestion that the matter be considered in the light of whether it was now counter-productive to continue to pursue this form of attack. In general, the Chiefs of Staff accepted this view, but did not rule out the need for area attacks in support of the ground troops. Thus, on 16 April, Portal sent Harris a message in advance of a fresh directive, which was not issued until 5 May, somewhat after the event, because of a wrangle between London and Washington as to whether it should come out under the signatures of Portal and Arnold, or Bottomley and Spaatz. After praising Bomber Command for its work to date, Portal ordered that:

> Henceforth the main tasks of the strategic airforces will be to afford direct support to the allied armies in the land battle and to continue their offensive against the sea power of the enemy which they have already done so much to destroy.[27]

For Harris, the last phase meant concentration chiefly on airfields and railway centres, as well as naval targets, and the biggest operation was by day on 18 April, when 969 bombers struck Heligoland, the naval base, airfield and the island in general. Harris also offered, as late as 27 April at a SHAEF Conference, to deliver attacks on towns in northern Germany in order to help the land forces take them more quickly, mentioning Bremen, Hamburg and Kiel in particular. Tedder felt that this was unnecessary as it was supply problems which were slowing the armies down rather than casualties or strong defences.[28] However, Harris did attack Hitler's retreat at Berchtesgaden on the 25th. This was not through personal whim, but because it was feared that fanatical elements were preparing to make a last-ditch stand in the Bavarian Alps – a fallacious belief that coloured much of Eisenhower's planning during the last weeks of the war. Then came more pleasant tasks, the bringing back to Britain of liberated prisoners-of-war and the dropping of food supplies to the starving Dutch.

The night of 2/3 May marked Bomber Command's last attack on Germany, when 128 No 8 Group Mosquitoes attacked Kiel, with sixteen further Mosquitoes bombing the airfields at Weggebek and Husam. To support them, No 100 Group flew no less than 155 sorties, and it was among these that Bomber Command's last casualties were suffered, with three Halifaxes failing to return. One No 100 Group Squadron Commander, who might easily have joined them, describes this last raid of the war:

> Knowing this was to be more than likely the last operation of the war I took an entirely new crew with me, except for Flying Officer Bates, my navigator. I thought it would be nice for newly trained aircrew who hadn't done an operation to have the experience and excitement of a raid for the last time. Thank God in many ways that I did this, for it probably saved my life! We were attacked over Kiel by a Ju88 and I had great difficulty in shaking him off. Twice he attacked and twice I weaved out of his cannon fire but this was a tough fighter pilot and he wasn't put off. Trust my luck, I thought, to get shot down and killed within sight of VE day! I eventually managed to get out of range of the searchlights and the next time the Ju88 attacked he hadn't the advantage of seeing me brightly coned in the sky and missed us by miles . . .
>
> We eventually shook him off and set course for home having dropped our 'window' and bomb load over Kiel. At last I felt relaxed and the fear whilst being attacked was gone . . . I put 'George' [automatic pilot] in and was happily sipping my coffee, when suddenly the rear gunner screamed at the top of his voice 'enemy fighter coming in astern'. I dropped my thermos flask, spilling coffee everywhere in panic, pulled out the automatic pilot and thrust the control column forward in a sudden dive. As luck would have it, his first burst of cannon fire went over the top of us along the fuselage and holes were punched in my old Halifax. I was virtually panic-stricken at being caught napping and loathed the thought of being shot down into the North Sea miles from land, so I flung the Halifax about desperately and dived down to sea level in an attempt to shake the Ju88 off. We eventually lost him and all breathed again.[29]

Because it was a 'fresher' crew who were, as the writer admits, much more alert than his normal crew would have been at that stage of the war, they survived. None the less, it was an experience which most aircrew had undergone during the last few years and for many it had been their last.

CHAPTER ELEVEN

THE RECKONING

The Prime Minister and many other of your colleagues are not likely to forget that you held what was probably the most difficult command in the war . . . - Viscount Bracken

---

By the time the war in Europe had ended, Bomber Command had put up no less than 297,663 sorties by night and 66,851 by day, and had dropped almost one million tons of bombs on enemy targets. More than 8,000 bombers had been lost during operational sorties, and by night alone nearly 14,000 were damaged, of which some 1,200 were totally wrecked. In terms of human casualties, no fewer than 46,268 aircrew had lost their lives during or as a result of operations, and a further 4,200 had been wounded. In addition, on non-operational flights 8,090 had been killed and 4,203 wounded.[1] Put another way, out of every one hundred aircrew who joined an OTU, on average 51 would be killed in operations, nine would be killed flying in England, three would be seriously injured in crashes, twelve would become POWs, of whom some would be injured, one would be shot down but evade capture, and 24 would survive unharmed.[2] No other branch of the fighting services faced quite these awesome odds, and the question has often been raised since 1945 as to whether the sacrifice made by so many Bomber Command aircrew was worth the results achieved. Indeed, the whole conduct of the RAF's strategic bomber campaign, both in terms of operational soundness and morality, has come under constant attack, and much of it has been directed at Sir Arthur Harris himself.

1939–1941

The years 1939–41 were unhappy and frustrating for Bomber Command. The pre-war Trenchardist views that the bomber would always get through and that it was capable of producing a knock-out blow, were not recognised as being clearly wrong at the time. Indeed, 1917–18 and the limited experience of the years 1919–39 in air control and the use of air power in Spain, China and elsewhere seemed to confirm rather than detract from the theories of the air prophets, and it was only with the development of radar in the late 1930s that the omnipotence of the bomber began to be questioned.

The problems facing the Command at the beginning of the war were two-fold. First, its scope was severely restricted by a justifiable attempt to follow the Hague Draft Rules, and the belief that any bombing which might cause civilian casualties or even put civilian lives at risk would bring about retaliation in kind. More importantly, the rapid expansion of the Command came home to roost in that it lacked the means to bomb effectively. The emphasis on quantity rather than quality on the grounds that to match the Luftwaffe would deter German aggression was to have serious consequences. The ever-increasing size of the expansion schemes forced the Air Ministry to procure aircraft which were clearly inadequate for the role they were expected to perform, and even though the right types were ordered in 1936, the war came far too early for them to be brought into service in time. Even more serious was the lack of modern ancillary aids, navigational and bombing, which would enable the crews to find their way to the target and attack it effectively, and low standards of training resulted in only an imperfect competence to use such aids as did exist. All this was recognised by Ludlow-Hewitt, but the Air Ministry tended to hide its head in the sand, mainly because Governmental pressure gave little opportunity to pause and think. In any event, the expansion programme was like manna from heaven to a Service which had been constantly under threat from its birth. As Sir Maurice Dean wrote:

At the end of the First World War the Royal Air Force was the greatest air service in the World, victorious on every front. Then, for ten to fifteen years or so, it entered the wilderness amid many who would have gladly broken it up and destroyed it. When a man knows he is going to be hanged in a fortnight it concentrates his mind wonderfully. It was a bit like that in the Twenties and early Thirties. A dozen more times it had escaped death by the whisker and grown wary. The sole reason for the creation of the Royal Air Force had been the need to bring into being a strategic bombing force. Forget this and the Royal Air Force was lost.[3]

Since most of its bombers were designed for use by day, and it was accepted that the precision targets the Command was called upon to attack in the early days of the war would be hard to find by night, daylight attacks were initially the stock-in-trade. With little experience other than that of the First World War on which to draw, it was believed that the bombers would be safe, provided they kept out of the way of flak, which was considered the main enemy, and maintained formation, which would prevent fighters from attacking them.* As we have seen, this was disastrous, but the Air Ministry was not unique in going to war with fallacious ideas. The Admiralty was guilty, too, in its failure to treat the U-boat threat with the seriousness it merited, and the War Office was scarcely blameless in its equipping of the BEF for the type of war it was to find itself fighting in May 1940.

Although the raid on Sylt in March 1940 certainly worried Bomber Command as to the ability of crews to locate and accurately bomb a target by night, it was the optimism of the crews themselves, that made the Command believe it was being more successful than it was during the embryo raids on Germany in Summer 1940, as well as a belief that standards would improve. With photographic assets being meagre, most reliance was placed on the post-raid reports of the crews, and the tendency to paint a rosy picture of what they believed they had achieved was understandable. This optimism pervaded the organs responsible for target selection, hence the over-optimistic forecasts of what Bomber Command could do against such precision targets as oil. At the same time, in the mistaken belief that the Germans had initiated a terror bombing campaign, the concept of attacks against morale began to be put into practice. It is very clear, though, that the agitation to bring the war home to the people of Germany came not from the Air Staff or Bomber Command, but from the Prime Minister himself. Yet, he echoed the popular mood at the time, especially as gleaned from his tours of the blitzed areas of London. Even so, a May 1941 Mass Observation survey found that the cries for 'retaliation' came more from those in rural areas unaffected by the bombing than from the city dwellers themselves.[4] Nevertheless, it was the only means of hitting directly back at the enemy, and the population at large drew comfort from reports of British bombing raids on Germany.

Autumn 1940 did, however, produce the first doubts as to the real strength and potential of Bomber Command at the time. Churchill's own concern over the rising losses made him realise that the Command as yet lacked the means to be a decisive weapon, and that it would have to be carefully nurtured for the time being. Then, there was the growing realisation, brought about by the Spitfire PRU reports, that perhaps the bombing was not as accurate as the crews claimed. It was this that led Portal to grow disenchanted with the oil target, and to argue for area targets instead, but Bomber Command under Peirse remained unrealistically confident. It took the Butt Report to drive home the point, and indeed, as a result, some of Churchill's earlier enthusiasm for the

*This did, however, disregard the experience of the Independent Force in 1918, which had to expend much of its effort on suppression attacks against enemy airfields.

bomber as a strategic weapon evaporated even more, hence the conservation policy introduced at the end of 1941.

At this stage, with no concrete experience of the effects of a fully-fledged strategic bombing campaign, target selection could only be made on the basis of theoretical calculation, and many assumptions had to be made, most of which turned out to be wildly optimistic. For a start there was the belief that the bombers were capable of achieving more than they were. This was not helped by the quality of Intelligence coming out of Germany at the time. Much of it unduly exaggerated the effects of the bombing, probably because those from whom it originated were anti-Nazi in their sentiments and wished to encourage Bomber Command in its efforts. That which was more accurate, especially when originated by Americans in Germany, caused momentary gloom, but there was still the belief that provided Bomber Command had sufficient means, it would be effective. Analysis of German raids on England provided some data on which to base arguments, but there was a naïve belief when it came to gauging the moral effect of bombing that the German people could not withstand it so well as the British. In some ways the planners were in a difficult position. Everyone realised that Bomber Command as it stood was not strong enough to have any decisive influence on the course of the war, but its resources could only be increased at the expense of other means of waging war and other theatres of war. Thus, in order to obtain War Cabinet agreement for further expansion, the pro-bombing lobby had necessarily to pitch their arguments high, and although Churchill was not wholly convinced by what they said, they did enough to regain his sympathy, and the result was Directive No 22.

It was at this point that Harris took over Bomber Command, although one historian has stated that by then area bombing was 'visibly unsuccessful and no longer necessary'.[5] While the first accusation was accepted at the time, the second is hard to fathom in that bombing, both area and precision, had not made much impression on the enemy because the resources with which to carry it out had been too slim or non-existent. Directive No 22, with its emphasis on attacks on morale, was based on the belief that GEE and the introduction into service of the heavy bomber in increasing numbers could make Bomber Command an effective bombing force. In view of the gloomy war situation, it is difficult even in hindsight to condemn the decision to resume the bombing campaign against Germany. It must also be remembered that there was intense pressure both from Russia and elements within Britain to invade the Continent in 1942, which was simply not feasible and, apart from the supply of munitions, bombing was the only means that could possibly take some of the pressure off the Russians.

Since efforts against oil, communications and other precision targets had appeared to have had little effect on Germany up until 1942, it was logical to concentrate on something which might. Furthermore, the whole basis of the argument of the champions of area bombing was that, apart from the mistaken belief in the ability of the German people to stand up to bombing in comparison with the British, the weight dropped by Bomber Command on Germany would exceed by many times that dropped by the Luftwaffe on Britain.

The debate over the course of the strategic bombing campaign of 1942–45 takes in several issues. They range from the correctness of allocating so much in the way of resources to it, often, especially during 1942–43, at the expense of other means of waging the war, through the area versus precision bombing argument, day or night bombing, and what the various parties hoped to achieve by it. Furthermore, there is the moral issue. In all of these, Harris's name looms large and it would be as well to gauge the influence that he himself had on the direction of the bombing campaign. The extent of this rests to a large extent on the relationships he had with others in positions of influence.

HARRIS'S WORKING RELATIONSHIPS

Throughout these years Harris's superior, as Chief of the Air Staff, was Portal. Much has been made of their great argument in late 1944 and early 1945 over the Oil Plan. Max Hastings, to quote one example, has accused Portal of 'indecision and weakness in handling Harris and the bombing offensive during the last eight months of the war'.[6] Yet, Portal's biographer puts a different complexion on it: 'It was because of Portal's admiration for Harris, and his understanding of the latter's distinctive gifts and character, that he was prepared to argue with him at such length, and to regard Harris's exaggeration in a tolerant light as the manifestations of an intensely valuable enthusiasm and energy.'[7] Indeed, studying the correspondence between them, taken with analysis of the targets attacked by Bomber Command, especially during the oil debate, there is nothing to suggest that Harris blithely ignored directives, even though he might not have agreed with them. Often, too, the directives were worded in such a vague way as to give Harris much latitude. Portal, as Denis Richards has said, fully recognised Harris's sterling qualities and viewed these as considerably outweighing his faults. He realised only too well Harris's tendency to see but one side of the argument and overstate it, but felt that it was important to try and convince Harris of his own and others' views rather than merely give him direct orders about which he knew he would be unhappy. Likewise, Harris was clearly unstinting in his admiration and friendship of Portal, and the fact that he was ably to state his case plainly to him showed not disrespect, but confidence in and a close relationship with him. As Harris later wrote of his commander: 'Portal had great strength, though he seldom showed it. His intellectual powers were outstanding; nobody could be more lucid; nobody could write a better minute. And he was a fighting man through and through, in spite of his quiet and modest manner.'[8]

As for Portal's staff, Harris undoubtedly got on well with Bottomley, although the latter often found himself in an invidious position of having to issue directives with which he knew that Harris would not agree, and it may have well been this that caused his directives to be what Harris later called 'confused and conflicting'.[9] At lower levels, however, relationships were not so happy, and Harris's view was that there were 'many individuals [who] thought that they enjoyed the privilege of running or trying to run a force without direct responsibility for the results which must, of course, remain with the Commander'.[10] Harris resented their interference, and nowhere was this better illustrated than over the Pathfinders. The fact that Harris viewed the idea as interference by the Air Ministry since it did not originate from within his Command was certainly a major reason why he dragged his feet over putting it into practice. He also had an unfortunate tendency to believe that officers like Bufton, because they were involved with bomber operations at the Air Ministry, should owe their first loyalty to Bomber Command. With his own considerable experience of working at the former, he should have realised that they were primarily answerable to the Air Staff and not to Harris.

There is no doubt that Harris enjoyed a special relationship with Churchill. He corresponded direct with him, and was a frequent visitor to Chequers, which was only half an hour by road from High Wycombe. Much of Churchill's change of heart over the bombing campaign in early 1942 was due to the immediate impact that Harris made, and in many ways, particularly in Harris's 'bulldog' determination, Churchill probably saw much of himself in him. Yet, Major Sir Desmond Morton, who, as Churchill's personal assistant throughout the war, was closer to him than most, has written that Churchill '. . . never cared for Harris as a person. I do not know why . . .'[11]

Others have asserted that Churchill turned his back on Harris and Bomber Command immediately the war ended. This could not have been farther from the truth, and is one of the myths which has been perpetuated since. For a start, on 15 May 1945 Churchill sent a letter to Harris:

Now that Nazi Germany is defeated, I wish to express to you on behalf of His Majesty's Government, the deep sense of gratitude which is felt by all the Nations for the glorious part which has been played by Bomber Command for forging the Victory. For over two years Bomber Command alone carried the War to the heart of Germany, bringing hope to the peoples of Occupied Europe and to the enemy a foretaste of the mighty power which was rising against him. As the Command expanded, in partnership with the Air Forces of our American Allies, the weight of the attack was increased, leaving destruction on an unparalleled scale to the German military, industrial and economic system. Your Command also gave powerful support to the Allied Armies in Europe and made a vital contribution to the war at sea. You destroyed or damaged many of the enemy's ships of War and much of his U-boat organisation. By a prolonged series of mining operations, you sank or damaged large quantities of his merchant shipping. All your operations were planned with great care and skill; they were executed in the face of desperate opposition and appalling hazards. They made a decisive contribution to Germany's defeat. The conduct of these operations demonstrated the fiery, gallant spirit which animated your aircrews and the high sense of duty of all ranks under your command. I believe that the massive achievement of Bomber Command will long be remembered as an example of duty nobly done.[12]

This was hardly the tone of one who was turning his back on the achievements of the Command. The main argument used to support the proposition that Churchill wished to distance himself from Harris is that Harris was not made a Peer, unlike other high commanders. For a start, he was advanced to a GCB in the Birthday Honours of 1945, and then on 1 January 1946, together with Sholto Douglas, who had been AOCinC Fighter and Coastal Commands, he was promoted Marshal of the Royal Air Force, specifically for their 'distinguished service during the war in Europe'. In Churchill's Resignation Honours List, which was reflected in the 1946 New Year's Honours List, only the three Chiefs of Staff, Cunningham, Alanbrooke and Portal, were elevated to the Peerage, all being made Viscounts. In addition, Tedder was made a Baron. No one of Harris's equivalent rank, seniority and level of command was awarded greater honours than he. Indeed, Attlee offered him a Peerage, but by then he was intent on going to South Africa, where he did not consider that a 'handle' would be of much use to him, and, in any event, his view was: 'I don't think that anyone should accept a Peerage unless you are prepared to do the work connected with it in the House of Lords and the very last thing I ever wanted to do was to get muddled up with politicians of any status.'[13]

When Churchill returned to power in 1951, attempts were made to get Harris to reconsider, and eventually he accepted a Baronetcy, which was announced in the New Year's Honours of 1953. Here, it is revealing to quote a letter written by Brendan Bracken to Harris on 6 January 1953. Viscount Bracken, as he was then, had been Parliamentary Private Secretary to Churchill during 1940–41, and

Minister of Information, and was as Desmond Morton wrote, one of Churchill's 'three real friends'.[14]

> Let me tell you, Bert, that W.S.C. [Churchill] was delighted that you should have the comparative modest honour that has come your way. Had you wished to join the morgue [House of Lords] to which Peter Portal, Tedder and I belong, your desire would have been fulfilled. The Prime Minister and many other of your colleagues are not likely to forget that you held what was probably the most difficult command in the war and that you and you alone as Commander-in-Chief were able to carry the war into Germany when the soldiers and sailors were unable to strike a blow at Hitler's warriors.
> And so there is no honour in the gift of the monarchy that you do not deserve. Putting aside your remarkable successes as Commander-in-Chief Bomber Command, I shall always remember with gratitude your willingness to look after all the visiting firemen whether they were neutral Americans [sic], Turks, Greeks and all the other strange folk inflicted on you by No. 10 [Downing Street] or the Ministry of Information. I remember telling you in 1942 that you were the best propagandist Britain possessed. The years that have passed have increased this belief.[15]

Perhaps, therefore, this particular myth will be laid to rest once and for all.

As for Churchill's views on Harris's strategy, like Portal, he was fully aware of Harris's proneness to overstatement, but he circulated many of Harris's papers not only within the War Cabinet, but on occasion to Roosevelt as well. The only definite instance where he clearly disagreed with Harris and, indeed with the Air Staff, was after Dresden, when he realised that further devastation of Germany would hinder the post-war occupation. In fact, at times he can be accused of bending too far in Harris's direction, especially during the conflict with the Admiralty in 1942 over diversion of aircraft to help in the Battle of the Atlantic.

One curious aspect of the relationship is that Harris seems often to have gone behind Portal's back, and this was most noticeable during the 1,000 Raids of 1942. Yet Portal does not appear to have taken umbrage, probably because at the time he and Harris were in total agreement on the bombing campaign, and he saw Harris's closeness to Churchill as a means of influencing the latter. In any event, it is another indication of the mutual regard in which Harris and Portal held each other.

For much of the period, Harris had little good to say about the other two fighting services. As in many of his RAF contemporaries, this attitude was inbred, stemming as it did from the constant threat to the RAF's existence before the war. As we have seen, it was the Admiralty rather than the War Office with whom he clashed most, because it was they who wanted to rob him of the means to wage a successful bombing campaign. In part, he deserves some sympathy in that the Admiralty would not for a long time accept Bomber Command's limitations with regard to precision targets, and never acknowledged the contribution it made to the war at sea with its GARDENING operations. Nevertheless, in the Admiralty's eyes, the Air Ministry, enthusiastically abetted by Harris, was remarkably obstructive, to such an extent that one view of it, in December 1942, was that:

Our fight with the Air Ministry becomes more and more fierce as the war proceeds. It is very much more savage than our war with the Huns, which is very unsatisfactory and such a waste of effort.[16]

Although Harris and the Air Staff can be justifiably accused of shutting their minds to the wider strategy of the war, and the vital importance of crushing the U-boat threat, without which the future successful conduct of the war was likely to be placed in jeopardy, Churchill must shoulder much of the blame. As Captain Stephen Roskill wrote:

These exchanges [between the Admiralty and the Air Ministry] show how very difficult it was to get from Churchill the priority to avoid losing, let alone winning the Atlantic Battle; and how he repeatedly accepted the needs *in principle* but refused as frequently to provide them at the expense of the bombing of Germany.[17]

Where the Army was concerned, Harris had little time for 'side-shows' and especially resented the drain on his resources to the Middle East, although much of the problem here lay in aircrews rather than aircraft, and imperfections in the Air Ministry posting system did at times lead to an excessive build-up of spare crews in that theatre.

In summary, therefore, it is clear that Harris was far too single-minded in his approach and lacked the necessary breadth of vision, at least up until 1944, to get on with the other two fighting services, but then, for much of the time he, as a subordinate commander, was merely following the attitude and policy of the Air Staff. As for his view of OVERLORD, like the rest of his generation who had fought in the First World War, he had a horror of the prospect that the ground forces might be forced to suffer the same level of casualties. Indeed, much of the rationale behind the pre-war theories of air power was to make war less costly than 1914–18. He thus genuinely believed that the invasion of France should be reduced at worst to a mere 'police action' and at best unnecessary if the strategic air forces could be given the means to batter Germany into submission beforehand. Hamburg showed how it might be done, but Berlin demonstrated that it was not, after all, possible. Once, however, the OVERLORD air support plans had been agreed, Harris did whole-heartedly follow them, even though he continued to argue that if there were too much of a running down of effort over Germany in the meantime, it would give her a valuable breathing-space. Indeed, many historians have used the fact that Germany's war production peaked, in 1944 to argue that this was proof of the failure of the ideas of the 'Bomber Barons', but they forget that for six months the pressure was taken off Germany. Thus, in March 1944 Bomber Command dropped more than 20,000 tons on the latter. This fell to 13,700 tons in April, 7,400 tons in May and went down to under 2,000 tons in June. During July–September 1944, the tonnage averaged out at just under 12,000 and only in October did it approach that of March again.[18] Further, the tonnage represented to a significant extent attacks on specific oil and transportation targets. On the other hand, only for two months did the total fall below 10,000 tons per month, which Harris believed was the minimum to prevent Germany making any form of industrial recovery. Yet, in spite of Harris's impassioned plea at the St Paul's Conference, Eisenhower was clearly delighted and surprised by the support which he gave to him. He attended SHAEF, at Bushey Park, near Kingston, daily until it moved to France in mid September 1944, and then flew across twice a week, even though by that time Eisenhower had relinquished operational control of the strategic air forces, and then, in the final stages of the war, once a week. Harris's willingness to co-operate with the ground forces, even though, as with the Roer Dams, he was doubtful of his ability to tackle some of the targets requested, supports the contention that he genuinely wished to prevent the armies' casualties, and believed that bombing could do this.

In terms of Harris's handling of his own Command, a popular view is that:

> The air marshals followed the example of the World War I generals who stayed well behind the lines and sent their men to die in morasses they, the generals, did not know of and refused to admit existed.[19]

And:

> Bomber Command was very well served by its aircrew, and with a few exceptions very badly served by its senior officers, in the Second World War. The gulf between the realities in the sky and the rural routine of headquarters was too great for most of the Staff to bridge. Cochrane and Bennett were the only men among Bomber Command's leaders to do so. High Wycombe was fatally isolated both from the front and from sharp critical debate on policy. Even after all their bitter experience in the early years of the war, senior officers were unwilling to face unacceptable realities.[20]

And:

> . . . a great deal depended on how much the crews believed in their leaders. Some did, but there were many who nicknamed Harris 'the Butcher' not so much because he cared nothing for the lives of German civilians but because they believed that he cared nothing for their own either.[21]

How much truth is there in these statements?

Most accounts of life at High Wycombe during Harris's reign speak of the sombre atmosphere which pervaded the Headquarters, and the fact that Harris cut a remote figure to most who worked there. One recorded that: 'It didn't really matter whether he was liked, our feeling was that our Commander-in-Chief was not there to be liked, he was there to be respected, and perhaps slightly feared.' Yet another who came into close contact with him, his personal WAAF clerk stated: 'We all adored him. We would have crawled on our hands and knees from High Wycombe to London had he asked us.'[22] However, Air Vice-Marshal Kingston-McCloughry, who had known Harris well especially during the OVERLORD phase, wrote:

> Apart from operations any decision by Harris to sack, promote or decorate an officer was never challenged by the Ministry. Thus much of his power and the loyalty of his whole Command hinged on this unequivocal ability to sack, or to give and take away acting rank of many of his officers: also his ability to influence the award of honours and to discredit or disgrace any of his personnel was much feared. Thus a genuine fear of the power he wielded rather than popularity, admiration or any exultation extended from his Deputy at Bomber Command HQ down through the Group HQs to all the officers in his Command.[23]

Thus he meant different things to different people, but his gruff manner made him difficult to get to know, and yet, as we shall see, his presence dominated his Command in entirety.

Robert Saundby, as his senior Air Staff Officer and later Deputy AOCinC, fulfilled an invaluable role. Knowing Harris as well as he did, having served as a flight commander in two of Harris's squadrons in the Twenties, and being a permanent guest in Harris's house, meant that he was probably on very much closer terms than Kingston-McCloughry implies. More important, in character Saundby was the very antithesis of his commander, and in many ways behaved like an absent-minded professor. He had a passion for collecting butterflies and thoroughly enjoyed Eaker's model railway. Above all he was extremely approachable and got on well with everyone. Like de Guingand with Montgomery, he was often able to smooth the waves and curb some of Harris's wilder flights of fancy. As for the Group Commanders, Bennett and Cochrane had, of course, also served under Harris and knew him well. Among the others, there is little evidence to suggest that they were terrified of Harris and out of touch with their own commands. To quote but two examples: AOC No 4 Group, Air Vice-Marshal Roddy Carr, was certainly approachable and in close contact with his aircrew, if Michael Renaut, who flew a tour under him is to be believed.[24] Then, there was Baldwin, AOC No 3 Group, who had flown on the first 1,000 Raid against Cologne.

This question of senior commanders flying on operations has been much misunderstood by some aviation writers. Baldwin's participation on the night of 30/31 May 1942 was the last raid flown by a Group Commander. Although he recognised the quality of what Baldwin had done, Harris issued explicit instructions next day that no AOC was to fly on operations without his permission, and it was a rule that he enforced throughout the remainder of the war, even when Bennett asked him if he could fly on one or two of the Pathfinder operations.[25] Harris explained why this edict was in force, and detailed the operational experience of his senior officers in a letter to the Air Ministry on 14 February 1944. What had triggered this off was an article entitled 'Fresh Blood', which had appeared in *The Aeroplane* on the 11th of that month. This advocated that Bomber Command adopt a policy similar to that of the USAAF which 'encourages rather than discourages a commander from going to see for himself' and that there was necessity for 'young blood' to now take up more senior positions in view of the fact that 'there is a small band of senior officers holding high appointments that has for some years enjoyed a game of general post'. Harris's letter included the following:

6. Of the sixty station commanders in the five RAF operational groups,* only five who were lately promoted have no personal operational experience. The average number of operational sorties flown by the remainder is eighteen.
7. Of the Air Officers** in the RAF Operational Groups, the average number of sorties is thirteen.
8. . . .
9. It will be recalled that there is, and always has been (in my opinion quite rightly), an embargo upon personnel holding key appointments flying on operations. This, in my view, should apply to Group Commanders and Base Commanders when they hold these appointments. The reason, of course, is that while individual aircrew personnel may be in possession of considerable knowledge centering round their own limited activities, Group and Base Commanders are naturally in possession not only of much wider general knowledge on technical, tactical and strategic matters, but are necessarily 'au fait' with new methods and new technical equipment intended for future use.
10. It is known that the enemy has great skill and means of extracting such knowledge by legitimate, illegitimate and undoubtedly, where it suits him, by means to make resistance impossible.[26]

In view of the intensity of the technological battle during this stage of the war over Germany, it is hard to dispute Harris's reasoning, and clearly demonstrates that his senior officers had had operational experience themselves and therefore could relate to their aircrew.

---

*No 6 (Canadian) Group was excluded because 'for reasons concerned with politics rather than operational efficiency' it had been 'largely re-manned in its upper ranks by inexperienced personnel'.
**This included Group SASOs, who were Air Commodores and AOCs.

To portray Harris as impervious to the fate of his aircrews, could not be farther from the truth. As a Group Commander, he had got to know them well, as his personal assistant of the time can vouch.[27] Indicative of this was his choice of Gibson to lead the Dambuster Raid, even though he was not known to Cochrane, Gibson's Group Commander. As a Group Commander, too, he had insisted on being told, at whatever hour of the day or night, what the casualties from a particular operation had been.[28] But, as AOCinC Bomber Command, Harris was not able to enjoy a close relationship with his squadrons. His reason was:

> As CinC I had to lay on in every day in ever changing weather conditions a major battle whether this happened or not. There came a point every day when as CinC I had to say yes or no subject to various conditions including the Met report. In these conditions I could not jaunt around the country and keep everything in mind.[29]

In this statement is also reflected the fact that, in the ever-intensifying dual with the German defences, more and more factors had to be taken into consideration when deciding to attack on any given night and Harris was often called upon to justify his selection of a particular target. He believed that he alone could make the final decision.

As has been related, he constantly struggled to ensure that his crews received the recognition they deserved. Perhaps nothing illustrates better his attitude to all those under his command than his letter to Portal of 1 June 1945, asking that a Bomber Command medal be struck, not just for the crews, who were awarded the Air Crew Europe Star up until 6 June 1944, and the France and Germany Star thereafter, but for those who served on the ground as well:

> . . . it is apparent to me that few people appreciate the terrible miseries and discomfort and the tremendous hours of work under which the ground personnel of Bomber Command on the airfields have laboured for nearly six years . . .[30]

This is hardly the writing of a commander who was out of touch with his men. His request was turned down, not because of any disapproval of what Bomber Command had done but, as with his plea for increased pay for the Pathfinders, for reasons of equity in that many others had also suffered six years of discomfort in the course of their war service, but, having remained in the United Kingdom, were only entitled to the Defence Medal.

That he did not care about casualties is also untrue. His constant concern over the faults of the Stirling and Halifax is one indication of this, and his valediction to his crews in *Bomber Offensive* is another:

There are no words with which I can do justice to the air-crew under my command. There is no parallel in warfare to such courage and determination in the face of danger over so prolonged a period . . . It was, moreover, a clear and highly conscious courage, by which the risk was taken with calm forethought, for their air-crew were all highly skilled men, much above average in education, who had to understand every aspect and detail of their task. It was, furthermore, the courage of the small hours, of men virtually alone, for at his battle station the airman is virtually alone. It was the courage of men with long-drawn apprehensions of daily 'going over the top'. They were without exception volunteers, for no man was trained for aircrew with the RAF who did not volunteer for this. Such devotion must never be forgotten. It is unforgettable by any whose contacts gave them knowledge and understanding of what these men experienced and faced.[31]

And, as he later asked: 'Do you honestly think that I would have risked aircrew unnecessarily when I admired and valued them as much as I did?'[32] However, it was war, and an often quoted remark of Harris's was: 'You can't make an omelette without breaking eggs.'

As for the aircrew themselves, most would echo the comment of Leonard Cheshire, one of the bravest and most brilliant of them all, who said: 'I was a pilot just doing a job. It is impossible for me to assess the rights and wrongs of the policies that were imposed upon us, but if the facts bear it out, I would certainly be prepared to concede that area bombing was not worth the aircrew losses it featured.'[33] The bad times of late 1943 and early 1944 engendered a feeling of acceptance among the aircrews that they were not going to survive their tours, but there is no evidence to suggest that there was ever a serious degradation in morale. Indeed, although his crews never saw him, Harris's aura does seem to have penetrated to the humblest levels of his Command, and when an operation turned out a disaster, as at Nuremberg, very little evidence exists of blame being attached to Harris himself. Such was his invisible presence, that more than one airman to whom I have talked, recalls languishing in a POW camp, convinced that not the Allied Armies, Churchill or the Americans would be responsible for his liberation, but Harris himself. Some, it is true, have in retrospect turned against him, but many still revere his memory, as one attending an Air Gunners' Association reunion recalls:

When he came in he received a standing ovation. No one would stop clapping. When he made a speech no one would stop clapping. And had he said to his old lags, as he called us, 'Will you fellows go back to Dresden, or Nuremberg, or Berlin tonight?' every man there would have stepped forward and said, 'Yes, sir, we will go.'[34]

It is understandable why Harris made such an impact on his arrival at High Wycombe; the positiveness of his character was just what was needed after the seeming indecisiveness of 1941. The fact that the Lancaster and GEE arrived with him helped, of course, but his initial operations, culminating in the first 1,000 Raid on Cologne, made the crews aware that they might, after all, have a war-winning weapon in their hands. It is more difficult to establish how it was that he was able to maintain their faith in him during the dark days that followed – the failure of subsequent 1,000 Raids in 1942 and, more especially, the Battle of Berlin. Bomber Command's individual successes helped – the Dams Raid, GOMORRAH, the pre-OVERLORD transportation attacks – as did the continual introduction of new technical aids. Above all, it was his ability to continue to make his crews believe that provided they kept at it, Germany would eventually crumble. He has been accused of purposely making his crews think that they were achieving more than in fact they were. There is little concrete evidence that Harris did this wittingly, and we have also seen that he could be very frank if he considered that the crews were not performing as well as he expected. The secret perhaps lies in the fact that he was unwavering in his aim of bringing Germany to her knees. This, and the stories of his bluntness, which percolated their way down the chain of command, gave his crews the feeling that here was a straight-forward Commander who knew what he wanted of them and made it plain to them. He was entirely honest, and they always knew where they stood with him. This style of command influenced his subordinates to adopt a similar approach. There was no attempt, at any level, to dissemble as to the hazards; it was a job which, once completed, would bring the war to an end. In summary, one former Flight Sergeant said of Harris: 'We had all the confidence in the world in his strategy. We felt that we and we alone in Bomber Command were winning the war.'[35] Thus, Harris exercised a very individual and extraordinary style of leadership, which went against all the accepted tenets that a commander should be seen by his troops. Yet it worked – such was the dominating character and force of the man.

LACK OF MORAL FIBRE

Before leaving the subject of aircrew, it is important to cover one aspect of the bombing campaign which some historians have claimed as a blot on the Command's handling of flying personnel, the question of LMF. This book has shown the official concern over the problem, something which other writers seem to have ignored. Much heart-searching went on as to how to be fair to the individual, recognising that unwillingness to continue flying was, in the majority of cases, caused by medical problems. Indeed, only 20 per cent of aircrew referred to as Waverers were found to have no pyschological or medical problems, and, of the remainder, 50 per cent ultimately returned to full flying duties.[36] Those who were eventually placed in Category W, were more often than not men who should have been rejected for flying training, and who had slipped through the filter of the selection boards. They tended to have joined for the wrong reasons – boost to their own confidence, to impress the girls – and had little thought as to the implications. These were usually identified as Waverers during their first few operations. More worrying were those who cracked towards the end of their tours, but, often a good CO and MO could nurse them through and, indeed, good leadership at squadron level did much to keep the problem within bounds. Nevertheless, an Air Ministry directive issued in August 1944 did recognise that some used up their reserves more quickly than others.

> In some cases, owing to the less robust constitution of an individual or his subjection to special operational strain, earlier relief will be necessary and should be encouraged.[37]

Some have felt that it was unjust to take away a man's flying brevet, but as one squadron commander put it in his report on a Waverer:

> So long as this man is permitted to wear his air gunner's badge and hold NCO rank, he is an incentive to further similar difficulties, besides being an insult to the men doing the job.[38]

Fear is infectious and Leonard Cheshire put the point quite succinctly:

> I was ruthless with 'moral fibre cases', I had to be. We were airmen not psychiatrists. Of course we had concern for any individual whose internal tensions meant that he could no longer go on; but there was the worry that one really frightened man could affect others around him. There was no time to be as compassionate as I would like to have been. I was flying too, and we had to get on with the war.[39]

One aviation doctor, the late Dr. Roland Winfield, who flew no fewer than 98 operations with Bomber Command to observe stress in aircrew, and who was decorated with both the DFC and AFC, wrote that aircrew went through two stages. Initially, as Freshers, they were glad to be away from the restrictions of the OTU, believed bombing to be worthwhile, were ignorant of what they might be up against, and had pride in belonging to a good squadron. This engendered a feeling that 'it can't happen to me'. Then came the realisation that 'it can happen to me'. Some, the cream, such as Gibson, Cheshire, Martin and others, found the solution was to put the war above themselves, and meticulously plan each operation with the aim of hitting the enemy as hard as possible. Others hung on in the hope of reaching the end of their tour, but this could be very draining. The majority concentrated on hiding their fear. Some fell by the wayside, but of the others who carried on, 'no reward can repay them and no praise is too great for the indomitable spirit of these unrecognised airmen'.[40]

CONDUCT OF THE BOMBING CAMPAIGN, 1942–45

While the period 1939–41 can be regarded as a period of experimentation for Bomber Command, which established that it was only capable of area bombing by night, its strategic bombing campaign can be said to have started with Directive No 22. This laid down the primary objective as being attacks on specified 'industrial areas', but GEE was to be used to develop precision attacks. However, the latter failed as a blind-bombing device, because it was not sufficiently accurate. Hence, there was agitation to overcome the problem by instituting a special Target Marking Force. Harris has been generally criticised for his resistance to this idea; he and his Group Commanders were not in favour of a *corps d'élite*, which would cream off the best crews. His resistance, in that he preferred to improve the accuracy of bombing as a whole throughout the Command, is understandable. However accurate and efficient target marking became, there would always be a proportion of crews that would not take the trouble to bomb accurately on the markers, and Harris felt that the instilling of a healthy feeling of competition throughout all squadrons would reduce the problem to a minimum. As it was, he did bow to Portal's demand that Pathfinder Force be formed, and once it was, he gave it his qualified backing. Post-war Air Ministry comment that the Pathfinders were not effective in 1942 because of Harris's failure to ensure that they had the best crews, and that it was not a *corps d'élite* because it had a different role from the main force[41] makes little sense. If the Pathfinder Force were to cream off the best crews yet remain within Bomber Command it could not be anything but a *corps d'élite*. Conversely, Harris, after listening to his Group Commanders, sensibly formed it round particular squadrons, selected by Groups as being the best in their commands, which seems to be a more logical approach than the Air Ministry's implication that wholesale plundering of the Command should take place. If this had happened, the resultant disruption would have undoubtedly caused a drop in effectiveness. As it was, by mid 1944 virtually every Group had developed its own marking methods.

Area bombing, the main policy for 1942, was never directed at the killing of civilians *per se*, but to disrupt their lives to the extent that there was a wholesale lowering of morale. As Cherwell had argued, from observations of the blitz on Britain, it was de-housing rather than death which had the greater effect on civilian morale, but as yet, the bombing force was not large enough to have a significant effect, and the pattern of operations during Harris's early months in command were directed at demonstrating bomber potential, not just to Churchill and the other Chiefs of Staff, but to the Americans as well. This was successful in that agreement was reached, both for expansion of the Command and for a combined strategic bombing campaign. Furthermore, the Air Staff's wording of the aim of POINTBLANK was agreed virtually word for word at Casablanca, and Harris was allowed to continue with area bombing. Indeed, the American intention to carry out precision bombing by day combined with area bombing by night seemed to be the ideal course. As it turned out, the Americans were unable to defend themselves in the air during 1943 because of the lack of suitable long-range fighters and the bulk of POINTBLANK rested on Harris's shoulders.

Harris's 'cities plan' and his belief that, given a sufficient number of aircraft, bombing could make invasion of France unnecessary, or at least turn it into a mere police action was not shared by others. But the wording of the POINTBLANK directive, with its emphasis on the 'fatal' weakening of German armed resistance, and the fact that it made no mention of invasion of the Continent, was vague enough to allow Harris to think as he did, and Portal certainly did not disagree with his views at the time. The ever-increasing size of his Force and his apparent successes against the Ruhr and Hamburg reinforced his belief, especially with the resultant Intelligence estimates on enemy morale. Berlin, however, proved that morale was not a decisive target and demonstrated that Bomber Command was not an all-weather force and that it was struggling to even hold its own in what had become an increasingly technological battle. Yet the fact that he was allowed to pound away for so long was because of the generally held and mistaken belief that German morale would eventually crack. This, however, ignored two factors. First, the Third Reich was a highly disciplined state, much more so than Britain or the USA, and second, the policy of Unconditional Surrender, aided rather than hindered the Nazi leaders. They were able to put it across to the people that there was nothing to be gained by surrender, since they would lose everything. Hence, they would do better to fight on and, in any event, the 'miracle weapons' were coming which would drastically change the course of the war. Thus, German morale never did break until the very end.

There is no doubt that the strategic air forces did play a vital role in the success of OVERLORD. Their execution of the Transportation Plan and their crushing of the Luftwaffe was decisive, and Harris and his crews deserve the fullest praise for their willingness in supporting the ground forces and the skill with which they carried out their attacks. The US Eighth and Fifteenth Air Forces merit similar laurels. As for the choice between the Transportation and Oil Plans, while it is accepted that the latter eventually proved decisive, there was not enough time before OVERLORD for a campaign against it to bite sufficiently to get the troops safely ashore and firmly established in Normandy, towards which attacks on transportation undoubtedly made a decisive contribution.

Nevertheless, with Spaatz and Portal championing oil as the final objective, Tedder transportation and Harris area attacks, the post-war bombing surveys and the admissions of Albert Speer and others point conclusively to the fact that Spaatz and Portal were right to concentrate on this from September 1944 onwards, and Harris should by then have learned the lesson of the Battle of Berlin. In 1942 and for much of 1943 he could rightly argue on past experience that 'panacea targets' were a waste of time, especially since Intelligence estimates on them had proved wholly over-optimistic. By 1944 Harris did have the means to attack oil success-fully, and those responsible for target selection now had a wealth of experience on which to draw. Yet, Portal never did emphatically discourage Harris's area attacks, and neither did others, as HURRICANE, CLARION and THUNDERCLAP show.

Thus, area bombing *per se* was not decisive, but to say that it contributed nothing to the war could not be farther from the truth. It may not have had much effect on enemy morale, but it certainly helped British morale during the early, dark years and, apart from logistic support, was the only method of giving active assistance to the Russians until June 1944. Furthermore, even though Germany's war production did not peak until 1944, it must be realised that she did not go on to a full war footing until 1943, and after July 1944 production dropped dramatically. The bombing, too, tied down a significant proportion of enemy manpower and munitions and, indeed, prevented German industrial output increasing to an even higher level. In addition, the Combined Bombing Offensive as a whole played a decisive role in bringing the war to a close through ground support, the reduction of the Luftwaffe, and attacks on oil and communications, and the more meagre the resources devoted to it, the longer the war would have gone on.

THE MORALITY OF STRATEGIC BOMBING

There remains the question of morality – whether it was right to attack targets that would inevitably bring about the death of civilians. Before the war, and at the beginning, in the light of The Hague Draft Rules, both Government and the RAF were clear that it was morally wrong to attack anything other than military targets in the strictest definition of the word. Yet, both sides realised that a military target cannot be strictly defined. As Sir Robert Saundby later wrote:

> It is generally agreed, for example, that the man who loads or fires a field-gun is a military target. So is the gun itself, and the ammunition dump which supplies it. So is the truck-driver who transports ammunition from the base to the dump. So – in the last two World Wars – was the man who transported weapons, ammunition, raw materials, etc., by sea. But are the weapons and war-like stores on their way from the factories to the bases, and the men who transport them, not also military targets? And what about the weapons under construction in the factories, and the men who make them? Are they not also military targets? And if they are not, where do you draw the line? If they are military targets, are not the industrial areas and the services – gas, electricity – that keep industry going, also military targets? Or is it permissible to starve these civilian workers by blockade, or shell them if you can get at them, but not to bomb them from the air? This is surely a *reductio ad absurdum*.[42]

This illustrates the dilemma, but Saundby left out one vital point – that of discrimination. The area bombing of cities could not distinguish between workers and women and children, who could hardly be thought of as combatants, even if war workers were. It is this point which those such as Bishop Bell of Chichester, Richard Stokes and Vera Brittain during the war, and many since have seized upon. A. J. P. Taylor registered surprise at 'the readiness, by the British, of all people, to stop at nothing when waging war. Civilised constraints, all considerations of morality, were abandoned.'[43] Professor Geoffrey Best, who is highly respected for his expertise on the Laws of War, has condemned it utterly.[44] Even the Editor of the Journal of the Royal United Services Institute, on the publication of the Official History, launched into a scathing attack on the immorality of area bombing.[45] Evidence has been displayed in this book that not just Churchill, but the Air Staff as well had occasional qualms about its morality, and at times some aircrew were unhappy about what they were doing, especially during the later stages of the war.

The other side of the coin is that primarily it was a question of retaliation, which, in the earlier part of the war, was the main argument used to justify strategic bombing. However, as Michael Glover has written: 'Civilian air raid deaths in Britain throughout the war amounted to 60,000; in Germany 800,000. There can be little doubt that, considered as retaliation, the imbalance was overwhelming.'[46] If it could have been seen to deter the Germans from bombing British civilians, the argument might stand up, but Hitler's v-weapon attacks showed that this was not so. On the other hand, these indiscriminate attacks against morale were aimed at shortening the war, and it is very clear that Harris saw it in this light. In particular, once the Allies were ashore in Normandy, he saw it as a means of keeping ground force casualties down. His argument was that the German soldier would fight on no matter how short of *matériel* (the aim of oil and transportation attacks), but that concentrated area bombing could break the structure of his society and persuade him to surrender that much more quickly, and thus save Allied casualties. In his comments on Churchill's minute of 28 March 1945, Harris, while denying that Bomber Command had ever gone in for terror attacks, argued that attacks on cities were strategically justified if aimed at shortening the war and saving Allied lives. It was the same argument that was used to justify the dropping of the Atomic bombs on Hiroshima and Nagasaki, and is hard to refute, particularly near the end of a long bloody road and faced with the daunting prospect of possibly much more to come. As Dr. Noble Frankland, one of the historians of the Official History of the strategic bombing campaign, and himself a Bomber Command navigator, who won a DFC, once said:

> I think it is between a man and his conscience. It does not trouble my conscience that we struck at the Germans as hard as we could in 1940 and 1941 and until they were beaten. As to whether this had any effect on subsequent policies, I think it would be difficult to sustain. In the interval between wars there are various theories of international legality and morality, but these will become acutely modified in accordance with the crisis which prevails. I think that the big moral question is whether you will fight at all. If you will, I think one's proper duty is to win as quickly and cheaply as possible.[47]

In essence, therefore, it becomes a question of how many of one's own people one is prepared to sacrifice on the altar of ethics.

A very unfair, though popular, accusation is that the RAF wanted to win the war on their own by bombing, the implication being that this was for reasons of self-aggrandisement. Accepted that they believed, especially Harris, their contribution, given the necessary resources, would be decisive, it was in the genuine belief that they could save casualties. Furthermore, it was total war, and it had become accepted since 1915 that this meant that civilians, just as much as fighting men, were in the front line.

IMMEDIATE POST-WAR ATTITUDES

It is clear that there was embarrassment immediately after the war about the way that the bombing campaign had been conducted, but it was not manifested in the ways that some historians have depicted. The question over official recognition of Harris's own services has already been covered, as has that of the Bomber Command medal. It is also implied that Harris left the RAF in September 1945 because the Air Ministry would not offer him another post.[48] He had always yearned to go back to his beloved Africa[49] and with his task done, he could now do so. He left the

Service voluntarily and departed for South Africa, where he had an equally successful second career as Managing Director of South African Marine Corporation.

Harris and many of his crews, did have the feeling that their efforts and sacrifices were being ignored, and this was why he wrote *Bomber Offensive* immediately after the war so that the deeds of Bomber Command could be publicised. Unlike others, his Official Dispatch was never published, but merely placed on a very limited circulation. Although written in 1945, it was not until March 1948 that even this was allowed, and then only when accompanied by a long, written rebuttal by the Air Ministry of much of what he had said.[50] The grounds given were, the fact that Harris did not take into account the findings of the British and US Bombing Survey Reports, especially in his claims on the losses to German war production as a result of his area attacks, which were considered inflationary. Also, 'the drastic criticisms of certain policy decisions and other matters which appear [in the Dispatch] to give only one side of the picture, and that there are other aspects which need to be given equal prominence'. In other words, they considered it too biassed. What was particularly resented was his statement that Bomber Command's main task throughout the war was 'to focus attacks on the morale of the enemy civil population, and, in particular, of the industrial workers'. It was stressed that area attacks were only considered as a temporary phase, and that the intention was always to go back to precision attacks, but that Harris had dragged his feet over doing it. This last point is accepted, but a study of the directives issued to Bomber Command shows that area bombing always featured prominently right up until April 1945, and that it was the top priority from February 1942 until at least 1944. While Harris maintained that 'the enemy's sinews of war were to be found in his industrial cities', the Air Ministry commented with some tortuous argument:

> This is considered too drastic a statement. It is probably true that the great bulk of the enemy's armament production came from the industrial cities, (though this was not demonstrated, as stated, by the experience of war), but his *most vulnerable* sinews of war (oil and communications) were generally outside them. They were the ones that were severed and most patently brought about his collapse. It may be claimed, however, that the destruction of industrial cities, by forcing the enemy to disperse its industry, increased his dependence on communications and oil, and so rendered their ultimate destruction decisive.

Then, as if to confound their confusion as to whether any credit should be given to area bombing at all, they continued:

> . . . it cannot be denied that there was, in Bomber Command, a reluctance to attack specific targets, born partly out of operational inability and partly of an underestimate on the part of their own ability. This made it difficult to advocate

them any real target system other than industrial areas – which, as is demonstrated throughout the dispatch, they wanted most to attack.

There is much truth in this, but, at the same time, the statement was tantamount to using the excuse that because the Air Staff could not control Harris, area rather than precision bombing remained a high priority. It is difficult not to conclude that the post-war Air Ministry wanted to slough any responsibility they might have had for the policy on to the shoulders of Harris. Another indication that the Establishment wished to forget that area bombing had ever taken place concerns Harris's book. When *Bomber Offensive* appeared in early 1947, the Journal of the Royal United Services Institute did not carry a review of it. As this was the first published account of the war by a senior commander, and the RUSI was the most august defence institute in the country, it seems a surprising omission, although a copy was acquired for the library.[51]

On the other hand, Sir Robert Saundby was invited to address the RUSI in October 1945 on the attack on communications, and concluded:

> The experience of the war that has just ended, has thus confirmed that there are two chief ways in which a powerful bomber force can contribute to victory. One way is the destruction of the vital industrial centres of the country, and the other way is the systematic paralysing of all forms of communication.[52]

In February 1948, however, Sir Norman Bottomley, who had just retired from the Royal Air Force, lectured the RUSI on 'The Strategic Bomber Offensive Against Germany', with Sir Archibald Sinclair in the Chair. He considered that the area attacks which, he pointed out, represented no less than 46 per cent of Bomber Command's total effort in the war, 'had a considerable effect on the German war effort, but it is very questionable whether the effect in itself was ever critical'.[53] This is a fair judgement from one who was as deeply involved as any in the bomber offensive.

THE FINAL VERDICT

Throughout his lifetime, Sir Arthur Harris maintained that his area attacks were decisive, and, although he can rightly be accused of stubbornness in this respect, his chief concern remained to honour the memory of those young men of forty and more years ago, who climbed night after night into their aircraft to face the countless terrors of the air war over Germany. Blinkered, boorish and stubborn he may have been at times, but there is no doubt that no other leader could have extracted so much from his men in the face of such fearful odds for three long years. In hindsight, the rigid adherence for so long to the concept of area bombing has been shown to have been a mistake, but during much of the war there was no way of knowing this, and many of the arguments for it seemed very persuasive in the context of the exhausting struggle of the time. Nevertheless, the part played by RAF Bomber Command in the winning of the war did justify the 7 per cent of the national war effort spent on it, and much of the credit for this must go to Harris himself, especially in his dogged upholding of that principle of war, maintenance of the aim, and his ability to inspire those under him to carry it out.

LIST OF SOURCES

The following abbreviations have been used. SAO: Strategic Air Offensive, which refers to the four-volume Official History of RAF Bomber Command's work in the Second World War, written by Sir Charles Webster and Dr Noble Frankland. JRUSI: Journal of the Royal United Services (now Service) Institute. PRO: Public Record Office, Kew, London. Categories of papers preserved there are: AIR (Air Ministry), ADM (Admiralty), CAB (Cabinet Office), PREM (Premier, the Prime Minister's own files), WO (War Office).

CHAPTER ONE

1. Anon. *War Birds: Diary of an Unknown Aviator.* (Hamilton, London, 1927), p. 126
2. Raleigh, Sir Walter, and Jones, H. A. *The War in the Air.* (Oxford University Press, 1937), vol. VI, p. 10
3. Telegram to India Office 13 February 1920: PRO WO 32/5227
4. Harris, Sir Arthur. *Bomber Offensive.* (Collins, 1947), p. 19
5. *Ibid.*
6. *Ibid.*, p. 22
7. Quoted Divine, David. *The Broken Wing.* (Hutchinson, London, 1966), p. 162
8. Quoted Longmate, Norman. *The Bombers.* (Hutchinson, 1983), p. 41
9. Collier, Basil. *A History of Air Power.* (Weidenfeld & Nicholson, 1974), p. 96
10. PRO AIR 27/543
11. O'Brien, Terence H. *History of the Second World War: Civil Defence.* (H.M.S.O., London, 1955), pp. 15–16
12. Quoted Howard, Michael. *The Continental Commitment.* (Temple Smith, London, 1972), p. 94
13. Fuller, J. F. C. *The Reformation of War.* (Dutton, New York, 1923), p. 150

14. Liddell Hart, B. H. *Paris, Or the Future of War.* (Kegan Paul, London, 1925), pp. 42, 46–7
15. SAO, vol. IV, pp. 71–83
16. DC(M) (32)2 Minutes of Meeting 5 April 1932: PRO CAB 27/505
17. Hansard, House of Commons Debate, 10 November 1932
18. Bialer, Uri. *The Shadow of the Bomber.* (Royal Historical Society, 1980), pp. 29–30
19. Bennett, D. C. T. *Pathfinder.* (Muller, 1958), p. 47
20. Hansard, House of Commons Debate
21. PRO AIR 2/692 Minute 22
22. Quoted PRO AIR 41/39, p. 127
23. Memo dated 4 February 1936: CID Paper 1207B
24. SAO, vol. IV, pp. 86–95
25. PRO AIR 41/39
26. Harris, *op. cit.*, pp. 26–7
27. SAO vol. IV, pp. 96–8
28. PRO AIR 14/57
29. Quoted Hastings, Max. *Bomber Command.* (Michael Joseph, 1980) p. 53
30. *Ibid.*
31. Bennet to Newall 9 September 1938, and Air Council to Bomber Command 15 September 1938: PRO AIR 8/251
32. *Ibid.*, minute dated 27 September 1938
33. Harris, *op. cit.*, p. 31

CHAPTER TWO

1. Gibson, Guy. *Enemy Coast Ahead.* (Pan, 1979), p.23
2. Harris, *op cit.*, p. 33
3. Secretary of State's Expansion Progress Meetings, Minutes for 4 August 1939: PRO AIR 6/39
4. Harris, *op. cit.*, p. 36
5. PRO AIR 25/109A
6. PRO AIR 14/3556

7. Quoted Jackson, Robert. *Before The Storm: The Story of Bomber Command 1939-42.* (Arthur Barker, 1972), pp. 71-2
8. Minutes of this conference are found in PRO AIR 14/227
9. PRO AIR 9/79
10. PRO AIR 9/80
11. Figures taken from SAO, vol. IV, pp. 205-9
12. A good description of these factors is in SAO, vol. I, pp. 205-9
13. Kay, C. E. *The Restless Sky.* (Harrap, 1964)
14. Quoted SAO, vol. I, pp. 205-9
15. Harris, *op. cit.*, p. 35. A particularly good account of Ludlow-Hewitt's views and battles with the Air Staff is given in Smith, Malcolm. *Sir Edgar Ludlow-Hewitt and the Expansion of Bomber Command, 1939-40.* (RUSI Journal March 1981) pp. 52-56.
16. Harris, *op. cit.*, p. 39
17. PRO CAB 65/7 War Cabinet 117(40)
18. *Ibid.* War Cabinet 118(40)
19. *Ibid.* War Cabinet 123(40)
20. Drawn from figures quoted in SAO, vol. IV, p. 431
21. All quoted in SAO, vol. I, p. 217
22. Gibson, *op. cit.*, p. 92
23. PRO AIR 14/673
24. Air Ministry letter to Commands dated 22 April 1940 in PRO AIR 2/8038
25. Quoted Jones, R. V. *Most Secret War: British Scientific Intelligence 1939-1945.* (Hamish Hamilton, 1978), p. 183
26. SAO, vol. I, p. 152
27. *Ibid.*, p. 153
28. PRO AIR 20/8144
29. *Ibid.*
30. PRO AIR 2/8038
31. All the above letters are found in PRO AIR 14/1941
32. Harris, *op. cit.*, p. 49
33. SAO, vol. IV, pp. 124-7
34. SAO, vol. I, p. 157
35. Figures derived from SAO, vol. IV, pp. 431-34
36. PRO AIR 8/407
37. Quoted SAO, vol. I, p. 227
38. PRO PREM 3/14/2
39. PRO CAB 120/292
40. *Ibid.*
41. Harris, *op. cit.*, pp. 52-3
42. SAO, vol. I, p. 165
43. PRO CAB 120/300
44. *Ibid.*
45. PRO AIR 20/8144
46. PRO AIR 45/2, which gives a history of the Delegation
47. SAO, vol. I, p. 179
48. PRO AIR 8/1356
49. *The Daily Telegraph* 16 September 1941.

This was certainly taken note of by the Air Staff as a clipping of it was placed in a file on the effect of bombing on German morale. (PRO AIR 20/8143)
50. SAO, vol. I, pp. 180-1
51. SAO, vol. I, p. 183
52. This correspondence is found in PRO AIR 8/258
53. Figures derived from SAO, vol. IV, pp. 431-34
54. SAO, vol. IV, p. 142
55. Bennett, *op. cit.*, p. 137

CHAPTER THREE
1. Raymond, Robert S. *A Yank in Bomber Command.* (David & Charles, 1977), p. 119
2. Harris, *op cit.*, p. 73
3. Minute Churchill to Anderson, Lord President of The Council, 7 September 1941 Quoted in Longmate, *op. cit.*, pp. 166-7
4. Figures derived from Longmate, *op. cit.*, pp. 168-9
5. Quoted Gywer J. M. A., and Butler, J. R. M. *Grand Strategy.* (H.M.S.O.), vol. III, p. 528
6. PRO AIR 2/8038
7. Longmate, *op. cit.*, p. 179
8. Air Ministry correspondence on the subject is in PRO AIR 2/8591
9. PRO AIR 20/8145
10. SAO, vol. IV, pp. 143-5
11. Harris, *op. cit.*, p. 74
12. Hansard House of Commons Debates 24-25 February 1942
13. PRO AIR 8/619
14. Both letters found in PRO AIR 8/625
15. Hansard House of Commons Debates 4 March 1942
16. Report dated 13 March 1942 in PRO AIR 8/625
17. Bushby, John. *Gunner's Moon.* (Futura, 1974), p. 125
18. PRO AIR 14/10
19. Harris to Oxland, 3 March 1942, PRO AIR 14/3548
20. *Ibid.*
21. PRO AIR 14/3547
22. PRO AIR 19/187
23. PRO CAB 120/300
24. Harris, *op. cit.*, p. 105
25. SAO, vol. I, pp. 331-2
26. Quoted Hastings, *op. cit.*, p. 130
27. Quoted Longmate, *op. cit.*, p. 129
28. SAO, vol. I, pp. 333-5
29. PRO AIR 8/1015, which gives the Singleton Report complete, as does SAO, vol. IV, pp. 231-8
30. Harris's reasoning appears in a letter to Churchill dated 2 May 1942 in PRO AIR 14/3507. This was written to counter a complaint by the Ministry of Economic

Warfare (MEW) that the target was not one of their recommended ones. Churchill accepted Harris's explanation and the latter made his peace with MEW.
31. Quoted Barker, Ralph. *Strike Hard, Strike Sure.* (Pan, 1974), p. 42
32. Harris to AOC No 1 Group, 22 May 1942, PRO AIR 14/3542
33. Comments are found in PRO AIR 8/1015
34. SAO, vol. I, pp. 338–9
35. PRO AIR 14/2024
36. No 91 Group Operational Record Book (Appendices): PRO AIR 25/751
37. Quoted Price, Alfred. *Battle Over The Reich.* (Ian Allan, 1973), pp. 28-9
38. Copy in PRO AIR 28/517
39. A graphic description of this conference is given in Saward, Dudley. *The Bomber's Eye.* (Cassell, 1959), p. 126
40. PRO AIR 14/2024
41. Although the most normally quoted figures are 1,046 or 1,047, this figure has been arrived at by careful cross-checking of all Operational Record Books, and the actual breakdown by units and bases is given in my *Cologne: The First 1000 Bomber Raid.* (Ian Allan, 1982), pp. 48-51
42. Renaut, Michael. *Terror by Night.* (Kimber, 1982), p. 85
43. Letter dated 5 June 1942 by Sergeant E. A. Manson, and preserved at RAF Museum Hendon, under DC 74/81/1
44. PRO AIR 14/3443
45. *The Times,* 31 May 1942
46. PRO AIR 24/204
47. Both found in PRO AIR 14/2024

CHAPTER FOUR
1. PRO CAB 120/300
2. *Ibid.*
3. Portal to Harris, 16 June 1942: PRO AIR 8/864
4. *Ibid.*
5. PRO CAB 79/21 COS Meeting 180 (42)
6. PRO AIR 2/8039
7. Quoted Hastings, *op. cit.*, p. 174
8. Quoted Bond, Brian. *Liddell Hart: A Study of his Military Thought.* (Cassell, 1977), p. 145
9. *The Times,* 16 July 1942
10. PRO AIR 14/3507
11. PRO PREM 3/7
12. Harris to Churchill, 18 July 1942: PRO PREM 3/11/12
13. Alanbrooke Diary entry 22 October 1942. Quoted in Fraser, David. *Alanbrooke.* (Collins, 1982), p. 264
14. SAO, vol. I, pp. 419–20
15. Singleton Report: PRO AIR 8/1015
16. Harris to Bufton, 17 April 1942: PRO AIR 14/3523

17. PRO AIR 8/407
18. PRO AIR 14/2714
19. Harris to Churchill, 6 July 1942: PRO PREM 20/9
20. Wood to Churchill, 9 July 1942: *Ibid.*
21. Bennett, *op. cit.*, pp. 162-3
22. PRO AIR 14/2714
23. Harris to Sinclair, 10 August 1942: PRO 14/1571
24. Meeting 15 July 1942, AIR 14/1655
25. Joubert to Harris, 15 September 1942 and Harris's reply dated 19 September 1942 in PRO AIR 14/3548
26. Harris to AOCs Nos 1, 3, 4, 5 Groups, 4 August 1942: PRO AIR 14/3548
27. PRO AIR 14/3544
28. PRO AIR 14/2821
29. Bushby, *op. cit.*, p. 173
30. Air Ministry. *Operational Research in the RAF.* (H.M.S.O., 1963), p. 66
31. PRO AIR 14/3512
32. Winfield, Dr. Roland. *The Sky Shall Not Have Them.* (Kimber, 1976), pp. 129-30
33. PRO AIR 14/2821
34. Correspondence in PRO AIR 2/8039

CHAPTER FIVE
1. PRO PREM 3/11/6
2. Churchill to Lord Privy Seal, 19 October 1942: PRO PREM 3/7
3. *Time,* 7 September 1942
4. PRO AIR 8/424
5. Paper dated 28 September 1942: PRO AIR 20/8146
6. COS(42) 379(0) PRO PREM 3/11/7
7. Minute dated 17 August 1942: PRO AIR 9/424
8. Quoted Hastings, Max., *op. cit.*, p. 170.
9. Minute dated 6 November 1942: PRO PREM 3/11/7
10. Churchill to Air Ministry, 18 November 1942: AIR 9/424
11. COS(42) 478(0) dated 26 December 1942: PREM 3/11/7
12. PRO AIR 8/711
13. PRO PREM 3/11/6
14. Bottomley to Portal, 26 September 1942: PRO AIR 8/711
15. PRO AIR 14/3507
16. PRO PREM 3/11/6
17. Minute dated 16 December 1942, *Ibid.*
18. SAO, vol. I, p. 377
19. SAO, vol. IV, pp. 265-6
20. Gibson, *op. cit.*, p. 201
21. *Ibid.*, p. 211
22. SAO, vol. I, pp. 449-452
23. PRO AIR 7/722
24. Harris to Saundby, 17 December 1942: PRO AIR 14/1454
25. SAO, vol. I, p. 348
26. SAO, vol. IV, pp. 245-252

27. PRO AIR 19/288
28. Statistics from PRO AIR 22/309
29. Raymond, *op. cit.*, pp. 103-4
30. CCS 166/1/D dated 21 January 1943:
PRO CAB 99/24
31. Harris, *op. cit.*, p. 145
32. SAO, vol. II, p. 14
33. *Ibid.*
34. PRO AIR 8/723
35. PRO ADM 199/1787
36. First Sea Lord 22 March 1943, *Ibid.*
37. PRO AIR 8/723
38. *Ibid.*
39. PRO ADM 199/1787
40. SAO, vol. IV, p. 155

CHAPTER SIX
1. Harris, *op. cit.*, p. 144
2. SAO, vol. II, pp. 115-6
3. Harris, *op. cit.*, p. 147
4. Harris to Portal, 30 March 1943: PRO
8/833
5. Inglis to Portal, 8 April 1943, *Ibid.*
6. Harris, *op. cit.*, p. 149
7. Raymond, *op. cit.*, p. 135
8. PRO AIR 2/8039
9. *Ibid.*
10. SAO, vol. II, pp. 15-19
11. Plan dated 14 May 1943: PRO AIR
20/8150
12. Hansell, Major-General S. Jr. *The Air
Plan that Defeated Hitler.* (Hansell, 1972),
p. 171
13. SAO, vol. IV, pp. 156-7
14. *Ibid.*, pp. 158-9
15. Cooper, Alan W. *The Men who
Breached the Dams.* (Kimber, 1982) and
Sweetman, John. *Operation Chastise – The
Dams Raid: Epic or Myth.* (Jane's, 1982)
16. Quoted Sweetman, *op. cit.*, p. 42
17. Quoted *Ibid.*, p. 45
18. Gibson, *op. cit.*, p. vii
19. PRO AIR 41/43
20. Quoted Sweetman, *op. cit.*, pp. 173-4
21. PRO PREM 3/14/5
22. Figures extracted from PRO AIR 41/43
and AIR 22/309
23. PRO AIR 14/872
24. PRO PREM 3/14/5
25. Harris, *op. cit.*, p. 148
26. SAO, vol. II, p. 257

CHAPTER SEVEN
1. ASI Report No 16 dated 24 October 1942:
PRO 8/1247
2. *Ibid.*
3. SAO, vol. II, p. 143 fn2
4. Air Staff Memorandum dated 28 March
1943: PRO AIR 8/1247
5. Bomber Command Operation Order No
173 dated 27 May 1943

6. Quoted Longmate, *op. cit.*, p. 264
7. *Ibid.*
8. PRO 8/1248
9. Figures derived from Middlebrook,
Martin. *The Peenemunde Raid.* (Allen Lane,
1982), p. 209
10. PRO AIR 20/8147
11. SAO, vol. IV, p. 160
12. PRO AIR 8/435
13. PRO AIR 14/1979
14. Bennett to Harris, 25 September 1943:
PRO AIR 14/2701
15. Harris to Bennett, 1 October 1943, *Ibid.*
16. Quoted Morrison, Wilbur H. *Fortress
Without a Roof.* (W. H. Allen, 1982),
p. 157
17. Clostermann, Pierre. *The Big Show.*
(Chatto & Windus, London, 1951), p. 94
18. Harris to Lovett, 12 November 1943:
PRO AIR 14/3552

CHAPTER EIGHT
1. PRO AIR 14/3507
2. PRO AIR 8/1167
3. *Ibid.*
4. Harris, *op. cit.*, pp. 186-7
5. Anderson, William. *Pathfinders.*
(Jarrolds, 1946), pp. 76-7
6. PRO AIR 8/435
7. Quoted, SAO, vol. II, p. 204
8. Correspondence in PRO AIR 14/1961
9. Peck to Sinclair, 19 November 1943: PRO
19/393
10. PRO 14/365
11. PRO AIR 8/425 and SAO, vol. II, pp.
55-7
12. SAO, vol. II, pp. 57-9
13. *Ibid.*, pp. 59-60
14. PRO AIR 19/189
15. Harris to Bottomley, 28 December 1943,
Ibid.
16. SAO, vol. IV, pp. 160-2
17. Bufton to Bottomley, 22 January 1944:
PRO 20/8148
18. SAO, vol. IV, pp. 162-3
19. SAO, vol. II, p. 206
20. See especially Middlebrook, Martin. *The
Nuremberg Raid.* (Allen Lane, 1973); Irving,
David. *The Mare's Nest.* (Kimber, 1964);
and Campbell, James. *The Bombing of
Nuremberg.* (Allison & Bushby, 1973)
21. Quoted Revie, Alastair. *The Lost
Command* (Corgi, 1977), p. 253
22. Quoted Middlebrook, *The Nuremberg
Raid.*, *op. cit.*, p. 255
23. Harris, *op. cit.*, p. 187

CHAPTER NINE
1. Quoted Morgan, Sir Frederick. *Overture
to Overlord.* (Hodder & Stoughton, London,
1950), p. 64

2. Portal to Churchill, 6 November 1943: PRO AIR 8/1187
3. Air Staff COSSAC AEF Memorandum 2 November 1943: PRO AIR 37/516
4. CCS/398 dated 18 November 1943 in PRO 41/56
5. PRO AIR 8/1187
6. *Ibid.*
7. Portal to Harris, 3 January 1944, *Ibid.*
8. *Ibid.*
9. Harris's paper dated 13 January 1944 and AEAF/Air Staff comments in PRO AIR 37/752
10. Portal to Harris, 30 January 1944: PRO AIR 8/1187
11. Quoted Rostow, W. W. *Pre-Invasion Bombing Strategy.* (Gower, 1982), p. 14
12. Quoted Wynn, Humphrey, and Young, Susan. *Prelude to Overlord.* (Airlife, 1983), p. 84
13. SAO, vol. IV, pp. 166-7
14. Quoted Ambrose, Stephen. *The Supreme Commander: The War Years of General Dwight D. Eisenhower.* (Doubleday, New York, 1970), p. 370
15. Harris to Portal, 24 March 1944: PRO AIR 8/1188
16. Full minutes are given in Rostow, *op. cit.*, pp. 88-98
17. SAO, vol. IV, pp. 167-70
18. PRO AIR 41/56 p. 10
19. Harris, *op. cit.*, pp. 197, 266
20. Bennett, *op. cit.*, pp. 213-4
21. Harris, *op. cit.*, pp. 202-3
22. PRO AIR 8/1190
23. *Ibid.*
24. *Ibid.*
25. PRO AIR 41/56 p. 53
26. Quoted Ambrose, *op. cit.*, p. 398
27. Blumenson, Martin. *The Patton Papers 1940-1945.* (Houghton Mifflin, New York, 1974), p. 456
28. Quoted Bradley, Omar, and Blair, Clay. *A General's Life.* (Sidgwick & Jackson, London 1983), p. 241
29. PRO AIR 41/56 p. 37
30. For a particularly good account see Leonard Cheshire's version (617 Squadron carried out TAXABLE) in Foxley-Norris, Sir Christopher (ed.). *Royal Air Force at War.* (Ian Allan, 1983)
31. SAO, vol. III, p. 47
32. PRO AIR 41/56, p. 54
33. SAO, vol. III, pp. 164-5
34. Bishop, Geoffrey S. C. *The Battle: A Tank Officer Remembers.* (pubd. privately, no date) pp. 27-8
35. PRO AIR 41/56 p. 52
36. PRO AIR 14/3506
37. Ambrose, *op. cit.*, pp. 500-1
38. Harris, *op. cit.*, p. 213

CHAPTER TEN
1. SAO, vol. IV, p. 171
2. *Ibid.*, pp. 172-4
3. *Ibid.*, pp. 174-6
4. PRO CAB 120/301
5. SAO, vol. IV, pp. 177-9
6. SAO, vol. III, pp. 80-4
7. Figures derived from PRO 41/56
8. Harris, *op. cit.*, p. 253
9. PRO AIR 14/1436 and AIR 14/1431
10. Figures derived from PRO 41/56
11. This correspondence is found in PRO 8/1020
12. Richards, Denis. *Portal of Hungerford.* (Heinemann, 1977), p. 318
13. PRO AIR 41/56 p. 175
14. COS Meeting 220(0) dated 5 July 1944
15. Portal Memorandum dated 1 August 1944: PRO AIR 20/8152 and COS Meeting 261(0) of 5 August 1944
16. JIC(45)34(0) (Final) dated 25 January 1945: PRO 20/8152
17. SAO, vol. III, p. 99
18. *Ibid.*, p. 101
19. PRO AIR 41/56, p. 199
20. SAO, vol. III, pp. 104-5
21. Quoted McKee, Alexander. *Dresden 1945.* (Souvenir Press, 1982), p. 201
22. PRO AIR 41/56, pp. 202-3 and SAO, vol. III, pp. 113-4
23. Hansard House of Commons Debates, 6 March 1945
24. Harris to Portal, 29 March 1945: PRO AIR 41/56, p. 203
25. SAO, vol. III, p. 119
26. Quoted Longmate, *op. cit.*, pp. 345-6
27. SAO, vol. III, p. 119
28. PRO AIR 14/1431
29. Renaut, *op. cit.*, p. 165

CHAPTER ELEVEN
1. Statistics derived from SAO, vol. IV
2. Middlebrook, Martin. *The Nuremberg Raid. op. cit.*, p. 57
3. Dean, Sir Maurice. *The Royal Air Force and Two World Wars.* (Cassell, 1979), p. 99
4. Calder, Angus. *The People's War.* (Cape, 1969), p. 229
5. Longmate, *op. cit.*, p. 381
6. Hastings, *op. cit.*, p. 350
7. Richards, *op. cit.*, p. 326
8. Harris, *op. cit.*, p. 57
9. *Ibid.*, p. 214
10. *Ibid.*, p. 215
11. Thompson, R. W. *Churchill and Morton.* (Hodder & Stoughton, London, 1976), p. 48
12. HQ Bomber Command ORB
13. Harris to Peter Tomlinson, 24 May 1983
14. Thompson, *op. cit.*, p. 79
15. Harris's own papers: copy lent to author

by Peter Tomlinson
16. Admiral Whitworth to Admiral
Cunningham, 15 December 1942, quoted in
Roskill, Stephen. *Churchill and the
Admirals.* (Collins, 1977), p. 139
17. Roskill, *op. cit.*, p. 147
18. Figures derived from AIR 41/56
19. Travis, Ralph. *The Bomber War.*
(Military History, April 1982), p. 153
20. Hastings, *op. cit.*, p. 351
21. McKee, *op. cit.*, p. 116
22. Both quoted from Longmate, *op. cit.*,
p. 145
23. Kingston-McCloughry, Air Vice-Marshal.
*Leadership with Special Reference to World
War 2.* (RAF Quarterly, Autumn 1967),
p. 208
24. Renaut, *op. cit.*
25. Bennett to Harris, 25 September 1943;
Harris to Bennett, 1 October 1943: PRO
AIR 14/2701
26. PRO AIR 14/1451
27. Author interview with Peter Tomlinson,
13 October 1983
28. *Ibid.*
29. Harris in Tomlinson, 12 October 1983
from Tomlinson, *op. cit.*
30. Quoted to Richards, *op. cit.*, p. 325
31. Harris, *op. cit.*, p. 267
32. Quoted Revie, *op. cit.*, p. 254

33. Quoted, *Ibid.*, p. 249
34. Quoted Longmate, *op. cit.*, p. 380
35. *Ibid.*, p. 187
36. PRO AIR 49/357
37. Directive dated 19 August 1944: PRO
AIR 2/8040
38. PRO AIR 49/357
39. Quoted Revie, *op. cit.*, pp. 247–8
40. Winfield, Dr. Roland. *The Sky Belongs
to Them.* (Kimber, 1976), p. 153
41. PRO AIR 14/1252
42. Saundby, Sir Robert. *The Ethics of
Bombing.* (RAF Quarterly, summer 1967),
p. 97
43. Taylor, A. J. P. *From Sarajevo to
Potsdam: The Years 1914–1945.* (Thames &
Hudson, London, 1974), p. 178
44. *Humanity in War.* (Methuen University
Paperback, 1983), pp. 275–285
45. JRUSI May 1962, pp. 1, 2
46. *The Velvet Glove.* (Hodder &
Stoughton, London, 1982), p. 152
47. JRUSI May 1962, pp. 108–9
48. See Hastings, *op. cit.*, p. 347 for
example
49. Harris, *op. cit.*, pp. 19, 25
50. PRO AIR 14/1252
51. JRUSI February 1947
52. JRUSI November 1945, p. 483
53. JRUSI May 1948, p. 227

SELECT BIBLIOGRAPHY

Aders, Gebhard. *History of the German Night Fighter Force 1917-1945*. Macdonald & Jane's, London, 1979

Air Ministry. *Operational Research in the RAF*. H.M.S.O., London, 1963

Anderson, Wing Commander William. *Pathfinders*. Jarrolds, London, 1946

Barker, Ralph. *Strike Hard, Strike Sure: Epics of the Bombers*. Pan Books, London, 1974

Best, Geoffrey. *Humanity in Warfare: The Modern History of the International Law of Armed Conflicts*. Methuen, London, 1983 (University paperback edition)

Bialer, Uri. *The Shadow of the Bomber: The Fear of Air Bombardment and British Politics 1932-1939*. Royal Historical Society, London, 1980

Bond, Brian. *Liddell Hart: A Study of his Military Thought*. Cassell, London, 1979

Bushby, John. *Gunner's Moon*. Futura, London, 1974

Calder, Angus. *The People's War: Britain 1939-1945*. Cape, London, 1969

Cheshire, Leonard. *Bomber Pilot*. Hutchinson, London, 1943

Collier, Basil. *A History of Air Power*. Weidenfeld & Nicolson, London, 1974

Cooper, Alan W. *The Men Who Breached the Dams*. Kimber, London, 1982

Cooper, Matthew. *The German Air Force 1933-1945: An Anatomy of Failure*. Jane's, London, 1981

Dean, Sir Maurice. *The Royal Air Force and Two World Wars*. Cassell, London, 1979

Frankland, Noble. *The Bombing Offensive Against Germany: Outlines and Perspectives*. Faber, London, 1965

Fraser, David. *Alanbrooke*. Collins, London, 1982

Gibson, Guy. *Enemy Coast Ahead*. Pan, London, 1979

Hansell, Major-General Hayward S. *The Air Plan that Defeated Hitler*. Hansell, Atlanta Ga., 1972

Harris, Sir Arthur. *Bomber Offensive*. Collins, London, 1947

Hastings, Max. *Bomber Command*. Michael Joseph, London, 1980

Higham, Robin. *Air Power: A Concise History*. Macdonald, London, 1972

Irving, David. *The Mare's Nest*. Kimber, London, 1964

Jackson, Robert. *Before the Storm: The Story of Bomber Command 1939-42*. Arthur Barker, London, 1972

Jones, Neville. *The Origins of Strategic Bombing: A Study of the Development of British Thought and Practice up to 1918*. Kimber, London, 1973

Jones, R. V. *Most Secret War: British Scientific Intelligence 1939-1945*. Hamish Hamilton, London, 1978

Lawrence, W. J. *No 5 Bomber Group RAF*. Faber, London, 1951

Lewis, Peter. *The British Bomber since 1914*. Putnam, London, 1980
Longmate, Norman. *The Bombers: The RAF Offensive Against Germany 1939–1945*. Hutchinson, London, 1983.
McKee, Alexander. *Dresden 1945: The Devil's Tinderbox*. Souvenir Press, London, 1982
Messenger, Charles. *Cologne: The First 1000 Bomber Raid*. Ian Allan, London 1982
Middlebrook, Martin. *The Nuremberg Raid*. Allen Lane, London, 1973
— *The Peenemünde Raid: The Night of 17-18 August 1943*. Allen Lane, London, 1982
— *The Schweinfurt-Regensburg Mission: The American Raids of 17 August 1943*. Allen Lane, London, 1983
Morrison, Wilbur H. *Fortress Without a Roof: The Allied Bombing of the Third Reich*. W. H. Allen, London, 1982
Moyes, Philip R. J. *Bomber Squadrons of the RAF and their Aircraft*. Macdonald, London, 1964
Price, Alfred. *Battle over the Reich*. Ian Allan, London, 1973
— *Instruments of Darkness*. Kimber, London, 1967
Renaut, Michael. *Terror by Night*. Kimber, London, 1982
Revie, Alastair. *The Lost Command*. Corgi, London, 1972
Richards, Denis. *Portal of Hungerford*. Heinemann, London, 1977
Rostow, W. W. *Pre-Invasion Bombing Strategy: General Eisenhower's Decision of March 25, 1944*. Gower, Aldershot, 1981
Saundby, Sir Robert. *Air Bombardment: The Story of its Development*. Chatto & Windus, London, 1961
Saward, Dudley. *The Bomber's Eye*. Cassell, London, 1959
Streetly, Martin. *Confound and Destroy: 100 Group and the Bomber Support Campaign*. Macdonald & Jane's, London, 1978
Sweetman, John. *Operation Chastise – The Dams Raid: Epic or Myth*. Jane's, London, 1982
Verrier, Anthony. *The Bomber Offensive*. Batsford, London, 1968
Webster, Sir Charles, and Frankland, Noble. *History of the Second World War: The Strategic Air Offensive Against Germany 1939–1945*. 4 vols., H.M.S.O., London, 1961
Weighley, Russell. *Eisenhower's Lieutenants: The Campaigns of France and Germany, 1944-1945*. Sidgwick & Jackson, London, 1981
Winfield, Dr. Roland. *The Sky Belongs to Them*. Kimber, London, 1976
Wynn, Humphrey and Young, Susan. *Prelude to Overlord*. Airlife, Shrewsbury, 1983

SELECT GLOSSARY

ACAS: Assistant Chief of the Air Staff
AEAF: Allied Expeditionary Air Force
AI: Airborne Interception. Refers to radars installed in night fighters
AIRBORNE CIGAR (ABC): Airborne jamming system used to disrupt German night fighter communications
AOC: Air Officer Commanding
AOCINC: Air Officer Commander-in-Chief
ARP: Air Raid Precautions
ASI: Air Scientific Intelligence
BBSU: British Bombing Survey Unit
BLIND BOMBING: Bombing without being able to locate the target visually
BOOZER: Passive airborne early warning device
BULL'S EYE: Diversionary or 'spoof' raid to deflect German night fighters away from main target
CAS: Chief of the Air Staff
CAT W: Official designation for aircrew suffering from Lack of Moral Fibre (W = Waverer)
CHASTISE: Attack on the Ruhr Dams by 617 Squadron on 16/17 May 1943
CID: Committee for Imperial Defence
CIRCUS: Daylight bombing attacks on targets in France and the Low Countries carried out in conjunction with Fighter Command. The primary aim was to tempt Luftwaffe fighters into the air
CLARION: US plan for bombing the smaller German towns as yet untouched by the war in early 1945
CO: Commanding Officer

CORONA: Ground-based system designed to interfere with German night fighter radio frequencies and feed them with false information
CROSSBOW: Attacks on V-weapon launch sites
DD PLANS: Deputy Director of Plans (an Air Ministry post)
DR: Dead Reckoning (a navigation technique)
EUREKA: A ground-based target marking system
EXODUS: Flying back of liberated Allied prisoners-of-war at end of April 1945
FRESHER: Aircrew newly graduated from OTU
GAF: German Air Force
GARDENING: Bomber Command mine-laying operations at sea
GEE: Navigation device introduced into general service in early 1942
G-H: Combined navigation/blind-bombing device incorporating GEE
GLIMMER: Operation mounted on night of 5/6 June 1944 to make German radar believe that there was an invasion fleet heading for Boulogne
GOMORRAH: The Hamburg 'firestorm' attacks of late July 1943
GRAND SLAM: The largest bomb (22,000lb) in RAF Bomber Command's armoury. Used to particular effect by 617 Squadron in communications attacks during the closing months of the war
H2S: Navigation/blind-bombing radar device

HE: High Explosive
HIGHBALL: Barnes Wallis's anti-shipping bouncing bomb
HURRICANE 1: USSTAFE/RAF Bomber Command attacks on Ruhr in order to assist Allied ground forces
HURRICANE 2: USSTAFE/RAF Bomber Command attacks on oil targets outside the Ruhr during the last six months of the war
HUSKY: Invasion of Sicily in July 1943
HYDRA: The Peenemünde raid on the night of 17/18 August 1943
INTRUDER: Patrol over enemy airfields by night designed to catch enemy aircraft landing. Used by both sides
KAMMHUBER LINE: Belt of searchlights and radars stretching from the Baltic, through the Low Countries and France to the Swiss border. Named after General of Night Fighters, Josef Kammhuber who set it up
L OF C: Lines of Communication
LMF: Lack of Moral Fibre
MAIN FORCE: RAF Bomber Command squadrons with no specialist role – the bulk of the Command
MANDREL: Air- and ground-based radar jammer
MANNA: Dropping of supplies to beleaguered N Holland at the end of the war
MASTER BOMBER: A senior officer controlling bombing from the air in order to maintain the accuracy of the attack
MEW: Ministry of Economic Warfare
MONICA: Active tail-mounted airborne early warning device
NFT: Night Flying Test – undertaken by crews on their aircraft prior to a night operation
NICKEL: Leaflet raid
NO BALL: Offensive against the V-weapon launching sites June–September 1944
OBOE: Blind-bombing device mounted in a Mosquito
OBOE REPEATER: Repeating station designed to extend the range of OBOE
ORB: Operations Record Book
ORS: Operational Research Section
OTU: Operational Training Unit
OFFSET MARKING: Target marking system used when target was visually

obscured. Markers were placed on a visible point and bomb-aimers were instructed to adjust their sights so that bombs would hit the target
OVERLORD: Allied invasion of Normandy in June 1944
PFF: Pathfinder Force
POINTBLANK: Anglo-American strategic bombing offensive against Germany
QUADRANT: Allied conference held in Quebec in August 1943
RCM: Radio Counter-Measures
RDF: Radio Direction Finding (radar)
RE8: Branch of Home Office responsible for bomb damage analysis
RED SPOT FIRES: Marking device which ignited at 3,000 feet and then burned on the ground for ten minutes
ROUND UP: Build-up of Allied forces in Britain in preparation for the invasion of the Continent
SABS: Stabilised Automatic Bombsight
SASO: Senior Air Staff Officer
SCREENED CREWS: Aircrew who had completed an operational tour
SERRATE: Device used to detect German night fighter radio transmissions
SEXTANT: Allied Conference held in Cairo in November 1943
SHAEF: Supreme Headquarters Allied Expeditionary Force
SHAKER TECHNIQUE: Use of GEE-equipped aircraft to mark a target with flares
SHUTTLE RAID: Attack on Germany with the bombers flying on to North Africa
SMO: Station Medical Officer
SOE: Special Operations Executive
TALLBOY: 12,000lb bomb developed by Barnes Wallis for use against reinforced targets. It was especially effective against v-weapon launch sites and tunnels
TAXABLE: Operation using WINDOW mounted on night of 5/6 June 1944 to make Germans believe an invasion fleet was heading for Le Havre
THUNDERCLAP: Plan for the bombing of Berlin and German cities in the east in support of the Soviet January 1945 offensive
TI: Target Indicator (marker)
TIME-AND-DISTANCE BOMBING: Use of visible reference points in line with the

target for accurate blind bombing

TINSEL: System for jamming the radio frequencies used by the German night fighter ground controllers

TORCH: Allied invasion of North Africa in November 1942

TRE: Telecommunications Research Establishment

UPKEEP: Barnes Wallis's anti-dam bouncing bomb

USSTAFE: US Strategic Air Forces in Europe

VCAS: Vice-Chief of the Air Staff

WA PLAN: Western Air Plan

WINDOW: Strips of aluminium foil dropped from the air to confuse the German radars

W/T: Wireless Telegraphy

WURZBURG: German ground-to-air radar

CHRONOLOGY

1939

3 September	Great Britain declares war on Germany.
	139 Sqn Blenheim IV mounts first operational sortie of the war with a reconnaissance of the Schillig Roads. That night 51 and 58 Sqns drop the first NICKELS over Germany, visiting the Ruhr, Hamburg and Bremen.
4 September	Blenheims, Hampdens and Whitleys attack German shipping in the Schillig Roads and Kiel Canal. Five Blenheims and two Wellingtons are shot down.
14 September	Harris becomes AOC No 5 Group.
1/2 October	First Bomber Command sorties to Berlin, when three 10 Sqn Whitleys drop NICKELS on capital.
17 October	First Luftwaffe bombing attack on Britain, when bombs fall on Scapa Flow. No casualties.
14 December	Six of twelve 99 Sqn Wellingtons lost in attack on *Nürnberg* and *Leipzig* in the Jade Estuary.
18 December	Twelve of 24 Wellingtons lost in attack on shipping in Schillig Roads.

1940

16 March	First British civilian killed by bombing when Luftwaffe attacks Scapa Flow.
19/20 March	Fifty bombers attack Sylt in retaliation. All return safely.
3 April	Portal relieves Ludlow-Hewitt as AOCinC Bomber Command.
4 April	75(NZ) Sqn formed – first Commonwealth unit in Bomber Command.
9 April	Hitler invades Denmark and Norway. Bomber Command involved in anti-shipping and airfield strikes.
10 May	Germans invade the Low Countries.
10/11 May	First bombing attack on German mainland against L of C targets.
15/16 May	99 bombers attack industrial targets in Hamburg and the Ruhr.

Note: A date expressed with an oblique (eg, 1/2) indicates a night operation.

11/12 June	First Bomber Command raid on Italy – 36 aircraft attack Genoa and Turin, one failing to return.
1/2 July	First operational use of 2,000lb bomb, dropped by F/O Guy Gibson of 83 Sqn in attack on *Scharnhorst* at Kiel.
12/13 August	F/L Learoyd wins Command's first VC in an attack on the Dortmund-Ems Canal.
25/26 August	First bombs land on Berlin, when 81 aircraft attack in retaliation for Luftwaffe's dropping bombs on London the previous night.
25 October	Portal succeeds Newall as Chief of the Air Staff, being replaced by Peirse in Bomber Command.
14/15 November	Luftwaffe attacks Coventry causing extensive damage.
25 November	Harris appointed as Deputy Chief of the Air Staff.
16/17 December	Bomber Command's first 'area' attack, when 134 aircraft set off for Mannheim with instructions to aim at the city centre in retaliation for Coventry. 102 claimed to have attacked the target.

1941

10/11 February	Operational début of the Stirling (7 Sqn) in an attack on oil storage tanks at Rotterdam.
24/25 February	Manchester's operational début (207 Sqn) in attack against Brest.
10/11 March	Halifax (35 Sqn) makes its first raid, against Le Havre.
31 March/1 April	Modified Wellington Is of 149 and 150 Sqns drop the first 4,000lb bombs in attack on Emden.
May	Harris appointed to head the RAF Delegation to Washington.
8 July	First operational sortie by RAF B-17s in attack by 90 Sqn on Wilhelmshaven.
11/12 August	First operational trial of GEE by two Wellingtons of 115 Sqn in an attack on München-Gladbach.
25/26 August	Last Bomber Command B-17 operation, when 90 Sqn raids Emden.
7/8 November	169 aircraft attack Berlin (21 missing), seven out of 55 are lost against Mannheim and nine out of 43 in GARDENING operations. 133 aircraft also attack Cologne, Ostend and Boulogne without loss. As a result, conservation policy comes into force.
11 December	Germany and Italy declare war on the United States of America.

1942

January	Washington Conference agrees on principle of Anglo-American strategic bombing campaign against Germany.
23 February	Harris takes over as AOCinC Bomber Command.
3/4 March	Successful precision attack on Renault factory at Billancourt. Lancaster makes its operational début in GARDENING operations off Brest.
8/9 March	SHAKER technique used for first time in a raid on Essen.
10/11 March	First Lancaster bombing operation (44 Sqn) in attack on Essen.
27 March	First Bomber Command attack on *Tirpitz* in Trondheim Fjord.
28/29 March	Incendiary attack on Lübeck.

16 April	Singleton Inquiry into the strategic bombing campaign set up.
17 April	Daylight raid by twelve Lancasters of 44 and 97 Sqns on Augsburg. Seven are shot down, and S/L Nettleton is awarded a VC.
23–28 April	Four attacks by night on Rostock.
30/31 May	First 1,000 bomber raid. 1,050 aircraft take off for Cologne; 890 claim to have attacked and 40 fail to return.
31 May	Operational début of Bomber Command Mosquitoes (105 Sqn), against Cologne.
1/2 June	956 aircraft attack Essen, 31 missing.
25/26 June	1,006 aircraft take off for Bremen, 49 lost. Last operational sorties by Manchester and Whitley, although latter will still be used by OTUs in GARDENING operations.
11 July	44 Lancasters attack Danzig by day.
11 August	Pathfinder Force formally established.
17 August	First US Eighth Air Force attack over Europe.
18/19 August	First Pathfinder operation, against Flensburg.
14/15 September	Last Hampden operation (408(RCAF)Sqn) with Bomber Command in an attack on Wilhelmshaven.
17 October	94 No 5 Group Lancasters attack the Schneider Armaments Arsenal at Le Creusot. A big dog-leg over the Atlantic makes this, at 1,700 miles, the longest trip so far.
28/29 November	106 Sqn drop the first 8,000lb bombs, over Turin.
20/21 December	First operational use of OBOE, by 109 Sqn over Lutterade.
1943	
1 January	No 6 (RCAF) Group formed.
25 January	No 8 (PFF) Group formed.
January	Casablanca Conference.
30/31 January	First operational use of H2S, by No 8 Group Stirlings and Halifaxes over Hamburg.
4 February	Bomber Command issued with a new directive reflecting decisions made at Casablanca on the conduct of the joint strategic bombing campaign.
5/6 March	Battle of the Ruhr opens with 442 aircraft attacking Essen, 14 fail to return.
16/17 May	617 Sqn's attack on the Ruhr Dams.
23/24 May	826 bombers are launched against Dortmund, the biggest raid since the 1942 1,000 Raids.
1 June	No 2 Group transferred to AEAF.
10 June	POINTBLANK Directive issued.
20/21 June	First Bomber Command SHUTTLE raid. Sixty No 5 Group Lancasters attack Friedrichshafen and then fly on to N Africa.
9/10 July	Attack by 422 bombers on Gelsenkirchen marks the end of the Battle of the Ruhr.
24 July–3 August	The Battle of Hamburg (GOMORRAH). Bomber Command mounts 3,097 sorties against the city in four attacks by night, the first (24/25 July) marking operational début of WINDOW. US Eighth Air Force also carries out two

attacks by day. 87 Bomber Command and five US aircraft are lost.

August	At the Quebec Conference (QUADRANT) the Allies confirm that OVERLORD will take place in 1944.
17 August	US Eighth Air Force loses 60 of 376 B-17s in attacks on Schweinfurt and Regensburg.
17/18 August	RAF Bomber Command attacks the V-weapon research establishment at Peenemünde. 596 aircraft take off, 38 are posted missing.
23 August–3 September	Harris mounts 1,447 sorties against Berlin in three major raids, but improved German defences account for 126 aircraft.
15/16 September	First use of TALLBOY by 617 Sqn in an attack on the Dortmund-Ems Canal.
22/23 September	First use of the 'spoof target' technique, with Hannover as the main target and Oldenburg the 'spoof'.
7/8 October	First operational use of G-H (139 Sqn over Aachen) and ABC (101 Sqn over Stuttgart).
8/9 October	Last Wellington bombing attack (300(Polish) Sqn) by Bomber Command, against Hannover.
14 October	In a second major attack on Schweinfurt, US Eighth Air Force loses 60 aircraft of 291 dispatched.
22/23 October	First use of CORONA, over Kassel.
November	Allied Conference in Cairo (SEXTANT).
8 November	No 100 (Special Duties) Group formed.
18/19 November	444 Mosquitoes and Lancasters set out for Berlin to mark the opening of the battle. Nine fail to return.
1944	
22 January	Publication of Zuckerman's Transportation Plan paper.
23/24 January	The beginning of 'Big Week' when, during a six-day period, Bomber Command and US Eighth Air Force drop 15,200 tons of bombs on German aircraft-manufacturing plants.
3/4 March	Last Wellington GARDENING sorties, carried out by 300 (Polish) Sqn off Lorient.
24/25 March	Last Bomber Command Battle of Berlin attack. Fourteen major operations had been mounted against the city, involving 5,000 sorties, of which 456 failed to return.
25 March	Eisenhower accepts the Transportation Plan for the strategic bombing forces' direct support of OVERLORD.
30/31 March	Bomber Command's last POINTBLANK operation. In its most costly raid of the war 96 of 795 aircraft are lost in an attack on Nuremberg.
14 April	RAF Bomber Command and US Eighth Air Force are placed under Eisenhower's operational direction.
6 June	D-Day. The Allies invade Normandy.
12 June	First V-1 hits England.
14 June	Bomber Command resumes daylight operations; 234 aircraft attack shipping at Le Havre, all returning safely.
16/17 June	Opening of the attack on the V-weapon sites (NO BALL).
8 September	Last Stirling operation with Bomber Command, flown by 149 Sqn against Le Havre. First V-2s fall on Paris and London.

14 September	USSTAFE and RAF Bomber Command revert to control by the Combined Chiefs of Staff.
14 October	1,013 bombers attack Duisburg by day and a further 1,008 that night. 21 aircraft are posted missing.
12 November	9 and 617 Sqns attack *Tirpitz* with TALLBOY, bringing about her final destruction.
3–11 December	Five Bomber Command attempts to knock out the Roer Dams meet with no success.

1945

13/14 February	Bomber Command sends 805 aircraft against Dresden, with 400 US bombers following up next day, in the most controversial bombing attack of the war.
12 March	Largest Bomber Command attack on a single target when 1,107 bombers are sent against Dortmund by day. 4,851 tons of bombs are dropped and two aircraft are shot down.
14 March	First use of GRAND SLAM, by 617 Sqn against the Bielefeld Viaduct.
16 April	Portal orders Harris to cease area bombing, and to concentrate on support of ground forces and naval targets.
26 April	Bomber Command begins flying back liberated prisoners-of-war (EXODUS).
29 April	Bomber Command launches MANNA, dropping of food supplies to beleaguered northern Holland.
2/3 May	Bomber Command's last attack on Germany. 299 Mosquito and No 100 Group sorties are mounted against naval targets in the Kiel area. Three Halifaxes fail to return.

APPENDICES

RAF BOMBER COMMAND
FRONT-LINE 4-ENGINE BOMBER AVAILABILITY
DECEMBER 1942–MAY 1945

Month*	No of Heavy Squadrons	Aircraft	Aircraft with Crews	Quarterly heavy bomber production
Dec 42	26	283	264	
Jan 43	31	338	292	232
Feb 43	33½	318	290	
Mar 43	35	423	379	
Apr 43	35½	558	443	321
May 43	36	604	487	
Jun 43	37	717	653	
Jul 43	40	681	626	387
Aug 43	40	743	700	
Sep 43	43	641	616	
Oct 43	48	742	710	383
Nov 43	49½	878	802	
Dec 43	61	760	731	
Jan 44	60¾	774	725	428
Feb 44	63½	856	783	
Mar 44	66½	927	889	
Apr 44	66½	961	857	483
May 44	67	975	914	
Jun 44	67½	1061	1046	
Jul 44	71	1166	1147	481
Aug 44	71½	1037	1026	
Sep 44	71½	1187	1175	
Oct 44	74½	1364	1329	460
Nov 44	78½	1300	1292	
Dec 44	81	1314	1301	
Jan 45	79½	1326	1306	412
Feb 45	79	1396	1358	
Mar 45	78½	1338	1305	
Apr 45	80	1429	1398	350
May 45	76½	1419	1398	

*Totals are taken as at the beginning of the month.

RAF BOMBER COMMAND DAMAGE CLAIMS

Fifteen of the nineteen German towns and cities claimed by Harris to be 'virtually destroyed' in his minute to Churchill of 3 November 1943 are listed below. The level of damage estimated in each, as at late March 1944, by the German Ministry of Home Security is compared to estimates made by the British Bombing Survey Unit in 1945.

Target	German Ministry of Home Security as at March 1944 (percentage)	BBSU Summer 1945 (percentage)
Kassel	54	69
Remscheid	53	83
Hamburg	51	75
Hannover	44	60
Düsseldorf	41	64
Cologne	40	61
München-Gladbach	37	54
Mannheim-Ludwigshafen	37	64
Barmen-Wuppertal	33	58
Elberfeld-Wuppertal	32	94
Krefeld	25	47
Mulheim	23	64
Essen	20	50
Dortmund	19	54
Bochum	17	83

RANGES AND BOMB-LOADS

Ranges are given in terms of the aircraft's radius of action – the farthest point to which it could fly and return to its base without running out of fuel – carrying maximum bomb-load. With a reduced bomb-load the range could be increased substantially. Thus, the Stirling, with a bomb-load of just 2000lb could quadruple its range. In terms of the escorts, ranges are given for normal flying. To allow for combat during the flight to and from the target, the effective range would be at least one-third less than that shown.

Type	Range (miles)	Max bomb-load (pounds)
Hampden	600	4,000
Wellington III	600	4,500
Whitley V	315	8,000
Manchester	600	10,350
Halifax I	500	13,000
Stirling III	295	14,000
Lancaster I	830	14,000
Mosquito IV	825	2,000
Boeing B-17G	550	12,800*
P-47C Thunderbolt	625**	
P-51D Mustang	1,040**	
Spitfire Mk XIVE	425**	

*The B-17 very seldom carried a full bomb-load – usually 4,000–6,000lb, which doubled its range. **All with drop tanks.

RAF BOMBER COMMAND VICTORIA CROSSES

Name	Squadron	Date of action	Target	Date of award
Flight Lieutenant R. A. B. Learoyd RAF	49	12/13 August 1940	Dortmund-Ems Canal	20 August 1940
Sergeant J. Hannah RAF	83	15/16 September 1940	Antwerp	1 October 1940
Wing Commander H. I. Edwards DFC, RAF	105	4 July 1941	Bremen	22 July 1941
Sergeant J. A. Ward RNZAF	75	7/8 July 1941	Münster	5 August 1941
Squadron Leader J. D. Nettleton RAF	44	17 April 1942	Augsburg	28 April 1942
Flying Officer L. T. Manser RAFVR (Posthumous)	50	30/31 May 1942	Cologne	20 October 1942
Flight Sergeant R. H. Middleton RAAF (Posthumous)	149	28/29 November 1942	Turin	15 January 1942
Wing Commander G. P. Gibson DSO, DFC, RAF	617	16/17 May 1943	Ruhr Dams	28 May 1943
Flight Sergeant A. L. Aaron DFM, RAFVR (Posthumous)	218	12/13 August 1943	Turin	5 November 1943
Flight Lieutenant W. Reid RAFVR	61	3/4 November 1943	Düsseldorf	14 December 1943
Pilot Officer C. J. Barton RAFVR (Posthumous)	578	30/31 March 1944	Nuremberg	27 June 1944
Wing Commander G. L. Cheshire DSO, DFC, RAFVR	617	1940–1944	Various	8 September 1944
Flight Sergeant G. Thompson RAFVR (Posthumous)	9	1 January 1945	Dortmund-Ems Canal	20 February 1945
Squadron Leader R. A. M. Palmer DFC, RAFVR (Posthumous)	109	23 December 1944	Cologne	23 March 1945
Captain E. Swales DFC, SAAF (Posthumous)	582	23/24 February 1945	Pforzheim	24 April 1945
Squadron Leader I. W. Bazalgette DFC, RAFVR (Posthumous)	635	4 August 1944	Trossy Saint-Maximin	17 August 1945
Sergeant N. C. Jackson RAFVR	106	26/27 April 1945	Schweinfurt	26 October 1945
Squadron Leader L. H. Trent DFC, RNZAF	487	3 May 1943	Amsterdam	1 March 1945
Pilot Officer A. C. Mynarski RCAF (Posthumous)	419	12/13 June 1944	Cambrai	11 October 1945

RAF BOMBER COMMAND OPERATIONAL GROUPS
AND SQUADRONS 1939–1945

26 SEPTEMBER 1939
No 2 Group
21, 82, 107, 110, 114, 139 Sqns
101 (Reserve) Sqn
All with Blenheims
No 3 Group
9, 37, 38, 99, 115, 149 Sqns
214 (Reserve), 215 (Reserve) Sqns
All with Wellingtons
No 4 Group
10, 51, 58, 77, 102 Sqns
78 (Reserve) Sqn
All with Whitleys
No 5 Group
44, 49, 50, 61, 83, 144 Sqns
106 (Reserve), 185 (Reserve) Sqns
All with Hampdens
No 6 Group
7, 76 Group Pool Sqns with Hampdens
75, 148 Group Pool Sqns with
Wellingtons
97, 166 Group Pool Sqns with Whitleys
90, 104, 108 Group Pool Sqns with
Blenheims
35, 52, 63, 207 Group Pool and 98
(Reserve) Sqns with Battles

9 JANUARY 1942
No 1 Group
12, 103, 142, 150, 300(Polish),
301(Pol), 304(Pol), 305(Pol),
458(RAAF), 460(RAAF) Sqns
All with Wellingtons
No 2 Group
18, 21, 82, 105, 107, 110, 114 Sqns
with Blenheims
88, 226 Sqns with Bostons
No 3 Group
9, 40, 57, 75(NZ), 99, 101, 115, 214,
218, 313(Czech), 419(RCAF) Sqns with
Wellingtons
7, 15, 149 Sqns with Stirlings
No 4 Group
51, 58, 77, 78, 98, 102, 104, 105 Sqns
with Whitleys
10, 35, 76 Sqns with Halifaxes
138(Special) Sqn with a miscellany of
aircraft for SOE duties
No 5 Group
49, 50, 83, 106, 144, 408(RCAF),
420(RCAF), 455(RAAF) Sqns with
Hampdens

61, 97, 207 Sqns with Manchesters
44(Rhodesia) Sqn with Lancasters

4 MARCH 1943
No 1 Group
12, 100, 101, 103, 460(RAAF) Sqns
with Lancasters
166, 199, 300(Pol), 301(Pol), 305(Pol)
Sqns with Wellingtons
No 2 Group
88, 107, 226 Sqns with Bostons
105, 139 Sqns with Mosquitoes
21, 464, 487 Sqns with Venturas
98, 180 Sqns with Mitchells
No 3 Group
15, 75(NZ), 90, 149, 214, 218 Sqns
with Stirlings
115 Sqn with Lancasters
138, 161, 192 Special Duties Sqns with
miscellaneous aircraft for SOE work
No 4 Group
76, 77, 78, 102, 105, 158 Sqns with
Halifaxes
196, 429(RCAF), 431(RCAF),
466(RCAF) Sqns with Wellingtons
No 5 Group
9, 44, 49, 50, 57, 61, 97, 106, 207,
467(RAAF) Sqns all with Lancasters
No 6(RCAF) Group
405, 408, 419 Sqns with Halifaxes
420, 424, 425, 426, 427, 428 Sqns with
Wellingtons
No 8(PFF) Group
7 Sqn with Stirlings
35 Sqn with Halifaxes
83, 156 Sqns with Lancasters
109 Sqn with Mosquitoes

19 APRIL 1945
No 1 Group
12, 100, 101, 103, 150, 153, 166, 170,
300(Pol), 460(RAAF), 550, 576, 625,
626 Sqns all with Lancasters
No 3 Group
15, 75, 90, 115, 138, 149, 186, 195,
218, 514, 622 Sqns all with Lancasters
No 4 Group
10, 51, 64, 76, 77, 78, 102,
346(French), 347(French), 466(RAAF)
all with Halifaxes
No 5 Group
9, 44(Rhod), 49, 50, 57, 61, 106, 189,

207, 227, 463(RAAF), 467(RAAF),
617, 619, 630, 83(PFF), 97(PFF) Sqns
with Lancasters
627(PFF) Sqn with Mosquitoes
No 6(RCAF) Group
408, 415, 420, 425, 426, 432 Sqns with
Halifaxes
419, 424, 427, 428, 429, 431, 433, 434
Sqns with Lancasters
No 8(PFF) Group
7, 35, 156, 405(RCAF), 582, 635 Sqns
with Lancasters
105, 109, 128, 139, 142, 162, 163, 571,
608, 692 Sqns with Mosquitoes
No 100(Special Duties) Group
23, 85, 141, 157, 169, 239, 515 Sqns
with Mosquitoes
171, 192, 199, 462(RAAF) Sqns with
Halifaxes
214 Sqn with Fortress IIIs
223 Sqn with Liberators

INDEX